POLITICAL IDEAS

for A-level

Liberalism, Conservatism, Socialism, Nationalism, Multiculturalism, Ecologism

Richard Kelly
Neil McNaughton

SERIES EDITOR:
Eric Magee

HODDER
EDUCATION
AN HACHETTE UK COMPANY

The Publishers would like to thank the following for permission to reproduce copyright material.

Acknowledgements

p.181, Cristina Odone, 'Immigrants love this country more than we do', *Daily Telegraph*, 10 August 2011; **p.187**, Trevor Phillips, 'White liberals have speeded segregation in the UK. The great struggle now is to reverse it', *Daily Telegraph*, 5 December 2016; **p.209**, Carolyn Merchant, interviewed in *California Monthly*, 2002.

Photo credits

Photos reproduced by permission of: **p.9** Ian Dagnall/Alamy Stock Photo; **p.11** North Wind Picture Archives/Alamy Stock Photo; **p.26** matteogirelli/Fotolia; **p.27** Georgios Kollidas/Fotolia; History collection 2016/Alamy Stock Photo; **p.41** Bob Daemmrich/Alamy Stock Photo; **p.44** pixs:sell/Fotolia; **p.45** (top) Stephen Mulligan/Fotolia; **p.45** (bottom) Gang/Fotolia; **p.56** GL Archive/Alamy Stock Photo; **p.68** colaimages/Alamy Stock Photo; **p.69** dpa picture alliance/Alamy Stock Photo; **p.78** Sueddeutsche Zeitung Photo/Alamy Stock Photo; **p.82** dpa picture alliance/Alamy Stock Photo; **p.95** age fotostock/Alamy Stock Photo; **p.97** vkilikov/Fotolia; **p.104** World History Archive/Alamy Stock Photo; **p.108** Keystone Pictures USA/Alamy Stock Photo; **p.110** Jeff Morgan 12/Alamy Stock Photo; **p.120** Cultura Creative (RF)/Alamy Stock Photo; **p.129** Everett Collection Inc/Alamy Stock Photo; **p.136** Tetra Images/Alamy Stock Photo; **p.144** jeremy sutton-hibbert/Alamy Stock Photo; **p.156** Janine Wiedel Photolibrary/Alamy Stock Photo; **p.165** Peter Cavanagh/Alamy Stock Photo; **p.174** Sam Pantakhy/Stringer; **p.175** PA Wire/PA Images; **p.184** WENN Ltd/Alamy Stock Photo; **p.186** Xinhua/Alamy Stock Photo; **p.188** Sergejs Duncs/Fotolia; **p.198** Mats Lindberg/Alamy Stock Photo; **p.207** John Devlin/Alamy Stock Photo.

Orders: please contact Bookpoint Ltd, 130 Park Drive, Milton Park, Abingdon, Oxon OX14 4SE. Telephone: (44) 01235 827720. Fax: (44) 01235 400454. Email education@bookpoint.co.uk

Lines are open from 9 a.m. to 5 p.m., Monday to Saturday, with a 24-hour message answering service. You can also order through our website: www.hoddereducation.co.uk

ISBN: 978 1 4718 89516

© Richard Kelly, Neil McNaughton and Eric Magee 2017

First published in 2017 by

Hodder Education,
An Hachette UK Company
Carmelite House
50 Victoria Embankment
London EC4Y 0DZ

www.hoddereducation.co.uk

Impression number   10

Year   2021 2020 2019

Typeset by Aptara, Inc.

Printed in India

A catalogue record for this title is available from the British Library.

Get the most from this book

Learning outcomes
A summary of the learning objectives for each chapter

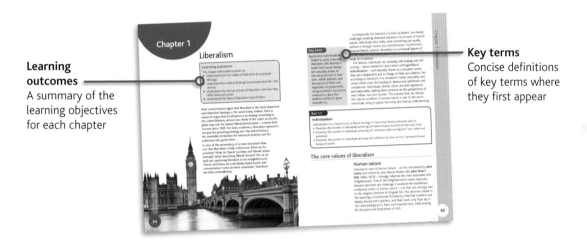

Key terms
Concise definitions of key terms where they first appear

Key thinker
Feature boxes giving details of the key people covered in the chapter

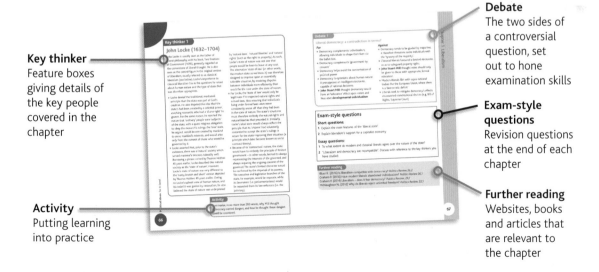

Debate
The two sides of a controversial question, set out to hone examination skills

Exam-style questions
Revision questions at the end of each chapter

Further reading
Websites, books and articles that are relevant to the chapter

Activity
Putting learning into practice

Contents

Answers to the exam-style questions at the end of
each chapter can be found at **www.hoddereducation.co.uk/
PoliticalIdeasNME**

Introduction

Four aspects of the course are considered here:

1 This part of the Government and Politics course is entitled 'Political ideas'. While this may seem self-explanatory, it is vital to understand what is actually meant by the terms 'ideas' and 'ideologies' and to distinguish them from political policies.

2 Each section is divided into four dominant themes: human nature, the state, society and economy. Answers to questions should take into account these themes wherever they are relevant.

3 The specification requires you to have knowledge about the beliefs of a number of key thinkers. Below is information on how you should use this knowledge.

4 It is important to employ appropriate vocabulary. The study of political ideas will challenge students to come to terms with new language, but it is important to meet that challenge in order to add clarity to your meanings.

Ideas and ideologies

We are used to discussing specific political policies but these refer largely to short-term, pragmatic decisions made by politicians, parties and pressure groups. Policies are developed to deal with particular problems which arise from time to time. Ideas and ideologies, meanwhile, look at longer-term issues and consider fundamental solutions to such questions. Furthermore, they are based on strongly held principles rather than pragmatic responses to short-term issues. Two examples can help here.

Let us consider the levels of taxation in a society. A policy to reduce income tax may be a short-term method of pumping more money into the economy, increasing spending and boosting economic growth. It cannot be undertaken permanently but it solves a problem in the meantime. Meanwhile, a party or group of politicians might believe that tax levels are generally too high, are a threat to people's economic liberty and individualism, and are a disincentive to work and enterprise, so they should be kept to as low a level as possible in the long term. A low-tax society is therefore a political idea.

Political ideologies are a stronger phenomenon altogether. Ideologies are sets of related political ideas which come together to create a vision of some kind of idealised society. Ideologies are based on strongly held, permanent principles and interlocking doctrines. In our example, the idea of a low-tax society connects with related doctrines such as opposition to high levels of welfare which, like high taxes, may be a disincentive to hard work, and free, unregulated markets which foster business enterprise. Put these three aims together — low taxation, low welfare and free markets — and we have an ideology, usually known as neo-liberalism.

We can now apply the same analysis to another set of ideas. These concern dealing with poverty and inequality:

- Raising the minimum wage is a short-term policy to reduce poverty.
- Reducing the gap in living standards between the rich and poor in the long term is a political idea.
- Creating a more generally equal society with equal rights, empowerment for the working classes, intervention by the state to avoid the 'excesses' of capitalism and public ownership of major industries to spread the fruits of their production more evenly are interlocking ideas, forming an ideology, which we know as socialism.

Put another way, policies come and go, while political ideas and ideologies have more permanence.

This book deals with political ideas and political ideologies but not with policies. There are three 'core' ideologies and five 'optional' ideologies. Apart from the fact that students must study all three core ideologies to be able to tackle the examination questions but have to study only one of the options, there is another distinction to be borne in mind:

- The core ideologies — liberalism, conservatism and socialism — have dominated western civilisation for more than 200 years. Political discourse and conflict therefore have largely been based on these three. However, they are largely based on western civilisation. Today we must look further afield in our study of political ideas, taking a world view and also considering those ideas that shape the relationships between minorities and the perspectives of alienated sections of society.
- The optional ideologies — nationalism, feminism, anarchism, ecologism and multiculturalism — have generally shorter histories than the core ideologies but often take their inspiration from different forms of consciousness of the world, ranging from eastern mysticism to gender awareness

to modern scientism. Some aspects of the optional ideas have also challenged the traditional ideas associated with liberalism, conservatism and socialism and as such can also be described as post-modern.

Four themes

These are guides as to how we can analyse and compare political ideas and the beliefs of the many key thinkers presented in this book. You do not have to apply them but you are advised to do so where you can. As a starting point they should be considered in the following ways:

- **Human nature.** This concerns beliefs about the fundamental nature of mankind's relationship with other people and with the world. In the political ideas presented here we will see that various thinkers have described human nature in enormously varied ways, from egocentric to social, from fundamentally good to fundamentally competitive, from gender obsessed to androgynous (having no gender identity), or from dominant over the natural world (anthropomorphic) to claiming to be only an equal part of nature.

- **State.** Nearly all people live under the jurisdiction of one state or another. Political ideas and ideologies therefore have adopted principles about the nature of the state, what part (if any) it should play in society, how it should be controlled and whether it is a force for good or evil.

- **Society.** All societies have a particular structure which has either evolved naturally or been imposed by the state and those who govern the state. Most ideologies therefore have developed some kind of vision of what their ideal society would look like. Sometimes this is very specific, as is the case with socialism, some multiculturalists and certain types of collectivist anarchism; sometimes it is more vague, as is the case with conservatism.

- **Economy.** Not all political ideas and ideologies contain a strong economic perspective, but some do and this should be reflected in analysis where it applies. Again, socialism is a clear example, while neo-liberals, as described above, base most of the ideas on economics and economic principles. Even some socialist feminists have been able to link most of their analysis to economic relations between the sexes. Many ecologists also see capitalism as the main culprit in the degradation of the natural environment and so propose to control or even abolish it.

7

Key thinkers

There are usually five key thinkers specified for each of the political ideologies in the specification. This book describes their main work, beliefs and importance in the development of political ideas. They are not exhaustive and you should also have knowledge of other key thinkers, but you are certainly advised to refer to them in your examination answers. Directly quoting them is not necessary, though you should do so if you can and if it helps to illustrate your analysis.

Every ideology comprises different themes and variations. Often the different thinkers in the text illustrate these variations most effectively. Thus the distinction between, for example, the liberals John Stuart Mill and John Rawls tells us a great deal about how liberalism evolved between the nineteenth and twentieth centuries. Similarly, Marx's fundamental version of socialism tells us much of how dramatically the ideology has been transformed by more recent left-wing thinkers such as Anthony Crosland and Anthony Giddens.

Political vocabulary

As we have said, you should use accurate and appropriate political vocabulary wherever possible. Fortunately, both this book and the examination specification contain key terms with their meanings. You should take time to understand these and practise using them wherever you can. They can also save you time in your writing as they have specific meanings, which will reduce the need for lengthy explanations.

You are strongly advised to learn those aspects of vocabulary with which you are not already familiar and to ensure that you are able to use them in the correct context.

Chapter 1

Liberalism

Learning outcomes

This chapter will enable students to:
- understand the core values of liberalism as a political ideology
- understand how liberal thinking has evolved since the seventeenth century
- understand the various strands of liberalism and how they differ from each other
- understand the ideas of liberalism's key thinkers

Introduction: a pervasive ideology

Most commentators agree that liberalism is the most important and influential ideology in the world today. Indeed, there is reason to argue that its influence is increasing. According to the United Nations, almost two-thirds of the states across the globe may now be classed 'liberal democracies' — a seven-fold increase since 1945. For many academics, liberalism represents not just the prevailing ideology but 'the end of history', the inevitable destination for advanced societies and the politicians who guide them.

In view of this ascendancy, it is more important than ever that liberalism is fully understood. What are its priorities? What do 'liberal' societies and 'liberal' states embody? What does being 'liberal' involve? Yet, as we shall see, explaining liberalism is not straightforward: 'liberal' politicians are a decidedly mixed bunch, and commentators' views on what constitutes 'liberalism' are often contradictory.

In the UK, the USA and much of western Europe, being 'liberal' usually denotes being at odds with the values of conservatism, while being closer to the values of socialism (hence the much-used term in politics, 'liberal-left'). This would explain why a self-proclaimed American liberal, such as Hillary Clinton, found herself seeking the same party's presidential nomination as a self-proclaimed socialist, Bernie Sanders, while strongly opposing aggressive conservatives in the Republican Party.

Yet if one turns to the states of the southern hemisphere and western Pacific, the term 'liberal' has rather different connotations. In Australia, for example, it is the Liberal Party that offers the main opposition to that country's Labor Party, while providing a home for many of Australia's self-styled conservatives.

Clearly, liberalism is not just hugely influential; it is also complex and potentially confusing. So, to make sense of it, let us examine the origins and core beliefs of this pre-eminent ideology.

The origins of liberalism

In many ways, the roots of liberalism lie in the Reformation, a religious movement affecting much of northern Europe in the late fifteenth and sixteenth centuries. Led by religious protestors such as Martin Luther, these founders of 'protestant' Christianity argued that individuals seeking to communicate with God, and to understand His commands, need no longer rely on priests, popes and other intermediaries. With the advent of the printing press and the printed word, and the wider literacy this promoted, Luther argued that Christianity could now assume a more individualistic character, with each man and woman undertaking their own private prayers and undertaking God's work in their own way.

However, it was the Enlightenment that sought to extend these religious ideas into the political and secular spheres.

John Locke: Enlightenment icon and classical liberal

The Enlightenment was an intellectual movement that emerged in the mid-seventeenth century (coinciding with the English Civil War and the subsequent overthrow of King Charles I), and one that had an especially profound effect upon politics in the eighteenth century (influencing, among other things, both the creation of an independent American republic after 1776 and the French Revolution of 1789). The Enlightenment was defined by a belief in reason rather than faith, and thus promoted relentless debate and inquiry, questioning and scrutinising almost anything that, hitherto, was unthinkingly accepted.

Among the radical ideas that emerged from the Enlightenment were that each individual is someone with free will, that each individual is the best judge of their own interests, and that each individual's life should be shaped by that individual's actions and decisions. More specifically, writers such as **John Locke** (1632–1704) (see 'Key thinker 1' box) — widely regarded as the 'father' of liberalism — began to question the relationship between individuals and governments, seeking to define just why and how individuals should defer to those who governed them.

Today, such an exercise may seem routine. But in the seventeenth century it had revolutionary potential. Until then, it had been assumed — by both rulers and ruled — that the natural form of government was monarchical; that a king (occasionally a queen) had been put in place by God; and that a king's decisions should be instinctively accepted by a king's 'subjects' — a doctrine later termed 'the divine right of kings'. Underpinning this agreement, of course, were a society and culture dominated by faith, religion and superstition.

Yet the Enlightenment was to challenge and eventually destroy such medieval attitudes. For Locke and other Enlightenment philosophers, human beings were uniquely endowed with the power of logic, calculation and deduction. And it was logical, they argued, that human beings should create, by themselves and for themselves, a political system based upon reason (a principle that political scientists now describe as **mechanistic theory**).

Key term

Mechanistic theory Linked to the writings of John Locke, this argues that mankind is rational and therefore capable of devising a state that reflects mankind's needs. It was a pointed rebuff to notions like the 'divine right of kings', which argued that the state reflected God's will and that obedience to the state was a religious duty.

John Locke (1632–1704)

John Locke is usually seen as the father of liberal philosophy, with his book *Two Treatises of Government* (1690) generally regarded as the cornerstone of liberal thought. He is also seen as the central figure in the original version of liberalism, usually referred to as classical liberalism (see below). Locke's importance to classical liberalism lies in the questions he raised about human nature and the type of state that was therefore appropriate.

- Locke denied the traditional, medieval principle that the state was part of God's creation. He also disputed the idea that the state had been created by a celestial power, involving monarchs who had a 'divine right' to govern. For the same reason, he rejected the notion that 'ordinary' people were 'subjects' of the state, with a quasi-religious obligation to obey the monarch's rulings: the 'true' state, he argued, would be one created by mankind to serve mankind's interests and would arise only from the *consent* of those who would be governed by it.
- Locke asserted that, prior to the state's existence, there was a 'natural' society which served mankind's interests tolerably well. Borrowing a phrase coined by Thomas Hobbes 40 years earlier, Locke described this natural society as the 'state of nature'. However, Locke's state of nature was very different to the 'nasty and brutish' version depicted by Hobbes. Owing to Locke's upbeat view of human nature, and his belief that it was guided by rationalism, he also believed the state of nature was to be underpinned by 'natural laws',

'natural liberties' and 'natural rights' (such as the right to property). As such, Locke's state of nature was not one that people would be keen to leave at any cost. The alternative 'state of law' (in other words, the modern state as we know it) was therefore designed to improve upon an essentially tolerable situation, by resolving disputes between individuals more efficiently than would be the case under the state of nature.

- For Locke, the 'state of law' would be legitimate only if it respected natural rights and natural laws, thus ensuring that individuals living under formal laws were never consistently worse off than they had been in the state of nature. The state's structures must therefore embody the natural rights and natural liberties that preceded it. Similarly, Locke's ideal state would always reflect the principle that its 'citizens' had voluntarily *consented* to accept the state's rulings in return for the state improving their situation (a principle which later became known as 'social contract theory').
- Because of its 'contractual' nature, the state would have to embody the principle of limited government — in other words, limited to always representing the interests of the governed and always requiring the ongoing consent of the governed. The state's 'limited' character would be confirmed by the dispersal of its powers. The executive and legislative branches of the state, for example, would be separate, while its lawmakers (i.e. parliamentarians) would be separated from its law enforcers (i.e. the judiciary).

Activity

Summarise, in no more than 200 words, the type of state John Locke prescribed.

The core ideas of liberalism

Human nature

Liberalism's view of human nature — as first articulated by John Locke and refined by later liberal thinkers such as **John Stuart Mill** (1806–73) (see 'Key thinker 3' box) — strongly reflected the view associated with the Enlightenment. One of the Enlightenment's most important features had been the challenge it issued to the established, medieval notion of human nature — one that was strongly tied to the religious doctrine of original sin. This doctrine, rooted in the teachings of traditional Christianity, held that mankind was deeply flawed and imperfect, and that man's only hope lay in him acknowledging his flaws and imperfections while praying for the grace and forgiveness of God.

Drawing upon the writings of Locke and other Enlightenment philosophers, liberalism has always denied this bleak view, offering instead a more optimistic view of human nature. Liberalism duly argues that human nature has a huge capacity to bring about progress, and an unending ability to forge greater human happiness. At the heart of this optimistic view is a belief that individuals are guided principally by reason or rationalism, and thus are able to calculate answers to all sorts of problems.

Liberals believe that mankind's innate reason is manifested in debate, discussion, peaceful argument and the measured examination of ideas and opinions. Rather than meekly accepting whatever life offers — perhaps on the grounds that it is the 'will of God' or simply 'fate' — individuals have the capacity to plan their own future and effect a preconceived outcome. Indeed, the concepts of both planning and the subsequent 'plan' itself are central to the rationalist idea and the cheery liberal belief that human nature allows us to shape our own destiny.

Consequently, for liberalism, human 'problems' are merely challenges awaiting reasoned solutions; on account of human nature, individuals who really want something can usually achieve it through reason plus determination. Furthermore, because liberals assume rationality is a universal feature of human nature, they usually assume that reasoned discussion leads to consensus.

Activity

Explain, in approximately 200 words, why liberalism is said to have an optimistic view of human nature.

For liberals, individuals are naturally self-seeking and self-serving — hence liberalism's association with **egotistical individualism** — and naturally drawn to a situation where they are independent and in charge of their own destiny. Yet, according to liberalism, it is mankind's innate rationality and virtue that stop this leading to destructive selfishness and competition. Individuals, liberals claim, are both egotistical *and* reasonable, making them sensitive to the perspectives of their fellow men and women. This ensures that, for liberals, the natural condition of human nature is one of self-aware individuals, living in peace, harmony and mutual understanding.

Society

Liberalism's optimistic view of human nature, particularly our capacity for reason, informs the liberal view about whether 'society' can ever exist without a state. In his classic work *Leviathan* (1651), Thomas Hobbes argued that human nature is so brutally selfish that no society could possibly arise, or survive, until human nature is restrained by a strong, formal authority — in short, a state. But early liberal philosophers like Locke offered a very different view, citing the existence of 'natural' society, with 'natural laws' and therefore natural rights (including the 'right' to life, liberty, property and happiness), all of which preceded the state. So, for liberals, life before the state was created was not 'nasty, brutish and short' (as Hobbes famously asserted) but potentially pleasant, civilised and long.

This liberal belief in a 'natural society', where certain 'natural rights' are enjoyed, helps explain why liberals place so much importance upon the individual (see Box 1.1). Indeed, as John Stuart Mill emphasised during the mid-nineteenth century, the main purpose of any civilised society — 'natural' or manufactured — is to facilitate individualism. In making this claim, Mill and other liberals argued that each individual has a unique personality and peculiar talents; that individuals are rational in pursuit of their self-interest; and that individuals are egotistical, driven by a wish to fulfil their potential and a desire to be self-reliant and independent. In view of all this, each individual therefore seeks freedom. For Mill, in his critical work *On Liberty* (1859), this specifically meant freedom from any dependency on others and the freedom to live one's life in a way that maximises self-reliance and self-fulfilment.

For this reason, liberals believe that the 'default setting' of any society is a focus upon individual freedom and that any society which seeks to deny individualism is dysfunctional.

In this respect, the 'right' to property — defined by Locke as 'that with which Man has mixed his labour' — is regarded by liberals as particularly important, as it is seen as the tangible expression of an individual within society. Furthermore, for later liberals like Mill, property is also the 'prism' through which individuals develop their potential, providing an opportunity, within civilised communities, for men and women to nurture their taste and judgement.

Box 1.1

Individualism

Individualism is a vital principle of liberal ideology. It means that individual needs should be at the heart of political thought, economic life and social organisation, and that society should prioritise the improvement of diverse, individual lives. Its implications are that liberal politicians seek to:

- maximise the number of individuals achieving self-determination (control of their own lives)
- maximise the number of individuals achieving self-realisation (discovering their 'true' selves and potential)
- maximise the number of individuals attaining self-fulfilment (a sense of one's 'personal mission' being achieved).

The economy

In addition to shaping its view of society, liberalism's devotion to private property informs its approach to the economy. Given its belief that property is a natural right, it is inevitable that liberalism should support an economy that puts private property at the heart of all economic arrangements. In short, it is inevitable that liberals should support capitalism.

Ever since the liberal economist Adam Smith enunciated his theory of markets in his seminal work *The Wealth of Nations* (1776), liberalism has been strongly associated with private enterprise and private ownership of the economy. Indeed, this explains why capitalism is routinely described as **economic liberalism**, and provides a key difference between liberalism and many forms of socialism. Although liberals and socialists share many assumptions and objectives, and criticise many of the same things, liberals will still ultimately defend a market-based economy and stridently refute the anti-capitalist message of 'fundamentalist' socialism (see Chapter 3).

Activity

Explain in approximately 200 words (and with reference to the chapter on conservatism) how John Locke's view of the state of nature differed from that of Thomas Hobbes.

Key term

State of nature This was a philosophical device used in the seventeenth century by both Thomas Hobbes and John Locke to justify the very different types of political state they were proposing. It referred to what life might have been like before laws, formal rules and governments came into being.

As with the stress on individualism, liberalism's endorsement of capitalism is strongly linked to its positive view of human nature. In making the case for free-market economics, Adam Smith had asserted that if obstacles to free trade were swept away, the 'invisible hand' of market forces would guide traders towards success, resulting wealth would 'trickle down' to everyone, and 'the wealth of nations' would be promoted globally. In making these confident assertions, Smith was clearly reflecting the optimistic tone of liberalism's core values — and, in the view of many non-liberals, being rather naïve about the efficacy of market forces.

The state

Although individualism and capitalism are central to liberalism's view of society and the economy, it is important to remember that this does not render liberalism unique among political ideologies — this also applies, for example, to several branches of anarchism (known as 'individualist anarchism').

What makes liberalism distinctive is that whereas anarchists see the state — any state — as the eternal enemy of individualism, liberals, from John Locke and Adam Smith onwards, believe that individualism and capitalism work best when accompanied by a certain kind of state. But to understand why, it is necessary to explain how liberals think the 'ideal' state originates, what it seeks to achieve and how it should be structured.

The liberal state: origins

To appreciate liberalism's belief in a state, it is important to remember that, while liberalism takes an optimistic view of human nature, it still accepts that, within the **state of nature**, there would have been clashes of interests between individuals pursuing their own, egocentric agendas. Locke was especially worried that without the sort of formal structures only a state can provide, the resolution of such clashes — particularly clashes concerning property — might not always be swift and efficient. As a result, individualism in the state of nature could have been impeded by stalemated disputes between competing individuals. So a mechanism — a state — was required, to arbitrate effectively between the competing claims of rational individuals.

To provide a sporting comparison, most footballers would accept that, in the absence of a referee, some kind of football match could still take place, with both teams self-regulating on an ad hoc basis (think in terms of a 'kick-around' among friends). Yet, even though it would result in their restriction and occasional punishment, most footballers would also accept that the match would be fairer, more efficient and more rewarding for individual players if a referee was present — especially if the referee officiated according to pre-agreed rules. For liberals, this is analogous to their argument that the state of nature, tolerable though it may be, is still inferior to the particular 'formalised' state liberals recommend.

The liberal state: objectives

Although their root justification for the 'liberal state' was that it allowed the more effective resolution of disputes between individuals, Locke and later liberals were also keen to show that the kind of state they wanted embodied wider and grander principles. These principles were to be significantly developed by England's Bill of Rights of 1689, the American Constitution of 1787 and the first French Republic of 1789. From these historical events emerge various objectives, which are central to any understanding of what the liberal state seeks to achieve.

Rejection of the 'traditional' state

The liberal state is founded upon an explicit rejection of the type of state common in Europe prior to the Enlightenment — a state marked by monarchical, absolutist and arbitrary rule. In other words, the liberal state renounces the sort of state where power is concentrated in the hands of one individual and where that power is exercised randomly. The liberal state would be especially contemptuous of any government that claimed a 'divine right' to govern, according to a subjective and thus irrational perception of God's will.

Government by consent

Following on from its rejection of 'the divine right of kings', liberalism insists that the state is legitimate only if those under its jurisdiction have effectively *volunteered* to be under its jurisdiction: in other words, governments must have the consent of the governed.

   This doctrine has a profound effect upon the relationship between politicians and people. Far from being the 'subjects' of the government — as the traditional state had asserted — the people in the state would now have ultimate control over it. As Locke maintained, 'government should always be the servant, not master, of the people'.

For this reason, 'government by consent' can be linked to the notion of 'government by contract' — what Enlightenment theorists such as Jean Jacques Rousseau (1712–78) later dubbed a **social contract**. In simple terms, individuals who 'contract out' of the state of nature and 'contract in' to the formal state of law agree to accept the latter's authority and restrictions, but are promised something in return. But *what* are they promised in return? This leads us to the remaining objectives of the liberal state.

Promotion of natural rights/individualism

Liberals always assume that, before any formal state was created, individuals enjoyed 'natural rights' that enabled self-realisation, self-determination and — therefore — individualism. So it would be irrational for individuals to abandon both natural rights and individualism by submitting unconditionally to any state. The only rational reason to submit to the state would be if it not only respected but promoted natural rights, ensuring they were more safely and easily exercised than in the state of nature.

Promotion of tolerance

Linked to its devotion to natural rights, the liberal state is also concerned to ensure tolerance towards all those individuals who exercise their natural rights in various ways. Obviously, tolerance was closely linked to individualism — how could an individual seek self-determination if his actions and opinions were to be forbidden by others? It was with this dilemma in mind that the French philosopher Voltaire (1694–1778) issued his famous clarion call for freedom, claiming 'I detest what you say but will defend unto the death your right to say it.'

This notion was to be developed a century or so later by John Stuart Mill, who insisted that the state should tolerate all actions and opinions unless they were shown to violate the **harm principle** — the principle that individuals should be free to do and say anything unless it could be proved that this 'harmed' the rights and freedoms of other individuals within the state.

Although liberalism is an individualistic creed, it has usually recognised that individuals do not necessarily seek isolation and detachment from their fellow men and women (thus creating an 'atomised' environment) but are instead drawn to societies that accommodate their individualism. So, when emphasising tolerance, for example, early liberals were aware that individuals were inclined to congregate into religious communities. It was therefore important that the state should show tolerance towards such communities, especially those representing the religious views of a minority. So, in the wake of the Glorious Revolution of 1688, which cemented the Protestant supremacy in England, Locke was particularly keen that the post-Revolution state should extend tolerance towards Roman Catholics.

Since then, tolerating minorities has been an ongoing passion for those seeking to support and advance the liberal state. Since the mid-twentieth century, American liberals such as the feminist **Betty Friedan** (1921–2006) (see 'Key thinker 5' box) have sought to update Locke's belief in the tolerance of minorities, campaigning for the state to improve the lot of individuals allegedly hindered by ethnicity, sexuality, physicality or (in the case of Friedan's campaigns) gender.

Meritocracy

Given the liberal state's stress on individualism, the next principle of a liberal state is that political power should be exercised only by those who show themselves worthy of it. In other words, government should be conducted by individuals who, through their own efforts and talents, have won the trust of the governed. Consequently, there is no guarantee that such responsibility will be conferred upon the descendants of those who govern — unless they, too, can demonstrate competence and integrity.

In this respect, the meritocratic liberal state again stands in contrast to the traditional state. In pre-Enlightenment regimes, power was largely hereditary and aristocratic, with circumstances of birth trumping individual ability. As Thomas Paine (1737–1809) remarked, when justifying the French Revolution's overthrow of the nobility in 1789, hereditary rule was 'beyond equity, beyond reason and most certainly beyond wisdom'. Aristocracy thus had no place in the meritocratic liberal state commended by Locke, Mill and other liberal thinkers.

Equality of opportunity

For liberals, it is an article of faith that all individuals are born equal, have equal natural rights and are of equal value — a belief often referred to as **foundational equality**. Within the liberal state, all individuals must therefore have equal opportunity to develop their potential and achieve control of their own lives. If an individual fails to fulfil their potential, they must be able to assume total responsibility for this failure — and not somehow attribute it to the state.

Activity

Exemplify, in approximately 100 words, how the liberal state promotes tolerance.

Key term

Foundational equality/ legal equality This refers to the liberal belief that every individual is born equal, with equal natural rights. Such individuals are therefore entitled to legal equality in a liberal state. This would involve equality before the law and an equal recognition of individual rights.

Justice

Linked to **equality of opportunity** is a belief that the state should embody justice: there must be an assumption that it will treat individuals fairly, or justly, without regard to their 'identity' (as defined, for example, by their occupation, religion, gender or ethnicity). As a result, individuals within the liberal state must be able to assume a just outcome from any complaints they express and therefore a satisfactory resolution to any grievances they have with other individuals.

The liberal state: methods and structures

Having clarified the aims of a liberal state, it is now important to examine the methods whereby such objectives are guaranteed. For liberals, the structure of the state must embody three features:

■ constitutional/limited government
■ fragmented government
■ formal equality.

Constitutional/limited government

Consistent with its faith in government by consent, liberalism holds that the 'contract' between government and governed (see above) should be cemented by a formal constitution. Furthermore, in keeping with its faith in rationalism, this constitution should be preceded by extensive discussion and consensus over what government should do and how it should do it. In this way, constitutional rule is in stark contrast to the arbitrary rule characteristic of monarchical states, where rulers often did whatever they pleased, using whatever methods they wished.

For this reason, constitutional government may be described as **limited government**, with a liberal constitution imposing upon government two broad limitations. First, it ensures that governments must govern according to prearranged rules and procedures, and not in a random, ad hoc fashion. Second, a liberal constitution is designed to prevent governments from eroding the natural rights of their citizens — a restriction often brought about via mechanisms like a Bill of Rights (see Box 1.2).

Fragmented government

The focus on limited government produces another key feature of a liberal state's structure, namely the dispersal or fragmentation of state power. Again, this was brought about largely as a reaction against pre-Enlightenment states where power was concentrated in the monarchy. As Lord Acton (1834–1902) famously observed, 'power tends to corrupt...and absolute power tends to corrupt absolutely'. Fragmented government also reflects liberalism's belief in the rationality of mankind: if individuals are generally reasonable, and inclined to self-determination, it seems logical to empower as many individuals as possible in the exercise of a state's functions.

This idea of fragmented political power has its most celebrated embodiment in the Constitution of the United States. Heavily indebted to the ideas of Locke, it introduces a series of 'checks and balances', designed to avoid power being concentrated. Since then, such checks and balances have become common in liberal states across the world, and are exemplified in Box 1.2.

> **Activity**
>
> Explain, in approximately 100 words, why liberals believe in the fragmentation of political power.

Box 1.2

The liberal state: how is power dispersed?

- A formal 'separation of powers', between the executive, legislature and judiciary.
- A separation of powers within the legislature itself, so as to produce a 'bicameral' (two-house) legislature.
- A Bill of Rights, immune to the short-term decisions of governments.
- A Supreme Court, to uphold any Bill of Rights, and whose decisions override those of elected governments.
- A federal system of government, whereby many of the state's functions are delegated to various regional governments.

Formal equality

Given the liberal belief in foundational equality (that all individuals are born with equal rights), it would be illogical for a liberal state not to reflect this in its own structures. As such, the liberal state strives for formal equality, where all individuals have the same legal and political rights in society. It places significant emphasis on the doctrine of the 'rule of law', which holds that laws passed in a liberal state are applicable to everyone, with no exemptions granted on the basis of status. In short, no one should be outside the law, but no one should be above it either. Likewise, the procedures whereby the law takes its course — as prescribed by a liberal constitution — will apply to all citizens.

Formal quality is also linked to the idea of equal political rights — for example, the equal right to petition a parliament, the equal right to invoke a Bill of Rights before the courts, or the equal right to criticise the state while exercising the 'natural' (and legally protected) right to freedom of speech and publication.

> **Activity**
>
> In no more than 200 words, outline the aims, structures and procedures of a liberal constitution.

Different types of liberalism

As indicated at the start of this chapter, liberalism may be seen as an ambiguous ideology. To see why, and to understand how liberals can differ, it is helpful to look at its two principal strands: classical liberalism and modern liberalism. It is important to remember, however, that both strands uphold the core values of liberalism examined earlier in this chapter. The variations occur merely in respect of how these values might be applied.

Classical liberalism (late seventeenth–late nineteenth centuries)

Given its timespan of two centuries, classical liberalism (or original liberalism) is itself somewhat ambiguous, and includes a diverse cast of politicians and philosophers. For this reason, it is helpful to divide it into two sections: early classical liberalism and later classical liberalism.

Early classical liberalism (late seventeenth century and eighteenth century)

Early classical liberalism represents the attempt, during the late seventeenth and the eighteenth centuries, to relate the ideology's core beliefs to the political and economic climate of the time. It had four distinctive features:

- revolutionary potential
- negative liberty
- minimal state
- **laissez-faire capitalism**.

Revolutionary potential

As we have seen, Locke's argument for government by consent, and the notion that a state should be driven by the representatives (not masters) of the people, is one of the most important 'core' principles of liberalism; it therefore applies to all strands of liberal thinking. Yet, in the context of the seventeenth and eighteenth centuries, it needs to be emphasised that such Lockean ideas — now commonplace in western democracies — required vigorous argument and sometimes revolutionary upheaval.

In repudiating the twin pillars of the traditional European state (absolute monarchical power and the 'divine right of kings'), Locke's philosophy became associated with England's Glorious Revolution of 1688, which duly secured constitutional government and the end of concentrated political power. Locke's blueprint for representative government also inspired both the American revolt against the British crown after 1775 and the

> ### Key term
>
> **Laissez-faire capitalism**
> Based on the liberal belief in private property, and the classical liberal belief in 'negative liberty', this is an economic system which allows private enterprise and capitalism to operate with little or no interference from the state.

subsequent American Constitution of 1787 — both of which reflected his insistence upon natural rights, the separation of powers and the principle of government by consent.

Similarly, the core liberal idea of rationalism — that humanity's prime characteristic was a capacity for reason and logic — was far from firmly accepted in the eighteenth century; neither was the central liberal idea that society should be geared to maximum individual freedom. Other key thinkers within classical liberalism, such as **Mary Wollstonecraft** (1759–97) (see 'Key thinker 2' box), argued that the treatment of women during this period was a general affront to reason and a particular affront to the individual liberty of half the adult population. Wollstonecraft duly contested that English society in the eighteenth century could only conceive of women as emotional creatures, suited to marriage and motherhood but little else. As Wollstonecraft observed, instead of developing their individual potential, Hanoverian society contrived to 'keep women in a state of listless inactivity and stupid acquiescence'.

Wollstonecraft's subsequent argument — that individual men *and* women required a formal education to release their innate powers of reason — would later be seen as indisputably liberal; yet during the eighteenth and early nineteenth centuries, such arguments were considered dangerously radical by most in authority.

Negative liberty

Early classical liberals, such as Voltaire (1694–1778) and Charles-Louis Montesquieu (1689–1755), were conscious that individual liberty — a crucial 'natural right' — was vital to self-determination and self-reliance, as well as being the condition of government by consent. In England, early 'liberal-feminists', like Wollstonecraft, also tried to relate such ideas to the individual liberty of women. However, early classical liberals were also conscious that 'liberty' was a somewhat vague term, which needed clarification if individualism were to be protected. So what was meant by 'liberty'?

The definition that emerged from classical liberal thinking would later be termed **negative liberty**, one which saw freedom as the absence of restraint. Individuals should therefore assume that they were 'naturally' free until something or someone put a brake on their actions. According to this definition, therefore, a man alone on a desert island might be lonely, but he could still exercise a high degree of personal freedom: an assumption complementing one of liberalism's core beliefs that individuals were potentially autonomous, atomistic and self-reliant. For early classical liberals, this definition would have consequences for both the size of the state and the emerging 'science' of economics.

Key term

Negative liberty A key feature of classical liberalism, this is a notion of freedom that involves individuals being left alone to pursue their destiny. Any attempt to interfere with individual actions may therefore be judged an infringement of liberty.

Mary Wollstonecraft (1759–97)

While John Locke laid the foundations of liberal thought in the seventeenth century, one of those who developed classical liberal ideas in the eighteenth century was Mary Wollstonecraft. Her most important publication, *A Vindication of the Rights of Woman* (1792), remains a classic of political thought and is still strongly linked to feminist ideology. Yet, though gender was crucial to her work, her arguments were actually rooted in liberal philosophy.

■ Wollstonecraft's primary claim was that the Enlightenment's optimistic view of human nature, and the assumption that it was guided by reason, should apply to all human beings, male and female. She went on to argue that in eighteenth-century England, both society and state implied that women were not rational, and they were thus denied individual freedom and formal equality. Women, for example, were rarely allowed land ownership or remunerative employment and sacrificed what little individualism they had in order to become wives. Once married, a woman had little legal protection against violence inflicted by her spouse, and no recourse to divorce. Furthermore, women could not vote for those who governed them — a blatant violation, Wollstonecraft pointed out, of 'government by consent'.

■ Yet Wollstonecraft was not simply a spokesperson for women's interests. She argued that as a result of fettering female individualism, nations like England were limiting their stock of intelligence, wisdom and morality. As Wollstonecraft observed,

'such arrangements are not conditions where reason and progress may prosper'. She asserted that the effective denial of liberty to an entire gender left society vulnerable to doctrines that threatened the whole spirit of the Enlightenment.

■ Like many upholders of 'classical' liberal ideals, Wollstonecraft welcomed both the American Revolution of 1776 and the French Revolution of 1789. Indeed, her other major work, *A Vindication of the Rights of Men* (1790), attacked Edmund Burke's critique of the French Revolution and his related defence of custom, history and aristocratic rule (see Chapter 2). Wollstonecraft thus stressed her support for republican government and formal equality, involving a constitutional defence of individual rights. But such formal equality, she restated, must be accorded to all individuals, and not just to men. For that reason, she applauded the French Revolution's emphasis upon 'citizens' and its apparent indifference to gender differences.

■ Wollstonecraft conceded that women themselves were complicit in their subjugation, generally desiring only marriage and motherhood. For this to be corrected, she argued, formal education should be made available to as many women (and men) as possible. Without such formal tuition, she contested, individuals could never develop their rational faculties, never realise their individual potential and never recognise the 'absurdity' of illiberal principles such as the divine right of kings.

Activity

Summarise, in no more than 200 words, how Wollstonecraft's early feminism relates to liberalism's core values.

Minimal state

The notion of negative freedom defined the answer to another key question facing early classical liberals: just how much governing should the new constitutional states undertake? Given that liberty was now seen as the absence of restraint, the answer became obvious: governments should not just be limited in terms of how they could act, but also limited in terms of what they would do. In other words, the limited state should co-exist with the **minimal state**.

The case for the minimal state was perhaps best summarised by Thomas Jefferson (1743–1826), one of the USA's Founding Fathers, who noted:

> 'The government that is best is that which governs least... when government grows, our liberty withers.'

The notion of a minimal state also served to strengthen classical liberalism's faith in the dispersal of political power: a state with assorted checks and balances, after all, would be one where bold state action was fraught with difficulty — and therefore infrequent.

Laissez-faire capitalism

Negative liberty and a belief in minimal government eventually led classical liberalism into the realms of economic activity. More specifically, it became linked to the issue of how the state should respond to the emergence of capitalism in the eighteenth century.

The most famous response, that of Adam Smith's *The Wealth of Nations* (1776), became one of the most important expressions of classical liberalism and, arguably, the original economics textbook. Smith duly argued that capitalism, via the 'invisible hand' of market forces, had a limitless capacity to enrich society and the individuals within it. The wealth acquired by individuals would accordingly 'trickle down' to the rest of the population — just as long as the state took a laissez-faire (let-it-happen) approach to the workings of a market economy.

Smith therefore advocated the end of tariffs and duties, which had 'protected' domestic producers, and the spread of 'free trade' between nation-states and their commercial classes. In the UK, these ideas were radical in 1776, but became orthodox in the century that followed.

Key term

Minimal state A feature of classical liberalism, the minimal state was one that reflected the concept of 'negative liberty' by minimising state activities — for example, legislating and taxing as infrequently as possible, while confining its range to areas such as defence and the protection of private property.

John Stuart Mill feared 'the tyranny of the majority'.

Later classical liberalism (early–mid nineteenth century)

By the 1800s, countries like Britain and the USA looked very different to the societies surveyed by Locke and the Founding Fathers. They had become more industrialised; most individuals now worked and lived in an urban environment; individuals had a growing sense of class consciousness; and, as a result, there was growing interest in concepts like democracy and socialism.

In such a changed environment, classical liberals faced a serious challenge if their core ideas were to remain relevant. A response duly came, but it was far from uniform. The ideas of four 'late classical' liberals provide an indication of how variable the response was.

Jeremy Bentham (1748–1832), known as the father of utilitarian philosophy, developed a supposedly scientific alternative to natural rights theory, based on the idea that each individual would seek to maximise their own 'utility' by maximising personal pleasure and minimising personal pain. Yet Bentham also acknowledged that, in an industrialised society, this could produce more clashes between individuals than early classical liberals had envisaged. As a result, he suggested that the liberal state would need to be more proactive, using the algebraic formula of 'the greatest happiness of the greatest number' to inform legislation and government policy. In the process Bentham laid the foundations of 'political science' and provided liberalism with one of its earliest justifications for democracy: as Bentham observed, governments were more likely to follow the 'greatest happiness of the greatest number' if they were elected by and accountable to 'the greatest number' of voters.

Samuel Smiles (1812–1904), fearing that individualism was threatened by the advent of socialism, with its related calls for more state provision, argued in his influential book *Self Help* (1859) that self-reliance was still perfectly feasible for most individuals, including members of the new working class. Smiles acknowledged that industrialised societies made it harder for individuals to be self-reliant: an increasing number were faceless employees in a bulging factory system. Yet Smiles argued that, in seeking to overcome the new obstacles, individuals would merely be challenged more rigorously and, in the process, become more fully developed. If 'self-help were usurped by state help', Smiles argued, 'human beings would remain stunted, their talents unknown, and their liberty squandered'.

Herbert Spencer (1820–1903), a contemporary of Smiles, acknowledged the importance of self-help and echoed Smiles' contempt for more state intervention. However, in *Man Versus the State* (1884), Spencer questioned Smiles' belief that all individuals could rise to the challenge of self-help, noting the presence of 'the feeble, the feckless and the failing' in many Victorian cities. Fearing that this 'feeble' minority could justify the extension of state power, and therefore (what he saw as) an erosion of the majority's freedom, Spencer sought to apply the principles of 'natural selection', recently unveiled to science by Charles Darwin. In what became known as 'social Darwinism', Spencer restated the classical liberal belief in a minimal state and negative freedom, claiming that this would lead to 'the survival of the fittest' and the gradual elimination of those unable to enjoy the benefits of individualism. The eventual outcome would be a society where rational self-reliance was the norm and where individual freedom could thrive.

In terms of long-term importance, however, Bentham, Smiles and Spencer were eclipsed by John Stuart Mill. Mill's contribution to philosophy in general was immense, with some of his ideas summarised in the 'Key thinker 3' box. Indeed, some have suggested that Mill's ideas represent a separate strand of liberalism, known as transitional liberalism or developmental individualism. Mill's contribution to liberalism and political thought was crucial, given that it took place at a time — the mid-nineteenth century — when many liberals were struggling to work out how liberalism (with its stress upon individualism) could harness trends towards universal suffrage (with its capacity for what Mill himself termed 'the tyranny of the majority'). Mill's response to this dilemma would have a profound effect upon the way in which later liberals reconciled themselves to democratic governance.

Anticipating universal suffrage, Mill updated Locke's case for representative government into a case for representative democracy. Under this model, the enlarged electorate would not make policy decisions themselves but elect

Jeremy Bentham: author of utilitarianism

liberally minded representatives to make decisions for them. When making those decisions, such representatives would not simply side with the majority view, they would seek to aggregate the various opinions within society so as to produce the broad consent of all. In putting forward this particular model of democracy, Mill also equipped later liberals to rebut alternative models — such as 'direct' democracy — which he claimed were much more conducive to the 'tyranny of the majority'.

Mill was still concerned, however, that during the mid-nineteenth century most would-be voters were ill-equipped to choose 'intelligent' representatives to act 'rationally' on their behalf. With that in mind, Mill argued that universal suffrage must be preceded by universal education, hoping this would promote **developmental individualism**. By this, Mill meant the advancement of individual potential, so as to produce a liberal consensus in society; this in turn would safeguard tolerance, reason and individualism. Meanwhile, a vote would be withheld from the illiterate and unschooled, while those with a university education (like Mill) would receive more than one vote.

Once widespread education had been secured, Mill argued, democracy could actually further liberal values — promoting, for example, political education and opportunities for enlightening debate. Such a progressive society, Mill argued, could allow a pleasing refinement of Bentham's utilitarianism: 'the greatest happiness of the greatest number' could then be a calculation made by politicians *and* voters, thus encouraging ordinary citizens to consider and aggregate everyone's interests, not just their own, when forming a political judgement.

Despite his commitment to mass education, Mill remained vague about how it would be provided. As someone wedded to the classical liberal ideas of a minimal state and negative freedom, he was reluctant to countenance extensive state provision of schooling. But this key issue was one that his successors, the so-called modern liberals, were prepared to answer with more clarity and boldness — and not just in relation to education.

Key term

Developmental individualism This relates to the liberal philosophy of John Stuart Mill, who wished to focus on what individuals *could* become rather than what they *had* become. It explained Mill's strong emphasis upon the value of formal education within a liberal society.

Key thinker 3

John Stuart Mill (1806–73)

Regarded by many as one of the greatest English philosophers, John Stuart Mill's contribution to liberal thought is immense. The son of utilitarian philosopher James Mill, John Stuart was not just an intellectual but also, at varying points in his life, a politician and campaigner who served to develop the ideas posited by Locke, Wollstonecraft and others. He would also provide a valuable bridge between classical liberalism and the 'modern' liberalism that proved so important in the twentieth century, which explains why Mill's political ideas are often said to represent 'transitional liberalism' and 'developmental individualism'.

■ Mill's most enduring idea, outlined in his seminal work *On Liberty* (1859), was one which later became known as 'negative freedom'. Put simply, it argued that freedom mainly involved an absence of restraint. This connected to Mill's 'harm principle' — the notion that an individual's actions should always be tolerated, by either the state or other individuals, unless it could be demonstrated that such actions would harm others.

■ With a view to clarifying tolerance, Mill divided human actions into 'self-regarding' and 'other regarding'. The former (involving, for example, religious worship or robust expression of personal views) did not impinge on the freedom of others in society and therefore should be tolerated; the latter (involving, for example, violent or riotous behaviour) clearly did 'harm' the freedom of others in society and therefore should not be tolerated by a liberal state. The tolerance of diverse opinions was especially important, Mill argued, because it would ensure new ideas emerged while bad ideas were exposed via open, rational debate.

■ Mill's importance lay in the fact that many of his arguments represented something more sophisticated than that provided by early classical liberalism. He saw liberty, for example, not just as a 'natural right' and an end in itself but as the engine of ongoing human development. As such, Mill's human nature was never the 'finished article' (as it had been for earlier liberals); there was always room for improvement.

■ This naturally affected Mill's approach to the core liberal principle of individualism. Mill did not just want to liberate individuals as they were at present; instead, he pondered what individuals could become — a concept he termed 'individuality' and which has since been referred to as developmental individualism. As he famously stated, it was 'better to be Socrates dissatisfied than a pig satisfied', while any support for liberty had to be 'grounded on the permanent interests of man as a progressive being'.

■ Mill's distinction between 'individualism' and 'individuality' would have crucial implications for how he approached the looming issue of democracy. He was particularly concerned that the timeless liberal principle of 'government by consent' would be compromised if the wishes of some individual citizens were overwhelmed by the wishes of most individual citizens. In other words, Mill feared that a democratic state had the potential to create a 'tyranny of the majority'.

Activity

Summarise, in no more than 200 words, why Mill thought democracy carried dangers and how he thought those dangers could be countered.

Liberal democracy: a contradiction in terms?

Yes

- Democracy tends to be guided by majorities. It therefore threatens some individuals with the 'tyranny of the majority'.
- Classical liberals favoured a limited electorate, so as to safeguard property rights.
- John Stuart Mill thought votes should be given only to those with appropriate, formal education.
- Modern liberals flirt with supranational bodies like the European Union, where there is a 'democratic deficit'.
- Liberals seek to mitigate democracy's effects via assorted constitutional devices (e.g. Bill of Rights, Supreme Court).

No

- Democracy complements individualism, allowing individuals to shape their lives via the ballot box.
- Democracy complements 'government by consent'.
- Democracy helps avoid the concentration of political power.
- Democracy is optimistic about human nature: it presupposes an intelligent electorate, capable of rational decisions.
- John Stuart Mill thought democracy would have an 'educative' effect upon voters and thus abet developmental individualism.

Modern liberalism (late nineteenth century–present)

As suggested at the end of the 'Key thinker 3' box, Mill did not just offer solutions to the dilemmas of liberalism in the late nineteenth century; he also raised a number of possibilities that later liberals could develop.

In particular, Mill's notion of individuality began to prompt fresh questions about the precise nature of 'liberty'. In order to liberate an individual's potential, was it really enough just to leave them alone (as supporters of negative freedom would argue)? Was it enough for the state simply to guarantee equal political rights and equality before the law?

The answers to such questions would produce a new and radical interpretation of what liberty involved, one that would lead to a very different form of liberalism. It was one that had a number of distinguishing characteristics.

Positive liberty/social justice

During the late nineteenth and early twentieth centuries, a number of English philosophers — later known as the 'new liberals' — re-examined the core principles of liberalism and reached radical conclusions about liberty, individualism and society.

T.H. Green (1836–82), L.T. Hobhouse (1864–1929) and J.A. Hobson (1854–1940) were prepared to argue that modern, advanced societies made a mockery of the idea that individuals were innately autonomous. The nature of modern economics and society, they argued, meant individuals were increasingly subject to socio-economic forces beyond their control. Such forces would then make it impossible for affected individuals to seek self-determination and self-realisation, even though they might not have caused the socio-economic problems now restricting their liberty. As a result, these new liberals argued that social justice, as well as legal justice, was now required if individuals were to fulfil their potential.

This led Green and others to revise the meaning of liberty, so as to make it a less 'negative' concept. In other words, instead of freedom being seen merely as the absence of restraint, it would now be interpreted as something more cooperative and altruistic, namely some individuals enabling or empowering other individuals. This approach — helping others to help themselves — would then allow certain individuals to act in a way that would have been impossible had they simply been left alone: a concept that became known as **positive freedom**.

The new liberals thus asserted that individuals had to be enabled in order for them to be free from socio-economic problems (such as poor health care, unemployment or a lack of education) and for social justice to be secured. But this raised an obvious question: how might this 'enabling' take place? This leads to the second feature of modern liberalism.

Enlarged and enabling state

As we saw earlier in the chapter, classical liberalism was strongly associated with the idea of minimal government — one that was closely linked to a belief in 'negative' liberty. By contrast, modern liberalism had no qualms about claiming that only a larger state could repel the new, socio-economic threats to freedom and individualism. Consequently, modern liberals like **John Rawls** (1921–2002) (see 'Key thinker 4' box) found themselves justifying a substantial extension of the state in the name of individual liberty: more laws, more state spending, more taxation and more state bureaucracy. In short, this brand of liberalism became strongly linked to *collectivism*, some examples of which are listed in Box 1.3.

Key term

Positive freedom A vital aspect of modern liberalism, this term denotes the belief that individuals left alone are often inhibited rather than 'free'. Such individuals may need enabling so that they are 'free' to exercise their individual talents.

Activity

Examine, in approximately 200 words, the extent to which liberals disagree about freedom.

Box 1.3

The quest for social justice: examples of modern liberal collectivism

- Liberal government 1906–1910: in the UK, it was a Liberal government, led by Herbert Asquith (1852–1928) and his chancellor David Lloyd-George (1863–1945), that provided one of the earliest instances of modern liberalism in action. The most important illustration of this was the 'people's budget' of 1908, which introduced a state pension, designed to liberate people from the financial problems of old age and funded by increased taxation of property owners.

- The most influential liberal economist of the twentieth century, John Maynard Keynes (1883–1946), was a professed liberal, committed to the maintenance of a capitalist economy. But the economic depression of the 1920s and 1930s convinced him that neither individual freedom nor the survival of capitalist economies and constitutional states was served by the cyclical nature of laissez-faire capitalism. Mass unemployment, he feared, not only deprived millions of their individual freedom; it also paved the way for utterly illiberal doctrines such as fascism and communism.

- In his key work, *The General Theory of Employment, Interest, and Money* (1936), Keynes therefore argued that the state must constantly 'steer' the economy and manage demand so as to secure full employment, without which (according to Keynes) individual liberty would be difficult. Keynes's brand of dirigisme, or state-directed capitalism, duly influenced a series of western governments in the mid-twentieth century, shaping President F.D. Roosevelt's 'New Deal' in the USA in the 1930s and the economic strategy of every UK government between 1945 and 1979.

- The Beveridge Report: William Beveridge (1879–1963) was a liberal social scientist whose 1942 report, 'Social Insurance and Allied Services', proved the bedrock of Britain's post-war 'welfare state'. Developing the ideas first mooted by T.H. Green, Beveridge predicted that individuals in the post-war world faced 'five giants' threatening their freedom and individual potential: poverty, unemployment, poor education, poor housing and poor health care. In a powerful statement of modern liberal thinking, Beveridge argued that these threats could be overcome only through a major extension of state provision (such as a national health service).

Activity

Summarise, in approximately 200 words, the 'modern liberalism' of one presidency in the USA. (Those of F.D. Roosevelt, J.F. Kennedy and Barack Obama might be examples.)

Key term

Enabling state Linked to the notion of positive liberty, an enabling state was one that extended its activities so as to 'liberate' individuals from restrictive social and economic problems, thus 'enabling' them to fulfil their potential.

Having embraced collectivism, modern liberalism faced the charge (from liberal critics like Friedrich von Hayek) that it had betrayed the fundamental principles of classical liberalism and had seriously blurred the distinction between liberalism and socialism. Later modern liberals, notably John Rawls, resisted such a suggestion, arguing that only an enlarged state could guarantee the equality of opportunity necessary to enable individual freedom.

Rawls insisted, however, that while an enlarged state would require some individuals to sacrifice more of their earnings to the state in the form of progressive taxation, those same individuals could still be persuaded that this was a good and necessary thing (see 'Key thinker 4' box). That being so, Rawls argued, the **enabling state** was perfectly consistent with the liberal principle of government by consent.

Rawls also pointed out that, while modern liberalism wished to improve the lot of society's least fortunate (via extensive state intervention), it remained indifferent to inequality of outcome. For modern liberals, this was the inevitable side effect of individual freedom and was the key difference with socialism. The priority, Rawls insisted, was to ameliorate the social and economic condition of society's most deprived members and thus enable them to exploit their individual potential and achieve control of their lives. As long as this occurred, Rawls contested, the gap between society's poorest and most prosperous elements was of secondary concern (a claim most socialists would vigorously refute).

Key thinker 4

John Rawls (1921–2002)

An American philosopher, Rawls is thought to be the most important exponent of modern liberalism in the twentieth century. Rawls' major work, *A Theory of Justice* (1971), remains a key reference for students of liberal thinking. It had two principal objectives:

- First, to restate the idea that the core liberal principle of 'foundational equality' meant individuals required not just formal equality under the law and constitution but also greater social and economic equality. This was necessary, Rawls argued, to ensure the just society, where all lives could be rich and fulfilled. Yet this could be provided, Rawls stated, only by a significant redistribution of wealth via an enabling state, with extensive public spending and progressive taxation.
- Second, *A Theory of Justice* set out to show that such a redistribution of wealth was not (as Friedrich von Hayek had suggested) a 'surrender to socialism' but perfectly consistent with liberal principles. To do this, Rawls constructed a series of philosophical conditions. The first of these was termed 'the original position', whereby individuals would be asked to construct from scratch a society they judged to be superior to the one they lived in currently. Central to such an exercise would be questions about how wealth and power should be distributed. The second condition was one Rawls termed the 'veil of ignorance', whereby

individuals would have no preconceptions about the sort of people they themselves might be in this new society. They might, for example, be white or they might be from an ethnic majority; they might be rich or they might be poor.

- Rawls argued that when faced with such conditions, human nature — being rational and empathetic — would lead individuals to choose a society where the poorest members fared significantly better than in present society. From a liberal angle, Rawls argued that the key point here was that this 'fairer' society, where inequalities were reduced, was the one individuals would *choose*. So an enlarged state, with higher taxation and significant wealth redistribution, was indeed consistent with liberalism's historic stress upon government by consent.
- Rawls denied this was simply a fresh justification for socialism and egalitarianism. He noted that though most individuals would indeed choose to improve the lot of the poorest, they would still want considerable scope for individual liberty, self-fulfilment and, therefore, significant inequalities of outcome. So although Rawls argued that the lot of the poor should be improved by the state, he did not argue that the gap between the richest and the poorest should necessarily be narrowed — thus ensuring that his philosophy was still distinct from socialism.

Activity

Summarise, in no more than 200 words, how Rawls reconciled liberal principles to the growth of state intervention.

Constitutional reform/liberal democracy

The third feature of modern liberalism has been a passion for ongoing, constitutional change. Put another way, precisely because it has sought to extend the state, modern liberalism has also been keen to reform it. As Hobhouse observed: 'If the state is to be enlarged, it must also be improved.'

If only to secure the principle of government by consent, modern liberalism has been associated with ongoing constitutional reform, so as to update this key liberal principle. In the UK, such liberal demands for reform have included a written or codified constitution, devolution of power from central government to regional government, electoral reform (especially proportional representation), and a more accountable House of Lords.

Yet the most important facet of modern liberalism's interest in constitutional reform has been its support for liberal democracy — in other words, completing the link between core liberal values and universal adult suffrage. So, in the UK for example, it was a Liberal prime minister who (in 1918) oversaw the enfranchisement of most women and nearly all men, irrespective of property ownership. Likewise, since 1945, UK liberals have tended to champion a lowering of the voting age, first (in 1969) to 18 and more recently to 16.

However, modern liberalism's enthusiasm for democracy is not unqualified. It has shown little interest, for example, in direct democracy, fearing that referendums and initiatives threaten the 'tyranny of the majority', and has seemed willing to dilute even representative democracy in order to protect 'liberal' values. This has been demonstrated by modern liberals' support for the UK's Human Rights Act (which effectively transferred powers from elective representatives to unelected judges) and their widespread enthusiasm for supranational bodies like the European Union. Indeed, 'Eurosceptics' have often depicted the EU as a vehicle for 'liberal bureaucrats' afraid of democracy — allowing them, for example, to advance 'liberal' initiatives (such as tolerance and anti-xenophobia) without being hindered by accountability to voters. Meanwhile, many modern liberals certainly regarded the outcome of the UK's EU referendum of 2016 — in which 48 per cent of voters wished to 'remain' — as a particularly unfortunate example of 'the tyranny of the majority', and a vindication of Mill's argument that such vital decisions were best left to a more liberally minded parliament.

Activity

Explain, in approximately 100 words, the links between social liberalism and classical liberalism.

Debate 2

Has modern liberalism abandoned the principles of classical liberalism?

Yes

- Classical liberalism defined liberty as individuals being left alone (negative freedom). Modern liberals think individuals are not free unless they are actively 'enabled' via interference from others (positive freedom).
- Classical liberalism championed a minimal state. Modern liberals champion an enlarged, enabling state.
- Classical liberalism was inclined to see taxation as 'theft' and sought to restrict it. Modern liberals often see increased taxation as the key method for implementing positive freedom.
- Classical liberalism favoured laissez-faire capitalism from which the state is detached. Modern liberals favour Keynesian capitalism, where the state seeks to 'manage' market forces.
- Classical liberalism had an ambivalent view of democracy, prioritising instead the interests of property owners. Modern liberalism has championed representative democracy.

No

- Both classical and modern liberalism have an optimistic view of human potential.
- Both classical and modern liberalism believe in rationalism and insist upon tolerance of minorities.
- Both classical and modern liberalism see individualism as the goal of politics and society — they differ merely about how to achieve it.
- Both classical and modern liberalism believe in capitalism and oppose state ownership of the economy.
- Both classical and modern liberalism believe in a constitutional ('limited') state and 'government by consent'.

Social liberalism

The final aspect of modern liberalism is its attempt to update classical liberalism's stress on tolerance — especially the tolerance of minorities. This argument has since become known as **social liberalism**.

From the mid-twentieth century onwards, modern liberalism became strongly linked with calls for greater racial and sexual toleration, with key thinkers like Betty Friedan (see 'Key thinker 5' box) arguing that too many individuals in western society were held back on account of innate factors such as ethnicity, gender, sexual orientation and physical disability. Given their acceptance of positive liberty and an enlarged state, modern liberals like Friedan argued that the solutions to these problems lay in further legislation, further state regulation and, sometimes, 'positive discrimination' (known in the USA as 'affirmative action'). This involved the state and other employers correcting an historical imbalance, by discriminating in favour of individuals from groups that were said to have been discriminated against previously, thus securing greater equality of opportunity.

From the 1960s onwards, modern liberalism thus became associated with initiatives like President Kennedy's Equal

Key term

Social liberalism This represents an updated version of the historic liberal belief in tolerance. It involves legislation that may criminalise actions that discriminate against individuals on the grounds of race, gender, sexual orientation, disability and religious persuasion.

Employment Opportunity Commission (EEOC), which required those managing projects financed by the state to take 'affirmative action' in respect of hiring employees from racial minorities. In the UK, meanwhile, modern liberals gave strong backing to legislation like the Race Relations Act 1976 and the Sex Discrimination Act 1975, which criminalised various forms of negative discrimination against ethnic minorities and women respectively.

Betty Friedan's importance to modern liberalism lay in her insistence that such reforms were perfectly consistent in many ways with the liberal tradition. Citing Mill's 'harm principle', Friedan claimed that laws criminalising sexual discrimination, for example, were designed merely to prevent some female individuals having their freedoms 'harmed' by others. Consistent with modern liberalism's support for an enlarged state, these laws were usually accompanied by interventionist agencies like the EEOC. Yet, as Friedan explained, these agencies were still consistent with the liberal state's original aim, namely the protection and advancement of natural rights.

Activity

Explain, in no more than 100 words, why Friedan's feminist views were consistent with liberalism in general and modern liberalism in particular.

Key thinker 5

Betty Friedan (1921–2006)

Betty Friedan is linked mainly to the development of feminist ideology, via her acclaimed work *The Feminine Mystique* (1963). Yet her ideas have also served to broaden liberalism's interest in equality of opportunity.

- As with all liberals, a concern for individualism lay at the heart of Friedan's philosophy. As such, she insisted that all individuals should be free to seek control over their own lives and the full realisation of their potential. Yet, in *The Feminine Mystique*, she argued — like Mary Wollstonecraft almost two centuries earlier — that gender was a serious hindrance to all those individuals who were female.
- Friedan argued that it was illiberal attitudes in society, rather than human nature, that condemned most women to underachievement. She contested that these attitudes were nurtured and transmitted via society's various 'cultural channels', notably schools, organised religion, the media, and mainstream literature, theatre and cinema.

These channels of 'cultural conditioning' left many women convinced that their lot in life was determined by human nature rather than their own rationality and enterprise. Friedan sought to challenge this 'irrational' assumption.

- Friedan's reputation as a liberal, as well as feminist, thinker was underlined by the fact that she always disdained violence or illegality as a means of pursuing change, arguing that significant progress was possible via legal equality, brought about by the procedures of a liberal state. She thus acknowledged the principles of the US Constitution (widely seen as a document inspired by the philosophy of John Locke) and endorsed its capacity to allow continuous improvement to individuals' lives. Consequently, she rejected the more radical feminist argument — that the state was 'patriarchal' and forever under the control of the dominant gender — in favour of a theory consistent with liberal constitutionalism.

Neo-liberalism: liberalism or conservatism?

By the end of the twentieth century, neo-liberalism was a widely recognised branch of political ideology, and a term often used by commentators to describe political thinking in countries like the UK and the USA. Yet there seems to be some confusion as to whether it is an expression of liberal or conservative thinking.

Friedrich von Hayek: doyen of neo-liberals

For neo-liberalism's most distinguished exponent, Austrian philosopher Friedrich von Hayek (1899–1992), there was absolute certainty that neo-liberalism represented the 'third strand' of liberal ideology. In his seminal work *The Road to Serfdom* (1944), Hayek was adamant that he was 'not a conservative', later arguing that he and like-minded philosophers such as Karl Popper, and like-minded economists such as Milton Friedman, favoured radical change, not conservative stability — a choice, Hayek argued, based upon their boundless faith in human potential.

As a self-proclaimed liberal, Hayek also had little time for conservatism's rigid defence of the constitutional status quo (especially when it involved a defence of hereditary influence), and was as passionate as most other liberals in respect of constitutional reforms that checked executive power. Recent neo-liberals, such as those at the Adam Smith Institute, have also opposed some of the social policies associated with conservatism. The Cameron government's promotion of marriage via the tax system, for instance, has been attacked as an unwelcome example of state intrusion into people's private lives (although neo-liberals would welcome the state's promotion of social liberalism, via the granting of equal status to gay couples).

So what makes neo-liberalism a distinctive branch of liberalism? First, it seeks to update the principles of classical liberalism within a twentieth- and twenty-first-century setting, aiming (for example) to reapply the ideas of Adam Smith and Thomas Jefferson to modern societies and modern, globalised economies. Second, it offers a liberal critique of modern liberalism, accusing it of a betrayal of individualism and a 'sell-out' to both socialism and conservatism. The Beveridge Report, for example, with its talk of the state supporting the people 'from cradle to grave', was criticised by Hayek for fostering a form of 'state paternalism', or 'dependency culture', while legitimising an endless extension of state restraint upon individual initiative.

Spurred on by the crises of the 1970s — when the efficiency of both Keynesian economics and welfare spending were brought into question — neo-liberals have thus re-advertised the merits of negative freedom and a minimal state, calling for politicians to 'roll back the frontiers of the state' and thereby 'set the people free'. Specifically, neo-liberals have demanded a reduction in public spending, often facilitated by the privatisation of public services, and much less state regulation of the economy. This, in turn, would allow lower rates of taxation and a gradual replacement of the 'dependency culture' with a new ethos of enterprising individualism.

Yet, despite their protestations of being 'real' liberals, neo-liberals have routinely been labelled as conservatives. This is partly because their views are thought to be reactionary rather than progressive, seeking to restore the economic arrangements of the nineteenth century as opposed to promoting innovative and novel ideas for the future. It is also undeniable that neo-liberal ideas have played a key role in the development of New Right conservatism, via politicians like Margaret Thatcher and Ronald Reagan. The relationship between neo-liberalism and conservatism will therefore be explored in more detail in Chapter 2.

The key liberals and their themes are summed up below.

Activity

Examine, in approximately 100 words, the links between classical and neo-liberalism.

Summary: key themes and key thinkers

	Human nature	The state	Society	The economy
John Locke	Human beings are rational, guided by the pursuit of self-interest, but mindful of others' concerns.	The state must be representative, based on the consent of the governed.	Society predates the state: there were 'natural' societies with natural laws and natural rights.	State policy should respect the 'natural right' to private property and arbitrate effectively between individuals competing for trade and resources.
Mary Wollstonecraft	Rationalism defines both genders: intellectually, men and women are not very different.	The monarchical state should be replaced by a republic which enshrines women's rights.	Society 'infantilised' women and thus stifled female individualism.	A free-market economy would be energised by the enterprise of liberated women.
John Stuart Mill	Though fundamentally rational, human nature is not fixed: it is forever progressing to a higher level.	The state should proceed cautiously towards representative democracy, mindful of minority rights.	The best society was one where 'individuality' co-existed with tolerance and self-improvement.	Laissez-faire capitalism was vital to progress, individual enterprise and individual initiative.
John Rawls	Mankind is selfish yet empathetic, valuing both individual liberty and the plight of those around them.	The state should enable less fortunate individuals to advance, via public spending and public services.	The society most individuals would choose would be one where the condition of the poorest improved.	Free-market capitalism should be tempered by the state's obligation to advance its poorest citizens.
Betty Friedan	Human nature has evolved in a way that discourages self-advancement among women.	The state should legislate to prevent continued discrimination against female individuals.	Society remained chauvinistic towards women, though women were complicit in their repression.	Free-market capitalism could be an ally of female emancipation, if allied to legislation precluding sexual discrimination.

Tensions within liberalism

- **Human nature:** all liberals believe that individuals are generally rational, intelligent, keen to prioritise their individual happiness and fulfilment, and respectful of other individuals' wish to do the same. However, early classical liberals like Locke, and neo-liberals like Hayek, believe that individuals are innately blessed with such qualities, while Mill and modern liberals like Rawls tend to think that such qualities are *potential* features of human nature, to be developed by enlightened liberal authorities. This is why modern liberals endorse Mill's concept of individuality — one that refers to what individuals could *become*, once 'enabled' to fulfil their potential.

- **Society:** classical liberals believe that human society predates the state, while all liberals see society as a collection of diverse and potentially autonomous individuals, seeking self-determination, self-realisation and self-fulfilment. Modern liberals like Rawls, however, believe that industrialised and urban societies are those where individuals are less autonomous and therefore require state support to be free ('positive liberty'). Neo-liberals often see society as one where individuals have been stymied by 'positive liberty' and that the 'dependency culture' must now be corrected by a radical reduction of the state. Some neo-liberals might see the ideal situation as one where 'there is no such thing' as society, just a collection of atomised individuals pursuing self-interest.

- **The state:** all liberals believe that the state should function according to prearranged rules and procedures, with power fragmented and authority subject to the consent of the governed. However, liberals vary on the extent of state activity. Classical liberals like Mill, in accordance with 'negative' liberty, believe state intervention should be minimal and individuals left unchecked (unless they hamper the freedom of others). Modern liberals like Friedan, in accordance with the concept of 'positive liberty', believe state intervention should be much more extensive so as to 'enable' individuals to reach their potential. Liberals have also varied over how democratic the state should be. Modern liberals are satisfied that representative democracy enhances constitutional government, whereas early classical liberals saw democracy as a threat to property rights.

- **The economy:** following Locke's assertion that property is a 'natural right', all liberals believe that the economy should be based on private property and private enterprise. However, while classical liberals and neo-liberals support Adam Smith's thesis (that the state should adopt a laissez-faire attitude to the economy), modern liberals have more sympathy for the view of John Maynard Keynes (that capitalism requires regular state management to ensure full employment). Modern liberalism's belief in 'managed' capitalism also explains its support for supranational organisations like the European Union, which many neo-liberals see as an obstacle to global free trade.

Do liberals have a coherent view of the state?

Yes

- Liberals are optimistic, believing that human beings are rational. It is therefore coherent that liberals believe in a constitutional state, drawn up as a result of rational discussion.
- Liberals believe in 'government by consent'. It is therefore coherent that their constitutional state should be seen as a 'contract' between government and governed.
- Because of the 'contractual' nature of the liberal state, it is therefore coherent that liberals believe in 'limited government', with politicians restrained by the rules of the constitution.
- Liberal philosophers like Locke speak of a 'natural society' in which all individuals enjoy 'natural rights'. It is therefore coherent for liberals to support a 'limited state' that embodies such natural advantages via mechanisms such as a bill of rights.
- The liberal state was a reaction against the medieval state in which power was concentrated in the monarch. It is therefore coherent that the liberal state should be one in which power is more dispersed.

No

- The liberal state supposedly supports foundational equality, in which all individuals are treated equally. Yet the liberal state was slow to adopt the principles of democracy, sexual equality and universal adult suffrage.
- The liberal state extols the natural right to property. But it fails to recognise that most individuals under the state's jurisdiction have not owned property.
- The liberal state defends 'government by consent', yet its constitution allows the consent of a majority to sometimes be defied via courts and assorted 'checks and balances'.
- The liberal state is supposed to be 'limited', yet modern liberals have advocated a significant extension of state intervention in the name of 'positive liberty'.
- Modern liberals have compromised their belief in 'government by consent' by supporting supranational bodies like the European Union, which arguably erode the authority of elective parliaments and elected representatives.

Conclusion: liberalism today

During the last decade of the twentieth century and the first decade of the twenty-first, liberals had several reasons to be optimistic. The collapse of Soviet communism in 1989, and the emergence of new capitalist states in eastern Europe, strengthened the idea (put forward by US academic Francis Fukuyama) that market economics and liberal democracy represented 'the end of history', the goals to which all states eventually aspire.

This was reinforced by recognition of 'globalisation' — in other words, the worldwide spread of economic liberalism — as hitherto illiberal states like China and Russia eagerly embraced market forces and modern capitalism. And, as many modern liberal economists pointed out (with reference to undemocratic countries like China), once individuals are given economic choices, it is increasingly hard to deny them political and philosophical choices as well.

Meanwhile, in established liberal democracies like the UK and the USA, society seemed to be assuming an even more liberal character. The liberal doctrine of individual choice and self-determination, already fuelled by the expansion of capitalism, was extended by the state-sponsored tolerance of diverse lifestyles (exemplified by the UK's legalisation of same-sex marriage) and by the revolution in communications. Widespread ownership of mobile telephones and personalised computers, for example, and the growing ease with which individuals 'express themselves' (via phenomena such as Facebook and Twitter), all served to make society increasingly orientated towards individualism.

Such developments in society and the economy inevitably affected the tone of political debate. In the UK, for example, 'New Labour' embraced economic liberalism by revising Clause IV of the party's constitution (that which had committed it to 'common ownership'), while David Cameron's Conservative Party embraced social liberalism by, among other things, promoting same-sex marriage. Meanwhile, a concern for improved constitutional government (another constant of modern liberalism) became a recurrent feature of UK governments after 1997, with both the Blair and Cameron governments undertaking various constitutional initiatives designed to bolster 'government by consent'.

However, other developments after 2000 gave liberals serious cause for concern. First, the atrocities witnessed in the USA on 11 September 2001, and in the UK on 7 July 2005, marked the rise and spread of Islamist terrorism, an aggressive and apparently irrational phenomenon, which blatantly challenges the most basic of liberal values. Liberal democracies were naturally forced to respond to such challenges. Yet the nature of that response — increased state security, heightened surveillance of suspected individuals, restrictions on immigration — seemed only to threaten liberal values (such as tolerance) even further. Fears were also expressed that among certain religious communities in western states, there was growing support for radical, faith-based politics that again defied the tolerant principles of the Enlightenment.

Such fears were related to the fact that while globalisation had brought benefits, it had also brought problems — notably that of increased migration. In both Europe and the United States, the changes this brought led to a backlash in many of the communities concerned and the emergence of attitudes which were at odds with the liberal mindset. This duly prompted increased support for parties like the United Kingdom Independence Party and, of course, politicians like Donald Trump — so-called 'populist' political movements that, with growing public support, effectively defied the liberal consensus. Indeed,

Donald Trump: populist assailant of liberalism

growing public concern about the effects of both economic liberalism (such as free movement of labour) and social liberalism (such as the emergence of more culturally plural societies) informed the outcome of both the UK's 2016 referendum on EU membership and, later that year, the USA's presidential election.

Yet there were other reasons why liberalism faced fresh scrutiny in the twenty-first century. The financial crash of 2008, and the economic crises affecting the Eurozone countries after 2013, revived fundamental criticisms about market economics while refreshing support for socialist politicians opposing capitalism. The public enthusiasm aroused by 'anti-austerity' parties in Greece, Spain and Portugal, the election of Jeremy Corbyn as leader of the UK Labour Party, and the surprising impact of Bernie Sanders (in the run-up to the US presidential election of 2016) all indicated that liberal economics were not as securely grounded as many had thought.

The social and economic problems besetting liberal states today should cause us to revisit the father of liberalism. John Locke's political philosophy, outlined more than 300 years ago, rested heavily upon an imagined 'state of nature', which depicted the default position of humanity. Yet the state of nature Locke described was one of peace, prosperity and reason. So when the world seems anything but peaceful, prosperous and reasonable, Locke's view of human nature — and the relevance of liberalism itself — becomes questionable.

Debate 4

Can liberalism be reconciled to conservatism?*

Yes
- Liberals and conservatives support private property and capitalism.
- Liberals and conservatives see inequality of outcome as a sign of liberty.
- Liberals and conservatives deny the inevitability of class conflict.
- Modern liberals and conservatives support gradual reform and reject revolution.
- Neo-liberals and New Right conservatives reject Keynesian economics and champion a more laissez-faire economy.

No
- Liberals have an optimistic view of human nature; conservatives are sceptical.
- Liberals see rationalism as central to human behaviour; conservatives stress habit, emotion, instinct.
- Liberals prioritise individual liberation; conservatives stress order and restraint.
- Liberals see individuals as potentially autonomous; conservatives see individuals as communal.
- Liberals extol free-market capitalism; traditional conservatives are more sceptical and protectionist.

*This debate is best addressed after reading both this chapter and the chapter on conservatism.
A similar debate about liberalism and socialism is to be found in the chapter on socialism.

Further reading

Bloor, K. (2016) Is liberalism compatible with democracy? *Politics Review*, 26,2.
Emmett-Tyrrell, R. (2011) *The Death of Liberalism*, Thomas Nelson.
Graham, P. (2016) Have modern liberals abandoned individualism? *Politics Review*, 26,1.
Gray, J. (1995) *Liberalism*, Oxford University Press.
Kelly, P. (2005) *Liberalism*, Wiley-Blackwell.
Rawls, J. (2005) *Political Liberalism*, Columbia University Press.

Exam-style questions

Short questions

The following questions are similar to those in examinations set by AQA. Each carries 9 marks.

1 Explain and analyse the main features of the 'liberal state'.

2 Explain and analyse liberalism's support for a capitalist economy.

Essay questions

The following questions are similar to those in examinations set by Edexcel (Pearson) and AQA.

Edexcel (24 marks) or AQA (25 marks):

1 To what extent do modern and classical liberals agree over the nature of the state? You must use appropriate thinkers you have studied to support your answer.

2 To what extent can liberalism be reconciled to collectivism? You must use appropriate thinkers you have studied to support your answer.

AQA only (25 marks):

3 'Liberalism and democracy are incompatible.' Analyse and evaluate with reference to the thinkers you have studied.

4 Analyses and evaluate the compatibility of liberalism and equality, with reference to the thinkers you have studied.

Conservatism

Introduction: the 'politics of maintenance'

As we shall see in the course of this chapter, conservatism is a durable ideology that has responded to a series of remarkable changes over two centuries. Yet despite this durability, it is widely misunderstood. This may arise from two paradoxes that are worth explaining at the outset of this chapter.

The first paradox is that conservatism is a form of change. In other words, conservatism is not just about conserving, and certainly not about avoiding reform at all costs; instead it is a case of **changing to conserve**. In this sense, it is useful to distinguish between conservative politics and reactionary politics: whereas the latter seeks to resist all change, to restore what has been lost and 'turn back the clock', conservatism argues that such objectives are at best futile and at worst counter-productive.

So, for conservatives, change is inevitable; what matters is that change occurs in an appropriate manner — namely, one drawing upon all that is good about what has gone before. In fact, conservatives would assert that a certain type of change is the *only* way to conserve that which is worth conserving. As **Edmund Burke** (1729–97) (see 'Key thinker 2' box) put it: 'A state without the means of change...is without the means of its conservation.'

The Church of England and Parliament – two institutions conservatives seek to maintain

To understand this paradox, we need only recall that no living organism can survive by remaining in a state of inertia: it needs constant attention, nurturing and renewal. Similarly, the preservation of an ancient building will not come about through inaction and an absence of interference; it requires ongoing maintenance. In fact, a useful starting point for any understanding of conservatism is to see it as a 'doctrine of maintenance': one that advocates change, but in the form of ongoing repair and development rather than outright demolition and the construction of something entirely new.

The other paradox we should consider is that, within the UK, conservatism is not Conservatism. In other words, conservatism is not synonymous with the ideas of the Conservative Party. But it is useful to understand why this is the case.

The basic reason is that the Conservative Party, like many other centre-right parties in the developed world, does not just uphold the principles of conservatism; the party also reflects many of the liberal principles described in Chapter 1 (such as support for free markets and individual aspiration). In short, the Conservative Party is not just conservative; it is ideologically eclectic (as are most electorally successful political parties).

Conversely, not all conservatives are Conservative; Many of those who fear change, for example, see their greatest enemy as free-market capitalism, with all its iconoclastic side effects (such as globalisation). Yet market-driven change often finds its loudest support in the Conservative Party and its sternest opposition within supposedly progressive parties like Labour. Indeed, in recent years, the policies of the Labour Party have become increasingly defensive (in short, conservative) — for example, in respect of the NHS, the welfare state and (for most Labour MPs) UK membership of the European Union.

Clearly, conservatism is a more subtle doctrine than many might imagine. It therefore makes sense to examine its provenance.

The origins of conservatism

Although conservative politics should not be confused with reactionary politics, it is fair to say that the origins of conservatism were themselves a reaction — or, more specifically, a reaction to the politics of the Enlightenment (as described at the start of Chapter 1).

It will be recalled that at the heart of the Enlightenment was a belief in reason and remorseless progress; the notion that there was an 'ideal' society towards which politicians should strive, underpinned by tolerance, equality and individual rights. Indeed, by the second half of the eighteenth century, and certainly after the American Revolution of 1775–1783 (when American colonists successfully defied British imperial rule), it became difficult for politicians and philosophers to argue against the principles of the Enlightenment without appearing regressive and intolerant.

In England, at least, this was the period historians have termed 'the Whig supremacy'. Early liberal politicians, such as those found in the Whig Party, were confident that the progressive principles embodied by England's Glorious Revolution (1689) and America's Declaration of Independence (1776) were intellectually unquestionable and politically irresistible. By contrast, any critique of the Enlightenment seemed rooted in outdated, theocratic thinking — associated, for example, with a defence of monarchical absolutism and the 'divine right' of kings.

At first, the French Revolution of 1789 seemed to vindicate the optimistic spirit of the Enlightenment. The rapid and dramatic overthrow of the despotic French monarchy, the rejection of the 'irrational' religious assumptions that went with it, and the creation of a new Republic founded on 'liberté, égalité, fraternité' were all greeted with enthusiasm by European intellectuals, thrilled that a huge continental power was embracing the ideas of Rousseau, Voltaire and other Enlightenment philosophers. As the English poet William Wordsworth recalled: 'Bliss was it to be in that dawn...but to be young was very heaven.'

By 1792, however, it was clear that revolutionary change, and the ruthless imposition of 'reason' and other Enlightenment ideals, could have shocking and horrific consequences. The public beheading of King Louis XVI was accompanied by what became known as 'the Terror' — a period when thousands of 'citizens' were persecuted and executed in the name of progress, and when genocidal violence became the means of securing an 'enlightened', revolutionary regime.

The course of the French Revolution, and the threat posed to peace across Europe by the new French regime, proved a watershed in political theory. Events in France now made it possible to assail liberal-Enlightenment principles without seeming reactionary, to criticise 'progress' without denying the spirit of the Enlightenment, and to accept reform while rejecting revolution. In this way, the savagery of the French Revolution paved the way for a new sort of political ideology, one that would respect the case for change while warning of its dangers. The political thinker who epitomised this new approach was Edmund Burke, the so-called 'father of conservatism'. (His arguments will be referred to throughout this chapter and are summarised in the 'Key thinker 2' box.)

The core ideas of conservatism

Human nature

The conservative view of human nature is defined largely by its response — and opposition — to those of rival ideologies, notably liberalism and socialism. Whereas these 'progressive' ideologies take an upbeat view of human nature, asserting that human beings have the capacity for endless achievement and improvement, conservatives are inclined to restrain such optimism by stressing human frailty and fallibility. Indeed, conservatism's view of human nature has led to it being described as 'a philosophy of imperfection'.

Conservatives thus deny any possibility of a perfect, utopian society, comprising flawless and rational individuals; their view of human nature tends to be descriptive, not prescriptive, highlighting humanity 'as it is' rather than as it could or should be. In this sense, conservatism rejects the malleable or 'plastic' view of human nature offered by socialism, and scorns the idea that humanity can be significantly remoulded given the 'correct' environment or society. For conservatives, human nature is pretty much fixed and constant, and the job of politicians is to accommodate, not alter, this reality. Yet conservatism's stress on **human imperfection** is more nuanced than many

Key term

Human imperfection
Drawing upon the Old Testament doctrine of original sin, this refers to the timeless flaws of humanity — flaws which make any quest for the 'perfect' society misguided and potentially disastrous.

47

imagine and comprises a number of interpretations from various conservative thinkers.

When assessing conservatism's view of humanity, it is certainly useful to reference **Thomas Hobbes** (1588–1679) (see 'Key thinker 1' box), whose view of life in the 'state of nature' was sharply different from that of liberal theorists such as John Locke (see Chapter 1). Regarding human nature as ruthlessly selfish, calculating and competitive, Hobbes argued that without the restraints of formal authority, relations between human beings would be marked by 'envy, hatred and war', leading to a life that was 'nasty, brutish and short'.

However, we should be wary of describing Hobbes as the quintessential conservative. As explained in the 'Key thinker 1' box, Hobbes went on to argue (in his classic work *Leviathan*) that underpinning human nature was a cold rationality; this would eventually lead hitherto warring individuals to forge a contract, which would in turn lead to a formal state. By admitting the possibility of such rational calculations and the concept of mankind achieving satisfactory outcomes, Hobbes thereby placed himself closer to liberalism in terms of explaining human nature — which explains why Hobbes is usually seen as an example, rather than a critic, of Enlightenment thinking.

For this reason, Burke has a much stronger claim than Hobbes to be the real 'father of conservatism'. Burke's historic diatribe on the French Revolution (*Reflections on the Revolution in France*) criticised not just recent events in France but the thrust of Enlightenment thinking — including the view of human nature that inspired it. Burke duly rejected the idea that human nature was guided mainly by reason and dismissed any notion that mankind could plan the near-perfect society. Drawing upon the biblical principle of original sin, Burke highlighted the 'chasm between our desire and our achievement' and thus stressed custom, habit and experience as signposts for how we should behave.

Both Burke and Hobbes exhibited scepticism in their view of human nature — they both ridiculed any idea that human nature was saintly or potentially flawless. Yet their definitions of human imperfection were distinct. First, Burke did not think that human beings were as brutally selfish as Hobbes alleged: fallible yes, terrible no. Second, Burke thought that human beings were capable of kindness and altruism, wisdom even, as long as their actions were rooted in history, tradition and the teachings of the Christian church — a possibility that Hobbes did not countenance. Third, Burke did not share Hobbes's view that human nature was ruthlessly individualistic. Instead, Burke argued that human nature was naturally communal, with individuals gaining comfort and support from the small communities around them (what Burke termed 'little platoons').

Burke's theory of human nature would be updated by various conservative scholars in the twentieth century, many of whom argued that the conservative view of human nature was, in fact, the essence of conservatism itself. **Michael Oakeshott** (1901–90) (see 'Key thinker 3' box) stated that conservatism was 'more psychology than ideology', claiming it articulated 'an instinctive preference for what is known, an innate fear of the uncertain'. Unlike Hobbes, however, Oakeshott believed that life without law would be 'not so much nasty, brutish and short...as noisy, foolish and flawed'. Human nature, Oakeshott conceded, was 'fragile and fallible', yet it was also 'benign and benevolent' when framed by routine, familiarity and religious principles.

Later conservative thinkers, notably those associated with the New Right, offered modifications to this view. **Robert Nozick** (1938–2002) and **Ayn Rand** (1905–82), for example, were keen to highlight human nature's yearning for individual freedom, and its subsequent capacity for enterprise and innovation (see 'Key thinker 4' and 'Key thinker 5' boxes). However, the New Right and traditional conservatives agreed that even the most enterprising individuals were still (in Nozick's words) 'freedom-loving pack animals', who need the periodic restraint of formal authority and deeply rooted communities. Indeed, this recognition provides a key link between New Right politics in the twentieth century and Hobbesian philosophy in the seventeenth century. Both Hobbes and the New Right took the view that human nature was driven by self-interest. Yet both also took the view that human nature must be contained in order to provide some peace and stability in human affairs.

Activity

In approximately 200 words, compare and contrast the views of human nature offered by Thomas Hobbes and Edmund Burke.

Thomas Hobbes (1588–1679)

Thomas Hobbes is considered one of England's most important political thinkers. Although widely seen as a 'conservative' philosopher, he is also linked to the liberal principle of government by consent and the philosophical artefact of a 'state of nature', later used to different effect by the liberal philosopher John Locke.

- In his most famous work, *Leviathan* (1651), Hobbes took a profoundly sceptical view of human nature, arguing that it was needy and vulnerable and therefore likely to commit destructive acts. Hobbes also asserted that, prior to the emergence of a state, there was no cooperation or voluntary arrangements between individuals and therefore none of the 'natural rights' later cited by liberals. Instead, the Hobbesian 'state of nature' was a place of scarce resources where individuals would be governed by ruthless self-interest. Human nature was thus shaped by a restless desire for the acquisition of goods, an immovable distrust of others and a constant fear of violent death. In Hobbes's own words, life in this state of nature would be 'solitary, poor, nasty, brutish and short'.
- For Hobbes, such 'natural chaos' stemmed from the absence of any formal authority, which could enforce an unquestioned code of right and wrong. In its absence, Hobbes noted, mankind in the state of nature was left to form his own version of acceptable and unacceptable conduct. Yet because each man's versions of right and wrong were likely to be different, this would lead only to uncertainty and war.
- Nevertheless, because Hobbes did not consider human nature wholly irrational, he believed that mankind would eventually realise that the state of nature was inimical to self-interest and thus agree to a 'contract'. Under this contract, individuals would render to a 'sovereign' (that is, a state) the right to make laws by which all were restrained and thus allow the sort of order and security absent in the state of nature. This would eventually lead to a 'society', where individuals could enjoy some security and progress.
- But for the state to accomplish its side of the bargain, Hobbes claimed it would have to be autocratic. If power were dispersed, Hobbes argued, then the conflicts within the state of nature would soon be replicated.
- In summary, Hobbes argued that the principal reason for the state was the creation of order and security; that without such a state there could be no civil society; and that for the state to be effective, it would have to be autocratic, intimidating and forbidding.

Explain, in no more than 200 words, Hobbes's view of the state's function.

Society

Conservatism's view of society is defined by a variety of themes, all of which are thought conducive to stability, security and orderly (as opposed to revolutionary) change.

Localism

When assessing conservatism's view of society, it is important to say at the outset that conservatives would certainly acknowledge its existence. Unlike some liberals, who see society as little more than a collection of atomistic individuals, conservatives see it as a collection of localised communities — what Burke described as 'little platoons'. These communities provide their individuals with security, status and inspiration, while acting as a brake upon the sort of selfish individualism extolled by classical liberals. Indeed, one of Burke's objections to the French Revolution was that it seemed to inaugurate a single, monolithic French society that would override local loyalties — a view reinforced by the new French Republic's development of a highly centralised state.

Organicism

For conservatives, society is not something that can be contrived or created but rather something that emerges gradually, organically, and therefore somewhat mysteriously. Here we see another illustration of conservative scepticism — this time in respect of liberal-style rationalism. For whereas liberals believe in the infinite possibility of planning and arrangement, based on a belief that mankind can determine its own fate, conservatives see the 'reality' of an unplanned organic society, proof that human life is subject to complex forces beyond the scope of reason. Consequently, conservatives view society as less like a machine, responsive to whichever levers are pulled by human hands, and more like a plant, growing in a way that can never be wholly predicted.

Empiricism

Because of its organic character, conservatives also look upon society in **empirical** terms. This means that conservatives will deal with society's issues in a practical, evidential, 'this is how it is' fashion, with no clear view of how society might evolve in the years and decades ahead. This empirical take on society is in sharp contrast to the **normative** view taken by **progressive** ideologies like liberalism and socialism, which have principled views of how society 'ought' to be and 'plans' for how to create it. As Oakeshott observed, the conservative society is one that merely aims to 'stay afloat' in uncertain waters, rather than sail steadily towards some specific destination (such as a fairer or more equal society) which may ultimately prove illusory.

Key terms

Empiricism This indicates a preference for 'evidence' over 'theory' and tends to emphasise 'what is' over 'what should be'.

Normative This denotes how arrangements theoretically 'should' be in future — a term conservatives disdain, given their stress upon the uncertainty of our existence.

Progressive Linked to the other ideologies (socialism and liberalism), this denotes a belief that problems invariably have solutions and that the future must always be superior to the past and present — an assumption about which conservatives are sceptical.

Key terms

Hierarchy This concept holds that equality of status and power is undesirable, that human affairs require leadership from a small number of individuals, and that the majority should accept their judgements. Hierarchy's apologists claim that successful structures, social and political, tend to have an unequal distribution of power.

Paternalism/noblesse oblige These terms refer to the 'fatherly' obligations that a ruling class — or 'nobility' — has to society as a whole. It can take the form of hard paternalism or soft paternalism.

In the case of *hard paternalism*, it involves elites deciding what is best for the rest, irrespective of what the rest want.

In the case of *soft paternalism*, power still rests with the elites but elite decisions will usually be preceded by listening carefully to what the non-elites want, with perhaps a degree of consultation involved.

Tradition

The effectiveness of an empirical, conservative society rests heavily upon the store it sets by tradition. Customs and habits are thus used to provide security in an uncertain world, with history and experience shaping whatever changes become necessary. It is here that tradition dovetails with organicism. As Oakeshott observed:

> 'Just as a plant's new leaves are connected to, dependent on and explained by the plant's roots and branches, so a society's present direction stems from its past development.'

As a result, conservatives argue that change and reform — though inevitable — must be slow not drastic; respectful not contemptuous of the past.

Hierarchy

While any liberal society would stress 'foundational' equality, or the notion that all individuals are born equal and are of equal worth, conservatives see society in a much less egalitarian way. For conservatives, the imperfections of humanity lead seamlessly to inequalities within human nature. This, in turn, leads to an unequal society, where (to quote Burke) 'the wiser, stronger and more opulent' establish a **hierarchy** of power and privilege. According to Burke, such hierarchies are so natural that even the smallest of 'little platoon' communities is likely to have a top-down structure, with a minority exercising some authority over the majority.

Conservatives are keen to stress, however, that with the privilege of power and authority comes responsibility. This compromise, known as **paternalism** or **noblesse oblige**, derives from the conservative principle that the relationship between society's stronger elements and its weaker elements is akin to the relationship between a father and his children, with the former having a natural — indeed organic — responsibility for the latter.

Judaeo-Christian morality

Unlike liberalism, which stresses rationality and humanity's capacity to control its own fate, conservatism has a much stronger attachment to religion, particularly Old Testament Christianity, with its belief in original sin. As a result, the conservative society often has an important role for the ethical guidance offered by Judaeo-Christian morality, which includes a strong emphasis upon marriage, self-contained

Activity

In approximately 100 words, cite examples of how Christian teaching supports the conservative view of society.

families, and individuals being held accountable for their own actions (conservatives refute the socialist contention that 'dysfunctional' individuals are merely the products of 'dysfunctional' societies). Consequently, in a typical conservative society, religious principles — such as the spiritual rewards of altruism and compassion — will help bind individuals together and curb the imperfections that both conservatism and Christianity see as inherent to human nature.

Property

Crucial to the conservative view of society, and the basis of the 'little platoons' or mini-societies lauded by Burke, is a respect for property. As we saw in Chapter 1, a stress upon property is not exclusive to conservatism: it is one of the main 'natural rights' espoused by liberalism and the root of liberalism's support for capitalism. For conservatives, however, property has different attributes.

First, the conservative view of property is closely tied to its support for tradition and continuity. Rather than being something acquired by autonomous individuals, property is often something inherited by one generation from another, thus providing a degree of stability in a shaky, imperfect world. Indeed, inherited and bequeathed property is seen as a tangible expression of Burke's belief that the ideal society is a 'partnership between those who are living, those who are dead and those who are yet to be born'.

The ongoing, practical maintenance of property could be seen as a metaphor for conservatism's belief in the ongoing maintenance of society — an illustration of its core belief that we must change to conserve. But there is also a connection between property and the paternalistic society conservatism supports. This is because those with property have a 'stake' in existing society and, if only to discourage revolution, should have some concern for those who are less fortunate (that is, those without property). Property ownership thus provides a platform and an incentive for property owners to exercise 'duty of care' towards others — and thereby maintain existing society.

New Right conservatives are even more zealous about property, wishing not just to preserve but to extend property ownership throughout society, thus creating a 'property-owning democracy'. For New Right thinkers like Rand and Nozick, those who own property are generally better placed to resist state-led incursions upon their liberty and will be emboldened to justify the sort of unequal society conservatives defend.

The New Right's overall analysis of society is somewhat distinctive, in that it places particular emphasis upon individual liberty. However, in line with traditional conservative thinking, it concedes that individualism is best pursued in a society that still values hierarchy and a traditional, Judaeo-Christian culture. In the New Right's view, such 'traditional' societies provide the security and discipline that individuals need to flourish.

The state

Order and authority

The conservative view of the state's purpose immediately provides a sharp distinction from liberalism and socialism. For whereas the two latter ideologies see the state as serving 'progressive' goals (such as the advancement of individualism or the creation of greater equality), conservatism sees the state as having more of a disciplinary function. Put simply, the main goal of the conservative state is to provide order, security and **authority**.

Like Hobbes, conservatives believe that without order there could be no liberty, and there could be no order until the emergence of clear, undisputed laws backed by firm authority. All this connects to the fundamental conservative belief that *the state precedes society* (and not, as liberals argue, vice versa) and that liberal notions of 'natural rights' are fanciful. Indeed, as Hobbes insisted, the feasibility of individual rights is entirely dependent upon law and order — which only the state can provide.

Organic origins

Although conservatives have a Hobbesian view of the state's function, the link between conservatism and Hobbes can again be overdone. As an early Enlightenment thinker, Hobbes was heavily committed to 'government by consent' and the notion of a state being 'rationally' created by a 'contract' between the government and governed. By contrast, conservatives are sceptical about states that arise momentously, from a formal 'rational' discussion. Such states, conservatives argue, are likely to be normative, not empirical, based on ideals rather than reality, and therefore likely to founder. Instead, conservatives prefer a state that emerges gradually, unpredictably and without fanfare: an 'organic' and pragmatic response to humanity's needs. For this reason, conservatives are less likely than liberals to demand a 'codified' constitution and more tolerant of UK-style arrangements, where unwritten constitutions have evolved organically in response to changing circumstances.

A ruling class

The structure of the state, at least for 'traditional' conservatives (see below), also differs from that advocated by liberalism and socialism. Unlike supporters of progressive ideologies, conservatives have been much more comfortable with a state that is overtly hierarchical, reflecting the elitist society they also endorse. Furthermore, the traditional conservative state is one that implicitly acknowledges the notion of a ruling class, whose power will often be aristocratic and hereditary rather than democratic.

Traditional conservatives, from Burke onwards, were therefore keen to signal the merits of a class that was born and trained to rule the state (mindful of its paternalistic responsibilities to society as a whole). For this reason, the traditional conservative state would again show pragmatic and empirical characteristics, legislating whenever there was evidence to show new laws were necessary and governing so as to ensure order and social cohesion. By such flexible means, the conservative state would avert social upheaval and revolution while maintaining traditional patterns of wealth and power in society.

The nation-state

From the mid-nineteenth century to the mid-twentieth century, conservatives tended to emphasise a state based on nationhood. For all conservatives, the nation became a mega-community, one that enfolded all classes and therefore provided a 'natural' basis for the state. For continental conservatives, such as those in Germany or Italy, there remains a powerful sense that the nation preceded the state, that the two are distinct, and that the latter is distinguishable from the former.

For British and American conservatives, however, nation and state are much more intertwined, with the state serving to define much of the nation itself — hence the importance of constitutions, monarchs and presidents as expressions of British and American identity. This would also explain why British conservatives have had a much greater attachment to the nation-state than their continental counterparts, and much less enthusiasm for European political union. Like American

Activity

Explain, in approximately 100 words, why conservatives might be wary of democracy.

conservatives, British conservatives tend to see any diminution of the nation-state as a diminution of the nation itself.

For New Right conservatives (again found mainly in the USA and the UK), the attitude to the state appears paradoxical: to strengthen the nation-state by 'rolling back its frontiers'. Yet for New Right thinkers like Nozick and Rand, the paradox is easily explained: if the nation-state is burdened by nationalised industries and welfare states, it is then harder for it to focus on its 'true' function of order and security. As Rand observed: 'When the state becomes flabby, it also becomes feeble.' So, for New Right conservatives, the aim is to streamline the nation-state's functions and to make it 'leaner and fitter' in the process.

The economy

Capitalism tends to nurture and widen economic inequalities and to sharpen the distinction between rich and poor. Conservatism, meanwhile, defends inequality and hierarchy. So it is unsurprising that 'conservative economics' have a pro-capitalist flavour. Indeed, Burke was a robust ally of Adam Smith, the father of **laissez-faire** economic theory.

Yet despite this overlap with liberalism, traditional conservatism's support for capitalism is nuanced. This is because conservatism worships order, stability and continuity. Yet free-market capitalism promotes risk, innovation and iconoclasm. The dynamic nature of capitalism might well excite liberals, with their optimistic view of human nature and residual belief that (to quote Voltaire) 'everything is for the best in this, the best of all worlds', but it can be quite frightening for conservatives, given their more sceptical view of human nature and their residual fear that radical change threatens dreadful outcomes.

With this in mind, traditional conservatives have sometimes been dubbed capitalism's 'reluctant supporters'. On the one hand, they recognise that any assault on capitalism is also an assault on property, inequality, hierarchy and the status quo. On the other hand, traditional conservatives are sceptical of the classical or neo-liberal belief that markets are at their most effective when left alone by governments. Supporting laissez-faire capitalism, after all, requires an optimistic view of market forces, and is therefore somewhat inconsistent with conservatism's scepticism and pessimism.

Traditional conservatives have tried to resolve this dilemma by supporting a moderated form of capitalism, in which free markets are tempered by state intervention. Under this conservative model of capitalism — sometimes referred to as protectionism — society and the economy would be insured

Laissez-faire This involves the state allowing market forces to operate freely. Though strongly associated with economic liberalism, laissez-faire economics has been supported by both traditional conservatives like Edmund Burke and New Right conservatives like Robert Nozick.

Adam Smith: father of liberal economics

Key term

Thatcherism This is essentially a synonym for New Right conservatism in the UK. Between 1979 and 1990, the governments of Margaret Thatcher pursued a controversial mixture of neo-liberal policies (such as privatisation and tax reduction) and neo-conservative policies (such as strengthened police powers, curbs on immigration and tax breaks for 'traditional' family structures).

Activity

Explain, in approximately 200 words, how conservatism's attitude to capitalism differs from that of liberalism.

against the vagaries of markets by state-imposed tariffs and duties. This 'protection' of national producers and consumers was also consistent with traditional conservatism's emphasis upon national identity and 'one nation' (see later), offsetting the globalising effects of free-market capitalism. Traditional conservatives in the twentieth century were also drawn to Keynesian capitalism, whereby the state 'managed' market forces in the interests of full employment.

Influenced by neo-liberal economists such as Milton Friedman (1912–2006) and Friedrich von Hayek (1899–1992), New Right conservatives have generally had a more sympathetic view of free-market economies. Indeed, in the USA during the 1980s, free-market capitalism was often referred to as 'Reaganomics', on account of the support it had in the Republican administration of President Ronald Reagan (1980–88). At the same time, the New Right governments of Margaret **Thatcher** (1979–90) aimed to 'free' the UK economy through the privatisation of formerly state-owned industries.

Yet New Right economics still manages to complement traditional conservatism in a number of ways. First, the New Right argues that by disengaging almost completely from the economy, the state could then focus on its true Hobbesian purpose of order and security. Second, the New Right believes that a free-market economy will be a prosperous economy. This might promote 'popular capitalism' and destroy socialism, but it would also fund greater state spending on the police, armed forces and other agencies vital to the defence of a conservative society.

Different types of conservatism

Unlike socialism, with its various tensions and subdivisions, there are just two strands of conservatism: traditional conservatism and New Right conservatism. Yet it would be wrong to conclude that conservatism is therefore a more straightforward ideology. Like classical liberalism, traditional conservatism is a creed that spans over two centuries; it is therefore an amorphous doctrine, evolving in accordance with changing circumstances.

Traditional conservatism (i): aftermath of the French Revolution

As explained in our review of conservatism's origins, the principles of conservatism were grounded in a reaction to the French Revolution of 1789 — an event that, by offering a radical interpretation of Enlightenment values, challenged established notions of state and society across Europe. Although conservatives were primarily concerned about the effects this would have upon their own security, it was the Whig politician Edmund Burke who offered the first philosophically coherent objection to what the French Revolution represented.

Edmund Burke (1729–97)

As a Whig MP, Edmund Burke was known as the champion of numerous radical causes during the mid to late eighteenth century. He was a firm supporter of the American Revolution after 1776, defended Irish tenants in their clashes with extortionate landlords, demanded the impeachment of the Governor General of Bengal (Warren Hastings) for alleged cruelty towards Hindustanis, and was a fervent advocate of Adam Smith's call for free trade. Yet despite this radical pedigree, Burke is widely considered the father of conservatism and one of the Enlightenment's most important critics. How did this arise?

- The answer lies in Burke's impassioned opposition to the French Revolution, via his famous text *Reflections on the Revolution in France* (1790). It was in this book that Burke defined various tenets of conservative thought, including human imperfection, empiricism, organicism, tradition, aristocracy and localism.
- In respect of human imperfection, Burke stressed mankind's fallibility and its tendency to fail more than succeed. He therefore denounced the idealistic society that the French Revolution represented, claiming it was based on a utopian — and thus unrealistic — view of human nature.

- Burke argued that while change was necessary to conserve, change should proceed on the basis of fact and experience — in other words, empiricism and tradition — rather than theory and idealism. Burke duly criticised the French Revolution for discarding what was known in favour of an entirely new society based on 'philosophical abstractions'.
- Burke claimed that both society and government were more akin to a plant than a machine. He thus argued that both had a mysterious dynamism that was beyond reason and planning. In the political and social context, Burke therefore insisted that change must be cautious and organic, and denounced the French Revolution for disregarding history and tradition.
- Burke was scathing about the French Revolution's stress on equality, asserting that within all 'organic' societies, a ruling class was inevitable and desirable. However, this class had a clear obligation to govern in the interests of all. For Burke, it was the French aristocracy's failure to do this that led to revolution.
- Burke condemned the new French Republic for its highly centralised structures, praising instead a society of 'little platoons': a multitude of small, diverse and largely autonomous communities, which would 'acknowledge, nurture and prune… the crooked timber of humanity'.

Activity

Explain, in no more than 200 words, Burke's view of how change should occur.

Debate 1

Is conservatism 'ruling-class ideology'?

Yes

- It was a claim regularly made by both fundamentalist socialists such as Beatrice Webb and revisionist socialists like Anthony Crosland.
- Those making such claims cited Burke — the 'father of conservatism' — who attacked the egalitarianism of the French Revolution while defending aristocratic rule.
- Since Burke, conservatives have always defended property, privilege and inequality.
- Conservative paternalism is merely an attempt to make inequality and elitism palatable to the majority.
- The stress on tradition and piecemeal change conspires to prevent *radical* change, which inherently threatens ruling-class interests.

No

- The prime purpose of the conservative state — the maintenance of order — is one with appeal to all sections of society.
- Conservatism's love of habit, custom and familiarity has echoes within all sections of society.
- Traditional conservatism has frequently promoted the interests of the poor in order to ensure the maintenance of 'one nation'.
- The conservative wish to avoid revolution is altruistic — during periods of revolutionary upheaval it is often society's most vulnerable members who suffer most.
- New Right conservatism is meritocratic, not aristocratic, identifying with ambitious and talented individuals from all backgrounds.

Key term

Tory Along with the Whigs, the Tories were one of the two main parties in England from the seventeenth to the early nineteenth centuries. They were linked to themes such as authority, tradition, hierarchy and religion. Following alliances with sections of the Whig Party, the Tories eventually evolved in the 1830s into a broader political grouping known as the Conservative Party.

Conservatism's opponents have since argued that Burke's thesis, as expounded in *Reflections on the Revolution in France* (1790), merely provided a sophisticated justification for existing society — one in which he, like other members of the 'ruling class', had a vested interest. Yet there can be no doubt that Burke's cogent analysis, based upon a web of philosophical principles, shaped not just the origins of conservatism but also its development in Britain during the early nineteenth century.

Tory prime ministers such as William Pitt (1759–1806), George Canning (1770–1827) and Robert Peel (1788–1850) were essentially conservative in their political practice. Like Burke, they displayed a reverence for order and property, showed an antipathy to revolutionary change, extolled tradition, endorsed the notion that society comprised a multitude of small communities, insisted that society and state emerged 'organically', praised experience and 'evidence' over theory and 'abstraction', and defended the principle of paternalistic, aristocratic rule.

Yet among such senior political figures, Burke's influence was most marked in their attitude to change. Once again, it is worth recalling the core conservative belief that we must 'change to conserve'. Within the UK, this principle was duly applied by a series of 'enlightened Tory' governments in the early nineteenth century — governments which sought to avert the spread of revolutionary ideas by embracing moderate reform in the name of continuity.

George Canning, for example, supported Catholic emancipation and, as prime minister, prepared legislation that allowed Roman Catholics to participate in Parliament (claiming that 'though emancipation carries dangers, civil strife carries even greater dangers'). Canning also championed the abolition of slavery, arguing that it brought property ownership into disrepute, while supporting demands from various Latin American countries for independence — all of which echoed Burke's support for the American Revolution of 1776 and his campaigns against corruption inside British colonies.

Within a decade of Canning's premiership, Robert Peel offered another example of changing to conserve, seeking to harness the interests of the new merchant and business classes to Britain's traditional constitution and society. To this end, Peel, along with other newly named 'Conservatives', supported the Great Reform Act of 1832, thus ensuring representation at Westminster for the new industrial towns. Peel's reasoning was that if the interests of the newly enriched were not harnessed to the existing social and political structure, there was a danger that those same interests would be harnessed instead to property-less forces with no vested interest in evolving the status quo (a conservative rationale for reform that was central to Burke's explanation for the French Revolution).

In addition to offering clear examples of 'changing to conserve' while prime minister (1841–46), Peel's political career offers a practical example of conservatism's belief in order and authority. As Home Secretary (1828–30), he established the Metropolitan Police Force in London, a measure which led to the creation of similar forces throughout the country. Peel's assertion that 'without security there can be no liberty' effectively updated Hobbes' justification for the state and strengthened the association between conservatism, order and authority.

Traditional conservatism (ii): the emergence of 'one nation'

Although the governments of Canning and Peel served to stem the effects of the French Revolution, the threat of disorder and insurrection persisted throughout the nineteenth century, fuelled by loud demands for greater democracy (and less aristocracy) within the UK's political system. All this required a further development of conservative thinking.

Of particular importance to this development were politicians like Benjamin Disraeli (1804–81) in Britain and Otto von Bismarck (1815–98) in Germany. Sensing that socialism, with its stress upon class conflict, was a new and grave threat to stability and tradition, conservatives like Disraeli and Bismarck understood that the case for orderly change would have to be refined. Likewise, they were aware that to ensure social cohesion and orderly change, new themes were needed to offset the class-conscious politics encouraged by early socialists like Marx.

It was at this point that the importance of the nation emerged in conservative thinking. This was ironic because, until the nineteenth century, nationalism had been associated with anti-imperialism and anti-monarchism. The French revolutionaries, whom Burke opposed so vehemently, were self-styled 'patriots', while subsequent revolutions across Europe (such as those of 1848) had frequently been hailed as 'patriotic' movements. In short, until the mid–late nineteenth century, 'the nation' was seen as anything but a conservative concept.

Disraeli and Bismarck, however, understood nationalism's conservative potential. Unlike contemporary liberals, whose individualistic outlook led them to deny social class, conservatives like Disraeli embraced class differences — but in a way that fostered unity rather than rupture. Against the rhetorical background of **one-nation conservatism**, Disraeli and Bismarck argued that a society's classes were, in fact, all members of the same national 'family' and that revolutionary politics (including Marxism) represented an attack on the nation itself. For Disraeli, 'the nation' was

Key term

One-nation conservatism
Dating from the 1870s, and linked to British politicians like Benjamin Disraeli, this term denotes a belief that conservatism should prioritise national unity by attending to the condition of society's poorer classes. It has been used by conservative politicians to justify greater state intervention in society and the economy, and thus higher levels of public spending and taxation.

not an alternative to the status quo but the *essence* of the status quo, with the existing nation-state being something that all classes had a vested interest in defending.

Conservatives like Disraeli therefore poured scorn on the supposed links between the workers of one nation and those of another (as suggested by Marx's call for 'workers of the world' to 'unite'). Instead these one-nation conservatives updated Burke's notion of an organic affinity between a nation's richer and poorer classes, arguing that the nation's aristocracy had a paternalistic duty to (in Disraeli's words) 'elevate the condition of the people'. Once this obligation was recognised by all classes, Disraeli and Bismarck asserted, social and political progress could be achieved harmoniously and without the horrors of class war and revolution. As Disraeli remarked: 'The palace is not safe when the cottage is not happy.'

However, in pursuit of this 'one nation' strategy, neither Disraeli nor Bismarck advocated mere philanthropy on the part of society's 'haves'. In a way that would never have occurred to previous generations of conservatives, they endorsed state-sponsored social reform, thereby distinguishing conservatism from the minimal-state principles of classical liberalism. (Indeed, they regarded laissez-faire individualism, like class-based socialism, as the enemy of 'one nation'.) As a result, the one-nation conservatism of the mid–late nineteenth century became associated with legislation that tempered the effects of laissez-faire capitalism, supposedly on behalf of the nation's working classes.

In England, this resulted in legislation such as the Factory Act 1874 and the Artisan Dwellings Act 1875, restricting the freedom of factory owners and landlords respectively, while Bismarck's chancellorship of Germany (1871–90) led to what some historians regard as the first welfare state, providing German workers with state-backed insurance against sickness, accident and destitution in old age. Bismarck's conservatism also led to the imposition of tariffs and import controls, thus confirming traditional conservatism's ambivalent attitude to free-market capitalism.

Activity

Explain, in approximately 200 words, why and how Disraeli promoted 'one-nation conservatism'.

Traditional conservatism (iii): response to egalitarianism and fascism

During the twentieth century, political debate was reshaped by two seismic events: the spread of socialism and communism after the First World War and the emergence of **fascism** prior to the Second World War. These developments were to have a profound impact upon the evolution of traditional conservatism.

For most of the twentieth century, conservatives regarded the existence of the Soviet Union as the most powerful example of the threat now posed by egalitarianism — an ideology, enfolding socialism and communism, which inherently challenged conservatism's belief in property, hierarchy and modest reform. In the UK, the conservative fear of egalitarianism was underlined by the extension of the franchise in 1918 (which flooded the electorate with working-class voters) and the accelerated growth of a new political party — Labour — committed to wholesale common ownership. Indeed, until the late twentieth century, it was common for conservatives to lament that socialism and communism were inevitable unless stern political action was taken.

With that in mind, traditional conservatism sought to temper the effects of a capitalist economy with a view to sustaining a society based on property ownership and inequality. Prominent inter-war conservatives, such as future Tory prime minister Harold Macmillan (1894–1986), spoke of a 'middle way' between capitalism and socialism, one that would address economic inequalities while respecting property rights, cultural tradition, national identity and other themes close to conservative hearts.

Although Macmillan did not become prime minister until the 1950s, as early as the 1930s it was clear that conservatism was now prepared to sanction a much greater degree of state intervention so as to protect privilege and stifle socialism. Between 1935 and 1937, for example, Conservative politicians supported Public Health, Housing and Factory Acts, all of which checked market forces in the name of social cohesion and 'one nation'.

After 1945, conservatism took further steps towards an acceptance of 'big government'. Across western Europe, conservatives seemed to yield to many of the ideas espoused by rival political ideologies, notably those of democratic socialism and modern liberalism, and thus embraced Keynesian

Key term

Fascism This was a revolutionary ideology which emerged in Europe during the 1920s and 1930s, finding its most devastating expression in the politics of Adolf Hitler's National Socialism in Germany and Benito Mussolini's nationalist politics in Italy. Because of its nationalistic and nostalgic character, it is sometimes seen as a form of 'ultra-conservatism'. Yet its belief in radical and immediate change, its contempt for traditional institutions and local diversity, and its glorification of dictatorship also make it abhorrent to orthodox conservatives.

economics, 'welfare states' and 'mixed economies' involving extensive state ownership of industries and services.

To a large extent, this was opportunistic and pragmatic. After all, to give effect to their views, conservative politicians in the twentieth century needed to win elections, and elections were now dominated by working-class, non-property-owning voters. This encouraged socialist theorists, such as Crosland, to argue that 'conservatives conserve no principles...they simply go along with whatever situation they inherit, in the interests of winning office and stemming the tide of change'.

Yet post-war conservatives denied such taunts and insisted they were evolving, rather than forgetting, their previous ideological positions. In his book *The Case for Conservatism* (1948), Quintin Hogg claimed that 'conservatism, unlike liberalism, has always recognised that unchecked laissez-faire can be destructive as well as creative', while R.A. Butler (in *The Art of the Possible*, 1971) argued that 'our support for state welfare, and the Keynesian principle of an economy based on full employment...were little more than updated expressions of our belief in one-nation and paternalism'.

Christian democracy

Outside the UK, traditional conservatism after 1945 evolved rather differently. The main reason for this was that other western European nations felt the effects of fascism much more acutely. Revolution, violent nationalism, totalitarian government, military defeat and national humiliation all had a huge effect on the psychology of continental conservatives like West Germany's Konrad Adenauer (1876–1967), France's Robert Schuman (1886–1963) and Italy's Luigi Sturzo (1871–1959). After 1945, such European conservatives therefore developed a variant of traditional conservatism known as Christian democracy.

However, this post-war European conservatism is not wholly dissimilar to traditional conservatism in the UK. In fact, there are numerous overlaps:

- There is the same belief in Judaeo-Christian morality as a force for binding society together.
- There is the same belief in authority and hierarchy (underlined, in Christian democracy's case, by its links to the Roman Catholic Church).
- There is the same commitment to social conservatism, the same emphasis upon marriage and family life, and the same scepticism towards socially liberal causes such as abortion and sexual equality.

Activity

Explain, in approximately 200 words, conservatism's contribution to the UK's post-war consensus.

■ There is the same scepticism towards free-market economics. Christian democracy thus stresses the 'social market', a form of capitalism that draws upon Roman Catholic principles of obligation and communal duty, but with echoes of Disraeli's 'paternalistic' conservatism.
■ There is the same acceptance of an enlarged state: like post-war conservatism in the UK, Christian democracy was comfortable with Keynesian (state-managed) capitalism, high public spending and an expansive welfare state.

What makes Christian democracy distinct from British (and American) conservatism is its attitude towards the nation-state. In countries like Germany, Italy and Spain, the experience of fascism left conservative politicians explicitly wary of nationalism and traditional notions of patriotism. (In Germany in particular, references to 'one nation' sat uncomfortably alongside its recent history of Nazism.) In other continental democracies too, the experience of invasion, occupation, collaboration and national shame deeply affected conservative attitudes towards national identity and national self-determination.

One crucial effect of this was to make post-war continental conservatives amenable to **supranationalism**, an idea first hinted at by Schuman's plan for limited economic integration in the 1950s and later embodied by the European Economic Community and the European Union. Here again the Roman Catholic influence within Christian democracy was helpful for continental conservatives, given that the Roman Catholic Church itself practises supranational authority.

For many British conservatives, meanwhile, the suspicion has always been that the real aim of Christian democracy's supranationalism is to eliminate 'the nation' as a feature of conservative philosophy and instead make 'the region' the main focus of communal identity (as it is now for many German and Italian conservatives). For this reason, many British conservatives — such as the philosopher Roger Scruton — regard Christian democracy as a form of 'no-nation conservatism' and therefore something for which they feel little affinity.

Michael Oakeshott (1901–90)

Michael Oakeshott is regarded as one of the most important conservative philosophers of the twentieth century, bringing a fresh perspective to the core themes of traditional conservatism. Oakeshott's key text on the subject, *On Being Conservative* (1962), is renowned for its fresh interpretation of how conservatives regarded human imperfection. In particular, it is remembered for its argument that a 'philosophy of imperfection' need not be a 'philosophy of pessimism' or indeed unhappiness.

- First of all, Oakeshott wished to qualify the negative view of human nature associated with Hobbes and, to a lesser extent, Burke. Most men and women, he argued, were 'fallible but not terrible' and 'imperfect but not immoral'. Though incapable of the 'perfect' societies linked to other ideologies, humanity was still able to secure 'both pleasure and improvement through the humdrum business of everyday life'.
- From this perspective, Oakeshott tried to make conservatism seem more optimistic than ideologies such as liberalism and socialism. He argued that such ideologies — with their clear views of how society 'should' be — produced impatience, intolerance and frustration. Oakeshott claimed that conservatives, who are reconciled to human imperfection, have a greater appreciation of the pleasures that already exist in life (from families and friends, for example). Conservatives, he claimed, 'prefer the familiar to the unknown, the actual to the possible, the convenient to the perfect…present laughter to utopian bliss'.

- Being dismissive of 'normative' politics, with its 'simplistic visions that overlook the complexity of reality', Oakeshott also affirmed the merits of an empirical and pragmatic approach to both politics and life generally — what might be termed 'the art of the possible'. He argued that it was through experience, trial and error, rather than abstract philosophy, that wisdom was achieved. In a memorable aside, Oakeshott remarked: 'In a kitchen, cook books are only useful after experience of preparing a meal.'
- These perspectives on human nature informed Oakeshott's views about the state. In his final work, *The Politics of Faith & the Politics of Scepticism*, he argued that the state existed to 'prevent the bad rather than create the good', restating that the best things in life normally emerge from routine, apolitical activity. This also led him to offer his celebrated 'nautical metaphor': that, during our lives, 'we all sail a boundless sea, with no appointed destination' and that the job of government is to reflect this by 'keeping the ship afloat at all costs… using experience to negotiate every storm, stoicism to accept necessary changes of direction…and not fixating on a port that may not exist'.
- Oakeshott's critics, especially conservative critics on the New Right, claim his philosophy is too fatalistic and underestimates our ability to shape circumstances. For New Right philosophers like Nozick, the 'Oakeshott mentality' was 'lazy' and had allowed socialist ideas to advance unchallenged after 1945.

Activity

Explain, in no more than 200 words, how Oakeshott's view of human nature differs from that of Hobbes.

Debate 2

Is conservatism merely the politics of pragmatism?

Yes

- The 'father of conservatism', Edmund Burke, made his attack on the French Revolution an attack on 'abstract philosophy', claiming it ignored human imperfection.
- Traditional conservatives have consistently advocated an 'empirical' approach to politics, one based on 'what is', not 'what should be'.
- Traditional conservatism prides itself on 'flexibility'. This has helped conservatism endure several centuries of dramatic change.
- Conservative pragmatism is shown by the different policies adopted by various conservatives at different times. Robert Peel, for example, supported laissez-faire capitalism, while (a century later) Harold Macmillan backed a more Keynesian (interventionist) approach.
- Michael Oakeshott therefore argued that conservatism is a short-term, 'getting by' approach to politics: unlike liberalism and socialism, it has no long-term objectives concerning society and the economy.

No

- Traditional conservatism, far from being philosophically neutral, is based on philosophically contentious assertions (for example, that slow change is preferable to radical change; that 'vision' and 'principle' are inferior to 'tradition' and 'evidence').
- Traditional conservatism does not reject revolution merely as a method of change; it does so to protect a society based on certain principles, such as hierarchy, inequality and private property.
- As a result, socialists see conservatism as 'ruling-class ideology', a changing set of biased policies, reflecting the evolving tactics of elites determined to preserve their privilege.
- Oakeshott described traditional conservatism as 'a psychology rather than an ideology', drawing upon humanity's 'instinctive love of the familiar'. Conservatives may therefore reject 'pragmatic' change if it conflicts with their instincts and emotions.
- New Right conservatism draws upon the neo-liberal/libertarian doctrines of philosophers like Hayek and Nozick, while New Right politicians, such as Margaret Thatcher, proclaimed themselves 'conviction politicians'.

New Right conservatism

An American export

For much of the twentieth century, conservatism in the UK — and most of western Europe — was defined by a combination of social conservatism and qualified support for economic liberalism. In other words, while conservatives stressed order, authority and traditional communities, their support for private property and capitalism was tempered by a fear that market forces could generate gross inequalities that would outrage the majority of (working-class) voters. As a result, traditional conservatives in Europe and the UK supported interventionist economic policies, such as Keynesianism, and high public spending on state welfare.

In the United States, however, conservatism had a rather different mixture. There, conservatives placed much more emphasis upon individual freedom, laissez-faire capitalism, private property and minimal government, largely because these values squared with different traditions (those of the USA), reflecting the communities that emerged organically after the discovery of the New World.

Many of these traditions were essentially liberal in character, stemming from the individualist values of the USA's Founding Fathers and a Constitution that owed much to the philosophy of John Locke. But it is important to remember that those values were quickly blended with other values that were more obviously conservative, such as traditional Christian morality, a respect for marriage and family life, intense patriotism and a belief in 'strong' (albeit limited) government.

In other words, American conservatism had always involved a synthesis between classical liberalism and social conservatism. From the 1970s onwards, conservatives in Europe were increasingly convinced that this (American) model of conservatism was one that they too should adopt.

The 'crisis' of traditional conservatism

To understand New Right conservatism, it is first necessary to appreciate that it was primarily an analysis of the 'crisis' engulfing states like the UK by the mid-1970s. This crisis was supposedly characterised by spiralling inflation, mounting unemployment, unsustainable welfare spending, increased crime rates, moral laxity and a growing sense that society was becoming ungovernable, largely on account of trade union militancy.

For the New Right, however, this crisis also represented an indictment of traditional conservatism. After 1945, traditional conservatives (like Macmillan, Hogg and Butler) had clearly endorsed a post-war consensus involving Keynesian economics, state welfare and social liberalism. According to the New Right, traditional conservatives were therefore complicit in a rapidly declining economy, a bloated welfare state, a 'permissive society' and an increasingly feeble country — one lacking in both moral and formal authority and struggling to resist both socialism at home and communism abroad. So, as well as new government policies, a new interpretation of conservatism was urgently required.

Harold Macmillan: Tory PM and practitioner of one-nation conservatism

In most of Europe, where conservatives remained faithful to the ideas of Christian democracy, such a reinterpretation was largely resisted. However, conservatives in the UK and the USA proved much more willing to challenge traditional conservative thinking. This was eventually expressed in the UK by the Conservative prime minister Margaret Thatcher (1925–2013) and in the USA by the Republican president Ronald Reagan (1911–2004).

Margaret Thatcher and Ronald Reagan: two leading advocates of New Right ideas

Debate 3

Is conservatism compatible with capitalism?

Yes

- Capitalism is based on private property, which historically conservatives support.
- Capitalism generates inequality, which conservatives defend as 'natural' and 'organic'.
- Capitalism has been at the heart of economic activity for several centuries and therefore squares with conservatism's support for tradition.
- Capitalism provides the ruling class with wealth that can then be used for paternalistic support for the less fortunate.
- New Right conservatism is keen to extend private property and market forces in the name of greater individual freedom.

No

- Capitalism is often described as economic liberalism — it is focused on individuals rather than the communities that conservatism champions.
- Capitalism creates economic and social divisions that threaten 'one nation'.
- Capitalism is dynamic and volatile, threatening the stability and continuity conservatives crave.
- Capitalism tends towards globalisation, undermining the national identity conservatives value.
- Capitalism promotes a meritocracy that challenges hereditary ruling classes.

New Right conservatism: a two-dimensional doctrine

New Right conservatism is best described as a merger between two distinct ideologies: neo-liberalism and neo-conservatism.

Neo-liberalism is principally associated with Austrian philosopher Friedrich von Hayek, whose 1944 thesis, *The Road to Serfdom*, is regarded as the 'bible' of neo-liberal thinking. Hayek's views were subsequently reinforced by American economist Milton Friedman and, in the UK, by think-tanks such as the Adam Smith Institute and the Institute of Economic Affairs. It also chimes with the libertarian philosophy of Robert Nozick and Ayn Rand.

Neo-liberalism's aims can be distilled into the following objective: to extend individual freedom by 'rolling back the frontiers of the state' in order to create a free market economy. According to thinkers like Nozick and Rand, such measures would not just promote freedom, they would also lead to the return of economic growth and a vibrant, prosperous society. In more specific terms, neo-liberals wished to see:

- a drastic reduction in taxation
- a much tighter control of government spending (along the monetarist lines prescribed by Friedman)
- an end to the dependency culture arising from expensive welfare states
- the deregulation and privatisation of services carried out by government
- the neutering of 'obstructive' bodies wedded to 'statist' ideas (such as trade unions and many local councils).

Neo-conservatism, meanwhile, is associated with American scholars like Irving Kristol (1920–2009) and British philosophers like Roger Scruton (1944–). Whereas neo-liberalism's concern was the salvation of individual liberty, neo-conservatism's main objective was the restoration of authority, national identity and a society informed by Judaeo-Christian morality. In more specific terms, neo-conservatives wished to see:

- a tougher approach to law and order, involving more powers for the police and stiffer sentences for offenders
- a more robust approach to national defence, including a less conciliatory approach to the nation's potential enemies (principally, in the context of the 1970s, the Soviet Union)
- a less tolerant approach to immigration (mainly because of its challenge to traditional national identity)
- **anti-permissive** social policies (in respect of issues like abortion and homosexuality) and the promotion of 'traditional' family structures via the state's tax and benefits system.

Key thinker 4

Ayn Rand (1905–82)

The sharp differences between traditional and New Right conservatism were highlighted by the writings of Ayn Rand, one of the USA's most provocative New Right thinkers.

- Rand's defining work, the novel *Atlas Shrugged* (1957), secured her status as one of America's most influential libertarians. Its theme was that talented individuals, rather than ambitious governments, lay at the heart of any successful society. The novel suggested that without the energy of such individuals, a society would quickly wither — no matter how much activity was expended by governments.
- This theme was restated in a non-fictional way through Rand's works of philosophy. *The Virtue of Selfishness* (1964) explained a philosophical system Rand described as 'objectivism', its core belief being that we should all be guided by self-interest and 'rational self-fulfilment'.
- For this reason, Rand became associated with the New Right's **atomism**, the term for a society defined by millions of autonomous individuals, each independently seeking self-fulfilment and self-realisation. Indeed, Rand's work provided a philosophical justification for the idea that society did not exist in any practical form, it was ideally just a loose collection of independent individuals.

- Although Rand's ideas are consistent with both classical and neo-liberalism, they gained political traction on account of New Right politics in the 1970s. Her 'objectivist' philosophy became strongly linked to the New Right's support for a more laissez-faire brand of capitalism and its renewal of negative liberty, thus providing a philosophical justification for 'rolling back the frontiers of the state' and projects such as tax cuts and privatisation.
- Rand was proud to call herself a libertarian, in that she defended not just free markets but also an individual's 'right to choose' in areas like homosexuality or abortion. But she firmly rejected any suggestion of anarchism, claiming that both free markets and cultural laissez-faire needed the parameters of a small state.
- In her later work, Rand strengthened her connection to conservatism by stating that liberty was impossible without order and security, which only a state could provide. Her conservative credentials were further strengthened by her support for the ultra-conservative Republican candidate Barry Goldwater in the 1964 US presidential election, during which she wrote: 'The small state is the strong state.'

Activity

Explain, in no more than 200 words, the connection between New Right conservatism and the philosophy of Ayn Rand.

Key term

Atomism This relates to the view that human beings seek autonomy and 'space', which therefore leads to only a vague sense of society. Conservatives traditionally reject this view, arguing that individuals are closely connected by their communities. However, New Right conservatives are much more atomistic in their view of human nature and society (see below).

Robert Nozick (1938–2002)

During the 1970s, Robert Nozick emerged as one of the key thinkers for New Right conservatism. His key work, *Anarchy, State and Utopia* (1974), remains a vital reference for modern conservative philosophy.

- Nozick developed many of the themes first raised by neo-liberal philosopher Friedrich von Hayek in *The Road to Serfdom* (1944). Like Hayek, Nozick argued that the growth of government was the gravest contemporary threat to individual freedom. More specifically, Nozick thought the growth of welfare states in western Europe fostered a dependency culture.
- Nozick's hostility to the state went beyond that of neo-liberalism. Unlike Hayek, Nozick became closely identified with libertarianism, a creed which argues that the individual should be 'left alone' not just in the economic sphere (as neo-liberals and all New Right conservatives would argue) but in the social and cultural spheres as well (an idea many on the New Right would find at odds with their social conservatism). As a result, libertarianism is tolerant of a liberal, 'permissive society' and takes a relaxed view of issues like abortion, divorce and homosexuality.
- Despite the title of his most famous work, *Anarchy, State and Utopia* (1974), Nozick was not a 'true' anarchist in that he believed in a minarchist state — one that mainly involved outsourcing public services to private companies.
- This minarchist prescription owed much to Nozick's optimistic view of human nature, which seems very different to that of Hobbes and Burke. Indeed, some have suggested that Nozick's philosophy has less in common with conservatism than with strands of anarchism. For example, his claim that 'tax, for the most part, is theft' indicates an upbeat view that individuals have self-ownership — that they are the sole authors of their talents and abilities and should be left alone to realise them, without the intervention of government. However, there are reasons why Nozick is considered a conservative.
- First, although he believed that society predates the state, Nozick's view of human nature was not wholeheartedly positive. He argued that while dishonesty, theft and violence were not the main characteristics of humanity, the preservation of life, liberty and property 'could not be taken for granted' without some formal authority enforcing laws: a vital concession to the legacy of Hobbes.
- Second, the purpose of Nozick's limited state was not simply to facilitate raw individualism and free-market capitalism. For Nozick, the minarchism he prescribed would allow a multitude of self-sufficient communities to emerge alongside the extension of individual freedom. In Nozick's minarchist society, each of these communities would be free to practise its particular moral codes and values, including values which might be seen as socialist or anti-Christian. This arguably represents an updated version of Burke's view that the best form of society is one comprising a variety of 'little platoons'.

Political ideas for A-level

Activity

Explain, in no more than 200 words, how Nozick's minarchist society is compatible with traditional conservatism.

New Right conservatism: a contradictory doctrine?

New Right conservatism proved to be one of the most controversial ideologies of the late twentieth century. Yet some of its fiercest critics were themselves conservatives. Some conservative commentators, for example Ian Gilmour in his book *Inside Right* (1977), argued that the New Right marked a 'betrayal' of traditional conservative principles. Other studies of conservatism, such as Anthony Quinton's *The Politics of Imperfection* (1978), contested that because it mixes neo-liberalism and neo-conservatism, the New Right enfolds a series of 'fundamental contradictions'. For example:

- While neo-liberals wish to 'roll back the frontiers of the state' (hence the Thatcher governments' promotion of privatisation), neo-conservatives wish to roll the frontiers of the state forward (hence the Thatcher governments' restrictions upon trade unions and local authorities).
- While neo-liberals wish to advance individual liberty (hence the Thatcher government's commitment to income tax cuts), neo-conservatives are prepared to restrict it (hence the Thatcher government's extension of police stop and search powers).
- While neo-liberals are relaxed about immigration (Rand saw it as a side effect of free markets and individual choice), neo-conservatives are much more wary (hence Thatcher's fear that immigration in the 1960s had 'swamped' traditional communities and Britain's traditional culture).
- While neo-liberals are keen to minimise government spending, in pursuit of what Nozick called the 'minarchist state'), neo-conservatives are prepared to increase it so as to strengthen the nation's profile (hence Thatcher's decision to upgrade the UK's nuclear deterrent, plus her government's ongoing financial commitment to the defence of the Falkland Islands).

Yet despite these tensions, there is reason to argue that New Right conservatism is a blend rather than a mismatch, and that neo-liberalism and neo-conservatism complement, rather than contradict, each other. This can be illustrated in three ways.

First, Irving Kristol famously observed that a New Right conservative was 'a liberal mugged by reality'. By that he meant that neo-liberals, with their optimistic view of human nature, fail to anticipate the tensions arising from a free-market capitalist society, where inequalityß flourishes. So to contain such tensions, they require a strong authoritarian state (of the sort favoured by neo-conservatives) to maintain order and protect private property.

Second, to achieve the low taxation they desire, neo-liberals would have to reduce dramatically levels of state spending on welfare. But for this to be viable, there have to be alternative sources of support for those blamelessly in need. So neo-conservatives provide an answer: the restoration of traditional morality (which neo-conservatism supports) and an end to the 'permissive society' should lead to the restoration of supportive families and altruistic voluntary communities, while reviving a sense of individual responsibility. All this will effectively 'privatise' compassion and social security and thus weaken the state's obligations.

Third, neo-conservatives wish to strengthen the state by reinforcing the police, security services and armed forces. All this requires extra state funding. But neo-liberals claim this will be easier once state spending has been reduced in other areas, following measures like privatisation and welfare reform. So neo-liberalism's wish to 'roll back the frontiers of the state' in economic and welfare policy effectively finances the more statist objectives of neo-conservatism. This arrangement was neatly summarised by the title of Andrew Gamble's study of Thatcherism: *The Free Economy and the Strong State* (1988).

Activity

Highlight, in approximately 200 words, the differences between neo-liberalism and neo-conservatism.

Summary: key themes and key thinkers

	Human nature	The state	Society	The economy
Thomas Hobbes	Cynical: individuals are selfish, driven by a restless and ruthless desire for supremacy and security.	The state arises 'contractually' from individuals who seek order and security. To serve its purpose, the state must be autocratic and awesome.	There can be no 'society' until the creation of a state brings order and authority to human affairs. Life until then is 'nasty, brutish and short'.	Constructive and enduring economic activity is impossible without a state guaranteeing order and security.
Edmund Burke	Sceptical: the 'crooked timber of humanity' is marked by a gap between aspiration and achievement. We may conceive of perfection but we are unable to achieve it.	The state arises organically and should be aristocratic, driven by a hereditary elite, reared to rule in the interests of all.	Society is organic and multi-faceted, comprising a host of small communities and organisations ('little platoons').	Trade should involve 'organic' free markets and laissez-faire capitalism.
Michael Oakeshott	Modest: humanity is at its best when free from grand designs and when focused on the routines of everyday life.	The state should be guided by tradition and practical concerns. Pragmatism, not dogmatism, should be its watchword.	Localised communities are essential to humanity's survival, especially when guided by short-term requirements rather than abstract ideas.	Free markets are volatile and unpredictable, and may require pragmatic moderation by the state.
Ayn Rand	'Objectivist': we are — and ought to be — guided by rational self-interest and the pursuit of self-fulfilment.	The state should confine itself to law, order and national security. Any attempt to promote 'positive liberty', via further state intervention, should be resisted.	In so far as it exists at all, society is atomistic: the mere sum total of its individuals. Any attempt to restrict individuals in the name of society should be challenged.	Free-market capitalism is an expression of 'objectivist' individualism and should not be hindered by the state.
Robert Nozick	Egotistical: individuals are driven by a quest for 'self-ownership', allowing them to realise their full potential.	The minarchist state should merely outsource, renew and reallocate contracts to private companies providing public services.	Society should be geared to individual self-fulfilment. This may lead to a plethora of small, variable communities reflecting their members' diverse tastes and philosophies.	The minarchist state should detach itself from a privatised and deregulated economy, merely arbitrating disputes between private economic organisations.

Tensions within conservatism

- **Human nature:** traditional conservatives, such as Burke and Oakeshott, take a sceptical view of human nature, drawing attention to the gap between aspiration and achievement while warning against the grand, utopian schemes of progressive politicians. For them, the horrors of supposedly idealistic movements — such as the French and Russian Revolutions — are not tragic accidents, they arise from a misreading and overestimation of human potential. By contrast, New Right thinkers take a more optimistic view, emphasising the possibilities of individuals with initiative and liberty. Key thinkers like Nozick and Rand take an especially positive view of what individuals can achieve in the economic sphere, arguing that the key to unlocking human potential lies in fostering a pro-capitalist environment where individual energies are unleashed.

- **Society:** traditional conservatives see society as a collection of small communities (what Burke termed 'little platoons'), overseen by a hierarchical structure in which 'paternalistic' elites exercise their inherited power in the interests of the majority. Such communities are considered organic, in the sense that they emerge in a natural and unplanned way, and place great store upon tradition and continuity. By contrast, New Right conservatives are ambivalent about society's very existence, drawing upon the libertarian belief that society is a mere collection of atomised individuals seeking self-determination. New Right conservatives are more sceptical about paternalistic communities, preferring a society defined by those who have achieved, rather than inherited, power, status and property — in other words, a society that is meritocratic rather than aristocratic.

- **The state:** traditional conservatives like Burke defend a state where political power is wielded by those who are 'born to rule'. As such, traditional conservatives believe the best states have a natural 'ruling class', reared according to the principles of duty and sacrifice, and instilled with a sense of responsibility towards the governed. Traditional conservatives are pragmatic about the extent of the state and are prepared to enlarge it in the name of social stability and 'one nation'. By contrast, New Right conservatives wish to 'roll back the frontiers of the state' (outside areas such as security and defence) so as to advance individual freedom and reverse the dependency culture. New Right conservatives are hostile to the principle of aristocratic rule — they fear that ruling classes have too much stake in the status quo and are therefore reluctant to admit the need for radical change by New Right governments.

- **Economy:** traditional conservatives, while keen to defend an economy based on private ownership, are sceptical about free-market capitalism, fearful that its dynamic effects exacerbate inequality, threaten 'one nation' and fuel support for socialism. As capitalism becomes more globalised, traditional conservatives also fear that market forces promote a more cosmopolitan society that erodes national identity and national culture. As a result, traditional conservatives have been prepared to countenance state intervention via Keynesian economics, higher taxation and high public spending on state welfare. By contrast, New Right conservatives like Nozick zealously advocate free-market economies where state functions are privatised and deregulated, and where levels of taxation and state spending are significantly reduced.

Can conservatism be reconciled with socialism?*

Yes
- Traditional conservatives and socialists play down the importance of individualism.
- Traditional conservatives and socialists stress the importance of communities.
- Traditional conservatives and socialists stress the importance of unity within communities.
- Traditional conservatives and socialists see capitalism as potentially problematic.
- Traditional conservatives and socialists are sceptical of meritocracy, highlighting 'fate' and 'chance'.

No
- Conservatives see inequality as natural, socialists see it as unacceptable.
- Conservatives are sceptical of progress, socialists see it as essential.
- Conservatives defend private property, fundamentalist socialists favour common ownership.
- Conservatives reject revolution, some fundamentalist socialists see it as desirable and inevitable.
- Traditional conservatives advocate noblesse oblige, socialists think paternalism is patronising.

* This debate is best addressed after reading both this chapter and Chapter 3. A similar debate about conservatism and liberalism is to be found in Chapter 1.

Conclusion: conservatism today

There is a case for saying that an ideology preaching order, stability, continuity and incremental change will always have some appeal. However, such an ideology is likely to have particular appeal during an era of economic, social and cultural volatility. For this reason, it could be contested that traditional conservative values are more resonant than ever as the twenty-first century progresses.

One illustration of this, in most of the developed states around the world, has been a shift in the focus of the state's responsibilities. During the late twentieth century, it may have seemed that the state's primary concern was the advancement of individual freedom. In the UK, for example, the first New Labour government (1997–2001) devoted much of its energies to devolving political power, establishing a Freedom of Information Act, and passing various laws that illegalised discrimination against individuals from minority backgrounds.

By the second decade of the twenty-first century, however, the growth of terrorism and the problems of mass migration had prompted a change of focus, with the state now giving precedence to order, safety and security. In short, the state's priorities, in both the UK and elsewhere, seemed to have regained an authoritarian character which traditional conservative thinkers — notably Hobbes — would readily understand and wholeheartedly applaud.

Another conservative trend in politics after 2010 was the growing interest in the concept of society and community. According to contemporary conservative theorists, such as Phillip Blond and Jesse Norman, this trend arose largely from a sense that liberal individualism spawned selfish, narcissistic cultures, devoid of collective identity or purpose. Of course, such trends may equally vindicate the case for socialism, given its timeless stress on solidarity and fraternity (see Chapter 3). Sadly for socialists, however, the renewed interest in society was not always accompanied by a resurgent faith in state intervention, akin to that which existed just after the Second World War.

David Cameron (PM 2010–16): a neo-Burkean conservative?

As a result, society and collectivism seemed to become decoupled within political debate. This development helped revive one of the key themes associated with Burke's conservatism — namely, a 'little platoons' society, comprising a vast assortment of local and voluntary communities. In the UK, Conservative prime minister David Cameron tried to advance this Burkean idea with his campaign for a 'big society'. Indeed, Cameron's defence of 'voluntarism', and his claim that 'there is such a thing as society...it's just not the same thing as the state', was a vivid illustration of how traditional conservatism can be both relevant to modern politics and distinct from both liberalism and socialism. In short, the 'big society' idea, and the continued attempts to foster 'a bigger society and a smaller state', provided evidence of a lingering conservative mentality in political life.

Yet it was another feature of that lingering mentality that led to the end of Cameron's political career. In the UK, the diminishing appeal of European, supranational authority (about which British conservatives have never enthused) was confirmed in 2016 by the electorate's decision to withdraw from the European Union. The reasons for this decision remain contentious. But it was hard to deny a yearning among voters for a greater sense of national identity and a form of government that was national, not continental, in character — yearnings which have been central to British conservatism for almost two centuries. Political trends elsewhere, in both Europe and the USA, show a similar wish to avert the sort of change that promotes cosmopolitan individualism, and the same preference for a different form of change, one that is more attuned to history, tradition and nationhood.

Even though the UK's Conservative Party has tried to reflect some of these changes — latterly by repudiating European supranationalism in order to reclaim national sovereignty and identity — we should remember two points made at the start of this chapter: Conservatism and conservatism are not indivisible (most Conservative MPs backed membership of the EU, for example), while conservatism in the UK is not confined to the Conservative Party.

Many of those concerned with the direction of the modern Labour Party, for instance (notably philosophers like Maurice Glasman), have argued for a new brand of politics dubbed 'Blue Labour', linking left-wing themes like equality and social justice to conservative themes such as 'family, faith and flag'. Similarly, in the USA, President Donald Trump (though fundamentally radical and iconoclastic rather than conservative) effectively exploited a number of themes that echoed the traditional conservative critique of liberalism — notably a wish to protect the US economy by curbing free markets, a desire to prioritise the national interest rather than global capitalism and individual rights, and a conviction that safety and security, rather than individual liberty, were the state's prime responsibilities.

Clearly, conservatism is a persistent and adaptable ideology, rooted in the importance of custom, habit, community and kinship. Change may be constant and inevitable, yet the desire to change in a certain way — one that is respectful, not contemptuous, of tradition and communal identity — will always be present and shows no sign of decaying. Maybe that was the real lesson of the UK's 2016 referendum: a Conservative prime minister was punished, perhaps, for not being sufficiently conservative in an increasingly conservative era.

Brexit: was the UK's 2016 referendum a 'conservative moment'?

Yes

- The UK's participation in a supranational political system was at odds with the UK's traditions.
- The decision to leave the EU was an attempt to restore national self-governance.
- The ability to take back control of immigration would help restore national identity.
- The EU was a contrived system of government, with normative principles (i.e. eventual political union within Europe), at odds with conservatism's preference for organic systems of government.
- The EU represented 'big government' and continental dirigisme, at odds with the 'leaner and fitter' state advocated by the New Right.

No

- Leaving the EU was a 'leap in the dark' — a radical change with highly uncertain consequences.
- Rejecting David Cameron's 'renegotiated membership' offer was a rejection of the case for gradual, incremental change.
- Leaving the EU was a rejection of an arrangement which, though imperfect, had worked for decades (the UK's 43-year membership was proof that its EU partnership had not been wholly ineffective).
- Leaving the EU was tied to a faith in global, laissez-faire capitalism — an historically liberal form of economics that defied traditional conservative scepticism.
- Brexit threatened 'one nation' by allegedly encouraging racism and xenophobia.

Further reading

Blond, P. (2010) *Red Tory*, Faber and Faber.

Grant, M. (2013) 'Conservatism — is it an ideology?', *Politics Review*, 23,1.

Heywood, A. (2015) 'Conservatism — a defence of the privileged and prosperous?', *Politics Review*, 25,1.

Honderich, T. (2005) *Conservatism*, Pluto Press.

Scruton, R. (2001) *The Meaning of Conservatism*, Macmillan.

Scruton, R. (2014) *How to Be a Conservative*, Bloomsbury Continuum.

Exam-style questions

Short questions

The following questions are similar to those in examinations set by AQA. Each carries 9 marks.

1 Explain and analyse how conservatives have justified private property.

2 Explain and analyse the grounds on which conservatives have supported tradition.

Essay questions

The following questions are similar to those in examinations set by Edexcel (Pearson) and AQA.

Edexcel (24 marks) or AQA (25 marks):

1 To what extent is conservatism a philosophy of imperfection? You must use appropriate thinkers you have studied to support your answer.

2 To what extent is conservatism a coherent ideology? You must use appropriate thinkers you have studied to support your answer.

AQA only (25 marks):

3 'The New Right has little in common with traditional conservatism.' Analyse and evaluate with reference to the thinkers you have studied.

4 'Less an ideology than a state of mind.' Analyse and evaluate this view of conservatism with reference to the thinkers you have studied.

Chapter 3

Socialism

Learning outcomes

This chapter will enable students to:
- understand the core values of socialism
- understand how socialism has evolved since the nineteenth century
- understand the various strands of socialism — from the works of Karl Marx to the influences upon Tony Blair
- understand the continuing relevance of socialism today

Introduction

Like liberalism, socialism is an ambiguous ideology, embracing followers with a range of competing views. Indeed, even the most basic knowledge of political history would indicate that socialism attracts an astonishing variety of champions: Karl Marx, Gordon Brown, Joseph Stalin, Harold Wilson, Chairman Mao, François Hollande, Fidel Castro, John Prescott, Che Guevara, Jeremy Corbyn, Pol Pot...these are just some of the people who have described themselves as 'socialist'. The issue of what, if anything, unites such an eclectic group will be an important focus of this chapter.

Just as socialism has some contradictory followers, it has also been linked to contradictory outcomes. On the one hand, it has been tied to what many see as the finest aspects of the human condition, such as fraternity, comradeship, altruism, compassion and a dedication to the interests of the underdog. On the other hand (in places like Russia, eastern Europe, China and Cambodia), 'socialist' reform has led to oppression, genocide and some of the most brutal societies ever witnessed. Far from being a glorious cause on behalf of the underdog, socialism in many parts of the world has become a by-word for tyranny and misery.

Of course, all political ideologies — especially the three 'core' ideologies covered in this book — contain contradictions and ambiguities. Yet those of socialism are particularly stark and controversial. This is why it is especially important for students of politics to understand the essence of socialism and the various ways it has been applied.

The origins of socialism

Like liberalism, socialism is an ideology that grew out of the Enlightenment (see Chapter 1). Indeed, socialism and liberalism have much in common. Both:

- take an optimistic view of human nature
- exalt reason over faith and superstition
- are 'progressive' — they believe in the possibility of reform and are always ready to challenge the status quo
- share a desire to liberate human beings from oppression
- believe in 'foundational' equality — men and women are born equal and deserve equal opportunities in life
- reject the 'traditional' state (defined by monarchical absolutism and the divine right of rulers)
- reject anarchism — in other words, both believe a certain type of state can secure significant progress in terms of freedom and foundational equality.

You will recall from Chapter 1, however, that one of liberalism's core features was support for private property, which liberals consider a natural right. Yet as early as the seventeenth century, there were those who were unsure about whether the principles of the Enlightenment could be reconciled to private ownership. During the English Civil War (1649–60), for example, one radical group of anti-monarchists, the Levellers, argued that God had given the land to all mankind, yet some had exercised greed so as to acquire that land for themselves.

Such ideas were developed by a small number of radical theorists during the eighteenth century. Jean-Jacques Rousseau, in his *Discourse on the Origin of Inequality* (1755), suggested that 'many crimes, wars and murders…many horrors and misfortunes' arose from the concept of private ownership, while during the 1789 French Revolution François-Noel Babeuf (1760–97) led a 'conspiracy of the equals', demanding the abolition of private property.

It was during the early nineteenth century that the term 'socialism' was first applied. The so-called **utopian socialists**, such as Charles Fourier (1772–1837) and Robert Owen (1771–1858), offered a radical response to the emerging problems of capitalism and industry. Fourier duly advocated independent communities based on communal ownership and production, involving the equal distribution of resources and a culture marked by tolerance and permissiveness. Owen, meanwhile, set up model 'cooperative' communities in Scotland and America, designed to promote shared ownership, shared responsibility and altruism.

Yet it was only during the mid-nineteenth century, when the pace of industrialisation began to quicken dramatically, that socialist ideas began to be taken seriously. For many of those otherwise sympathetic to liberal principles, liberalism now offered an inadequate response to the profound changes wrought by the industrial revolution. It was felt that liberalism was in denial about the effects of urban life and blinkered to the fact that in the new industrial areas there was little scope for individual autonomy and individual freedom. As a later socialist thinker, Eric Hobsbawm, wrote (in respect of conditions in mid-nineteenth-century England):

> 'For an individual living in a slum…paying rent to a rapacious landlord, while working in a factory for whatever wages his employer deigned to pay him, any notion of freedom or independence seemed utterly distant.' (*The Age of Capital, 1848–1875*, 1975)

As a result, the early socialists argued for a new approach, one that would make Enlightenment principles (such as self-determination) more achievable in an industrialised society — one where employment was much less individualistic and where individuals seemed to have much less autonomy in their everyday lives.

Key term

Utopian socialism Linked to philanthropists like Robert Owen, this refers to the earliest form of socialism, one based on a vision of the perfect human existence. For Karl Marx, however, its 'utopian' character stemmed from the absence of any clear method for bringing about such 'socialism'.

Activity

Explain, in approximately 200 words, how industrialisation led to socialist ideas.

The core ideas of socialism

As explained earlier, there is considerable overlap between socialism and liberalism. As a result, any explanation of socialism's core themes should take account of the core themes it shares with liberalism (see above). This section of the chapter, however, will largely examine the core themes that distinguish socialism from liberalism — although, as we shall see, there is also an overlap between the core themes of socialism and those of certain strands of anarchism.

Human nature

Like liberalism, socialists have an upbeat, optimistic view of human nature, which helps explain why both liberalism and socialism are seen as 'progressive' ideologies. Yet liberals and socialists differ as to *why* they are optimistic.

Whereas most liberals think individuals are naturally self-reliant and self-sufficient, socialists believe that individuals are naturally cooperative, generous and altruistic. So instead of forever seeking autonomy, independence and supremacy, as liberals claim, human beings (according to socialists) naturally seek solidarity, fraternity and comradeship, reflecting the claim of poet John Donne (1571–1631) that 'no man is an island'.

Socialism concedes, however, that mankind's true nature has been diluted by time and circumstance. So whereas liberalism takes an optimistic view of human nature as it is, socialists are more optimistic about how it could be. This is because socialism, unlike liberalism, sees human nature as malleable, or 'plastic', rather than permanently fixed at birth. Consequently, socialists believe that human nature can be adjusted, thus ensuring that men and women fulfil their true, fraternal potential while contributing to a more cooperative community.

The key issue, of course, is what determines human nature? And by what means can human nature be improved and mankind's potential realised?

Society

According to socialism, any understanding of human nature requires a clear understanding of society. Much more than liberalism, socialism — by definition — focuses upon an individual's social environment: in other words, the individual's society. Whereas liberals tend to see society as the sum of autonomous individuals, socialists see things the other way round — for socialists, individuals are the product of the society into which they were born.

Socialists thus see society as an independent construct, formed by impersonal forces (see below) and thereafter shaping the individuals inside it. Key thinkers like **Karl Marx** (1818–83) and **Friedrich Engels** (1820–95) thought these forces were primarily economic, with the 'means of production' — that is, the way a society's resources are determined and distributed — having a crucial impact upon the nature of society and, by implication, human behaviour (see 'Key thinker 1' box).

Socialists are therefore sceptical of the classical liberal claim that individuals can be masters of their own destiny — this will always depend, they claim, on the nature of society. Indeed, society is often cited as the main reason for individuals not fulfilling their potential. Yet for socialists, this is no cause for despair. In keeping with their faith in human potential, socialists argue that if only society can be improved, there will be a corresponding improvement to the prospects of its individuals.

So how can society be improved from a socialist point of view? Socialists argue that in order to prescribe a better society in future, we must first diagnose the society we have today. It is at this point that we see the importance to socialism of social class.

For socialists, the major consequence of the industrial revolution was the emergence of distinct social groupings — classes — based principally upon employment and an individual's source of income. According to socialism, these classes are central to an individual's fate. Rejecting the liberal view — that men and women are autonomous creatures, free to carve out their own identities and destinies — socialists argue that an individual's status, priorities and prospects are shaped by the social class he or she is born into. And as key socialist thinkers like Marx and Engels explained, an individual's social class is determined by their status within society's economy.

Marx and Engels — along with more modern socialist thinkers such as **Anthony Crosland** (1918–77) (see 'Key thinker 4' box): also noted that society's classes tend to be profoundly unequal in terms of power and influence: those in the working class, for example, are seen to earn less and therefore exercise less influence within their society. Put another way, individuals in some sections of society will have more opportunities to exploit their potential than individuals in other sections of society. This in turn leads to socialism's unique perspective on the issue of equality.

Key term

Class Social class is central to socialism — it defines an individual's circumstances, prospects and attitudes. Socialism's key thinkers have used various terms to describe society's class divisions: middle class/working class, bourgeoisie/proletariat, white collar/blue collar. All denote a certain type of employment, while indicating status and wealth within society.

You may recall from Chapter 1 that one of liberalism's core themes was foundational equality — or the notion that all men are born equal and are of equal value. This, in turn, relates to liberalism's belief in formal equality, equality of opportunity and therefore justice: in short, the state should treat everyone equally so as to ensure everyone has a level chance to fulfil their potential. Yet socialism, mindful of class differences, insists that such forms of equality are meaningless without another form of equality, namely greater equality of outcome within society — by which socialists mean a greater similarity between people's material resources and material circumstances. It is this additional emphasis, upon what socialists see as **social justice**, that explains why socialism and equality are more indivisible than liberalism and equality. It also explains why socialism — much more than liberalism — is regarded as an egalitarian doctrine.

In essence, socialists contest that to have equality of opportunity there must first be greater equality of outcome in society. Given that socialism stresses the importance of social class, this means that socialists seek a narrowing of the gap between society's poorer and richer classes. In justifying this position, socialists argue that irrespective of character, ability and intelligence, an individual born into a lower/working/blue collar-class background will have fewer opportunities than a similar individual born into a higher-class background.

As a result, socialists argue that a society which allows inequality of outcome in one generation will be a society that produces inequality of opportunity in the next generation. Socialists therefore argue that until we have a society where there is greater equality of outcome, the noble objectives of liberalism and the Enlightenment — such as self-determination and foundational equality — will never be realised. Unlike both modern liberals, such as John Rawls, and paternalistic conservatives, such as Disraeli, socialists think it is insufficient just to improve the condition of society's poorest — socialists claim that unless there is a narrowing of the gap between social classes, society will continue to lack fraternity, cooperation and solidarity, and instead will foster greed, envy, resentment and division.

Of course, the key question for socialism then becomes: how is greater equality of outcome to be brought about? This leads us to socialism's economic perspectives.

Key term

Social justice For socialists, legal and formal justice (as propounded by liberalism) is not enough to guarantee equality of opportunity. These things must be accompanied by social justice — involving, for example, health care and education accessible to all, or a minimum wage for employees. As such, the case for social justice usually leads to the case for collectivism (see below).

Activity

Explain, in approximately 200 words, the importance of social class to socialism.

The economy

As indicated in the section on 'Society', socialists have always argued that equality of opportunity was precluded by the inequalities existing between social classes. Furthermore, key socialist ers, from Marx and Engels onwards, have argued that social class is determined by the economic system underpinning society. So it has been impossible for socialists to address the fundamental issue of inequality within society without addressing the structure of the economy.

Socialists have always recognised that an economic system based upon private property and capitalism — as opposed to **common ownership** — can be hugely problematic. As explained in this chapter's section on 'Human nature', socialists believe that the 'natural' condition of mankind is one of cooperation and fraternity. Yet these attributes are said to be seriously threatened by both private property and **capitalism**, which are said to encourage competitiveness, ruthless egotism and the callous pursuit of self-interest. Free-market capitalism also generates huge inequalities of outcome, which for socialists, of course, are incompatible with equality of opportunity, self-determination and social justice.

Socialism seeks to rectify the problems caused by capitalism by championing an economy that provides for greater workers' control in employment, and a significant redistribution of wealth and resources within the economy generally. Indeed, socialism is routinely described by its proponents as a 'redistributionist' doctrine, practising what Tony Benn (1925–2014) wryly described as 'the politics of Robin Hood — taking from the rich and then giving to the poor'. For socialists, the 'redistributionist' economy will usually involve two broad principles.

First, there will be an emphatic rejection of the laissez-faire capitalism advocated by classical and neo-liberalism, whereby market forces are given free rein by a state that is disengaged and minimalist in relation to a society's economy. According to socialism, an economy where there is low taxation and little state interference will be one where unfairness and social injustice become exacerbated.

Key terms

Common ownership This represents an alternative to both private property and a capitalist economy, and a method of ownership seen (by many socialists) as conducive to equality and fraternity. It is synonymous with state ownership and public ownership.

Capitalism Sometimes referred to as economic liberalism, capitalism is an economic system based on private property, private enterprise and competition between individuals and individual organisations. Its tendency to produce unequal outcomes is of concern to most socialists.

Activity

Explain, in approximately 200 words, why many socialists treat private property with suspicion.

Second, and arising from the rejection of laissez-faire, socialists demand greater collectivism. This perspective on the economy claims to focus on the needs of society as a whole rather than on the abilities of a few enterprising individuals, as with economic liberalism. For socialists, economic collectivism can take various forms, for example:

■ Progressive taxation, whereby the state extracts wealth from its citizens but on a 'sliding scale', so that the richer classes contribute much more than the poorer classes.

■ Progressive public spending, whereby the state uses the economic resources it has acquired (via taxation) in a way that enhances the less fortunate elements of society — for example, via state benefits to the unemployed or elderly.

■ Extensive public services, whereby the state uses its yield from taxation to guarantee key public services, such as health care and education. Socialists claim that if left entirely to private enterprise, such services might prove inaccessible to less advantaged sections of society.

■ Extensive state regulation of capitalism, exemplified by various state regulations designed to prevent exploitation by the economy's richer and more powerful elements. A legal minimum wage for employees, equal pay legislation, health and safety directives, and guarantees of maternity leave are examples of such regulation that socialism would applaud.

■ State/common ownership, recommended when private enterprise is seen to fail parts (or all) of the economy, with grievous consequences for society and its more vulnerable citizens. The original Clause IV of the UK Labour Party's constitution — initially championed by socialists like **Beatrice Webb** (1858–1943) (see 'Key thinker 3' box) — was a controversial expression of this belief in a more collectivist economy, while the post-war nationalisation of industries such as coal, iron and steel is an example of it being given effect.

As well as its primary aim, of redistributing a society's wealth and resources, socialism believes that economic collectivism has two other benefits. First, progressive taxation, increased public spending, extensive public services and sometimes public ownership are seen as expressions of a more fraternal, more cooperative society with greater social justice. Second, such collectivist policies are thought to make the economy more efficient. As Marx and Engels were the first to point out, capitalism and market forces are inherently volatile and unpredictable — causing, for instance, periodic mass unemployment. A more collectivist economy, it is argued, will be more stable and manageable, and therefore more likely to provide the material resources society needs.

Activity

Explain, in approximately 100 words, why socialists have favoured collectivism.

The state

It needs to be emphasised that the core socialist values discussed so far — such as equality, fraternity, even collectivism — are not exclusive to socialists: they are also shared by certain anarchists, notably 'collectivist anarchists' like Peter Kropotkin (1842–1921) and Mikhail Bakunin (1814–76). What makes socialism distinctive from collectivist anarchism is that it also advocates a strong state.

Socialists believe that without a strong state, it will be impossible to bring about a fairer and more equal society. In the short to medium term at least, it would certainly be difficult to bring about a redistribution of wealth and greater social justice without a state that was expansive and dirigiste (actively seeking to direct a society's economy).

Some socialists (such as Marxists and orthodox communists — see below) argue that, eventually, the state will 'wither away' — a blissful moment in human evolution, which Marx described as 'the end of history'. However, all socialists agree that for the foreseeable future, a strong state is essential. They also agree it must be a certain type of state, and certainly not the sort that preceded the Enlightenment.

Socialism therefore rejects the monarchical state (one based on the absolute authority of one person), it rejects the theocratic state (one based on religious principles), and it rejects the aristocratic state (one based on a hereditary ruling class). Instead, socialists advocate a state where political power, as well as economic power, has supposedly been redistributed and where decision making reflects the principle of equality and an empowerment of 'the people'. In short, the socialist state will usually pay lip service, at least, to the principle of democracy.

Socialists also agree that the state must be an extensive one; socialists will therefore contest that any reduction of state power is likely to produce increased social and economic inequality. Nevertheless, among socialists, there are still significant differences about the structure of the ideal state, the extent of its activities and how it emerges. These differences, indeed, help explain why socialism has such a large number of variants and subdivisions, some of which will now be examined.

Different types of socialism

As explained at the beginning of the chapter, socialism is an ambiguous ideology. So it has produced a wide variety of views about how the core socialist themes (as outlined above) can be achieved. It is possible, however, to divide these views into two broad categories: **fundamentalist socialism** and revisionist socialism. Each of these categories is defined by the answer to a basic question: are the core themes of socialism compatible with private property and a capitalist economy?

Those socialists who argue that socialism is fundamentally at odds with private ownership and capitalism are described as fundamentalist socialists. Alternatively, those who believe that socialism can be achieved alongside private property, and that socialism and capitalism can co-exist, are usually labelled revisionist socialists.

Fundamentalist socialism

All fundamentalist socialists believe that capitalism, at some stage, must be abolished. However, there are significant differences about how capitalism should be abolished. Does it necessitate revolutionary change, which quickly destroys both the capitalist system and the state that supports it? Or can the elimination of socialism be done gradually, via evolutionary change, and within the confines of the existing state?

This section of the chapter, which examines five strands of fundamentalist socialism, ascertains — among other things — where each strand stands on the issue of 'revolution or evolution?'.

Classical Marxism

Classical **Marxism** refers to the writings of Karl Marx and his collaborator Friedrich Engels. Although it was not the earliest form of socialism, it was certainly the first form to set out its analysis in detail. Indeed, the term 'utopian socialism', used to describe previous socialist thinkers such as Owen and Fourier, was actually coined by Marx to denote the vagueness and superficiality of their views.

The definitive authors of fundamentalist socialism, Marx and Engels made it plain that capitalism must disappear before socialism — and then **communism** — could be established. Along with Engels, Marx contested that capitalism promoted 'exploitation', 'alienation' and the 'oppression' of one class by another and was therefore wholly at odds with key socialist principles such as fraternity, solidarity and equality.

Key terms

Fundamentalist socialism
This represents the earliest form of socialism, which holds that socialist values are fundamentally incompatible with capitalism. Originally asserted by Karl Marx and Friedrich Engels ('classical Marxism'), this form of socialism has since been associated with various strands of socialism such as orthodox communism, neo-Marxism, Euro-communism and democratic socialism.

Marxism and communism
Seen by Marx as the ultimate stage of human development, communism represents (for communists) the perfect society, based on communal ownership, communal living and the principle of 'each according to his needs'. Marxism reflects this prediction and also involves an 'episodic' view of history, a rigorous critique of capitalism and a justification for revolutionary politics.

Dialectic Associated with the philosopher Hegel, this refers to the clash of ideas and perceptions that will inevitably take place within each 'stage' of history and which eventually leads to the disappearance of existing society.

Historical materialism This refers to the view of Marx and Engels that each 'stage' of history was defined by a clash of economic ideas, relating to how society's resources should be produced and distributed.

Class consciousness According to Marx and Engels, this was a by-product of capitalism that would be especially pronounced among the downtrodden working class, or proletariat. It would eventually be the engine of revolution and capitalism's destruction.

Furthermore, drawing upon the philosophy of Friedrich Hegel (1770–1831), Marx and Engels argued that history was a series of stages, moving towards an inevitable and final destination ('historicism'). Within each historical 'stage' there was — eventually — an intellectual clash, which Hegel had described as **dialectic**. This dialectic occurred when the 'official' narrative about a society's aims and character — as propounded by its ruling classes — no longer corresponded to the perceptions of the majority, who then experienced what Hegel described as 'alienation'. For Hegel, this clash would eventually spawn a new society, a new orthodox mentality and a new stage of history that would survive until the next wave of alienation.

Marx and Engels, however, made a crucial adjustment to Hegel's historicism. For them, the prevailing mentality would always be defined by economics and the way a society's resources were generated and dispersed ('the mode of production'). For them, history was thus a series of economic stages (see Box 3.1), a process they termed **historical materialism**.

For Marx and Engels, the dialectic was not so much a clash of ideas as a clash of economic interests — a process they termed 'dialectical materialism'. Within the Marx–Engels dialectic, one particular class would be economically dominant, while others would be exploited for economic purposes. It was this logic that led Marx and Engels to believe that capitalism was 'historically doomed', given the **class consciousness** it would produce among an economically exploited and therefore 'alienated' workforce (or proletariat).

> ## Box 3.1
>
> ### Historical materialism and dialectical change (according to Marx and Engels)
>
> 1 Primitive societies with no economic organisation.
> 2 Slave-based societies — slaves are the main mode of production.
> 3 Feudal societies — land owned by the monarch is leased to lords, tenants and eventually serfs.
> 4 Emergence of capitalism.
> 5 Emergence of proletariat and class consciousness.
> 6 Revolution and destruction of capitalism.
> 7 Socialism (dictatorship of the proletariat).
> 8 Withering away of the socialist state.
> 9 Communism.
> 10 'End of history'.

Activity

Explain, in approximately 100 words, why Marx believed communism to be 'the end of history'.

The Marx–Engels philosophy was also heavily shaped by a belief in revolution. They argued that when capitalism became unsustainable (on account of its tendency to produce an exploited and 'alienated' workforce that was increasingly class conscious), it was necessary to 'smash' capitalism via revolutionary violence and replace it with an alternative economy and society. For Marx and Engels, such action could not be accomplished peacefully within existing liberal political systems, such as those present in the UK or the USA. According to Marx and Engels, these states were mere 'servants' of the very economic system that socialism must destroy. In short, Marx and Engels emphatically rejected evolutionary or reformist socialism, which they considered an inherent contradiction.

As a result, they insisted that a new economy and a new state, forged by revolution, were essential if socialist values were to be secured. The new state they commended, the 'dictatorship of the proletariat', would supposedly obliterate all traces of liberal-capitalist values and pave the way for a stateless communist society based on common ownership, one that would be so flawless that it would represent the peak of human achievement: what Marx and Engels termed 'the end of history'.

Marxism–Leninism (orthodox communism)

No history of socialism would be complete without reference to Vladimir Ilyich Lenin (1874–1924). Leader of Russia's Bolshevik party prior to the Russian Revolution of 1917, Lenin was a key figure during the revolution itself and the de facto leader of the new, 'socialist' state that emerged in its wake. Yet, in addition to being a major figure in Russian political history, Lenin made a pivotal contribution to the development of revolutionary socialism.

Prior to the revolution, Lenin had accorded great respect to the ideas of Marx. Yet he still sought to refine Marx's prescriptions for how communism should arise. In particular, Lenin was concerned by Marx's insistence that revolution, and a dictatorship of the proletariat, could occur only in societies where capitalism and the proletariat were well developed — a view vigorously disputed not just by Lenin but by German-based socialists such as **Rosa Luxemburg** (1871–1919) (see 'Key thinker 2' box). For both Lenin and Luxemburg, the unacceptable implication was that less developed countries would have to endure many more decades of oppressive rule, plus all the horrors of a developing capitalist economy, before the salvation of socialism could arrive.

Karl Marx (1818–83) and Friedrich Engels (1820–95)

No socialist thinker has had more impact upon both socialism and world history than Karl Marx. Aided by his lifelong collaborator Friedrich Engels, Marx propounded a series of revolutionary ideas that would have a seismic effect on political debate. Indeed, works like *The Communist Manifesto* (1848) and *Das Kapital* (1867) remain essential reading for any serious student of political science.

- Marx and Engels were the first socialist thinkers to offer a fulsome analysis of how humans were social and economic beings. Specifically, they argued that human nature had been contaminated by the prevailing economic system — capitalism — which encouraged selfishness, ruthlessness and greed. They argued further that capitalism had instilled in mankind a 'false consciousness' far removed from mankind's original nature — one that had been cooperative, selfless and fraternal. The task, they argued, was to create a new, non-capitalist economic system that would revive such noble characteristics.
- Marx and Engels were the first socialist thinkers to explain the centrality of social class. They argued that capitalism created two conflicted economic classes: the bourgeoisie (in effect, the ruling class, which owned and managed the economy) and the proletariat (in effect, the working class, which sold its labour to the bourgeoisie in return for wages). However, they also argued that class differences were far from harmonious: they involved harsh inequalities of wealth and power, and the exploitation of the proletariat. For this reason, capitalist societies were also unstable and would eventually be overthrown by an 'historically inevitable' proletarian revolution.
- Rejecting the liberal view that capitalism promotes prosperity and individual liberty for all, Marx and Engels explained how capitalism usually sought to be competitive by creating 'surplus value', whereas employers paid employees minimum wages, so as to allow most profits to be used for refining the means of production. Yet surplus value would also, they asserted, implant in capitalism 'the seeds of its own destruction' by nurturing resentful class consciousness among workers, who would eventually overthrow capitalism via revolution.
- Marx and Engels were also the first socialist thinkers to challenge the liberal notion that the state was politically neutral. Instead, they argued that the state would always serve the interests of whichever class controlled the economy. Consequently, the liberal state was 'merely a committee' for the ruling capitalist class and could therefore never provide an evolutionary road to socialism. This argument would inspire later fundamentalist socialists, such as Ralph Miliband (1924–94) and Tariq Ali (1943–), who ridiculed the 'parliamentary socialism' championed by organisations like the Labour Party.
- Marx and Engels thus became the first socialists to explain why revolution was not just inevitable but essential, and to describe what should happen once revolution had occurred. They asserted that, in the wake of revolution, an entirely new state should arise that would govern in the interests of the new, economically dominant class — one they called the dictatorship of the proletariat. Once this alternative state had cemented socialist values, it would 'wither away' and be replaced by communism: a stateless society involving common ownership and the principle of 'from each according to his ability to each according to his needs'. Such a scenario has never been realised, yet Marx and Engels' idea of a dictatorship of the proletariat proved hugely significant, justifying oppressive political systems in post-revolutionary societies such as the Soviet Union and China.

Activity

Describe, in approximately 100 words, the adult life of Karl Marx prior to his authorship of *The Communist Manifesto*, citing the key influences upon his thinking.

Lenin's vision, therefore, was accelerated revolutionary socialism — designed to ensure that socialism, and ultimately communism, could pre-empt the full development of capitalism. In his key work, *What Is to Be Done?* (1902), Lenin thus argued that revolution in pre-industrial countries should be the cause and not (as Marx argued) the effect of socialist ideas developing. Similarly, Lenin believed that revolution in early capitalist societies would prevent 'the masses' from developing any sympathy for capitalist values (a situation Leninists refer to as 'false consciousness'), which would then be a further obstacle to socialism.

Rosa Luxemburg: Marxist critic of Lenin

Luxemburg endorsed Lenin's argument, but only so far as economically under-developed societies were concerned. Although she admired Lenin's impatience for socialism, Luxemburg was concerned that Lenin's ideas could make revolutionary socialism irrelevant to the already industrialised masses in countries like Germany. Yet it was in respect of how the revolution should arise, and how it should be conducted, that led to the most serious dispute between followers of Lenin and supporters of Luxemburg.

To understand this dispute, it should be recalled that Lenin stressed the importance of a revolutionary elite — or vanguard — which would perform four vital tasks. First, it would plot and plan the overthrow of the existing regime (in Lenin's case, Tsarist Russia). Second, it would incite and organise the revolution. Third, prior to and during the revolution, it would start educating the masses into the basic virtues of socialism. Fourth, once the old regime had been toppled, the vanguard would form a new organisation: the Communist Party. This new party would embody Marx's dictatorship of the proletariat and direct all aspects of the new, post-revolutionary society — a doctrine that became known as **democratic centralism**.

Although some of Lenin's ideas, particularly about the dictatorship of the proletariat, were disputed by socialists like Luxemburg, they were aggressively upheld by a series of more important socialist leaders. Joseph Stalin (1879–1953) directed the Soviet Union in the 30 years after Lenin's death and constructed one of the most brutal, totalitarian regimes ever recorded, 'collectivising' agriculture, instituting a Five Year Plan for industrial development, and either relocating or murdering a whole peasant class in the process.

Stalin rejected the 'permanent revolution' theory of his fellow Bolshevik and arch rival Leon Trotsky (1879–1940), who had argued that any new socialist state could only entrench itself by encouraging similar revolutions in neighbouring capitalist countries. Instead, Stalin promoted the idea of 'socialism in one country', whereby the Soviet Union would effectively isolate itself from the outside world and thereafter promote a form of 'socialist nationalism' (a concept Luxemburg abhorred).

Activity

Explain, in no more than 200 words, how Luxemburg's revolutionary socialism differed from that of Marx, Lenin and Stalin.

Mao Tse-tung adapted Marxist-Leninism to peasant society

Having led the Chinese Revolution of 1949, after a prolonged civil war, Mao Tse-tung (1893–1976) applied similar ruthless methods during the first three decades of China's new 'socialist' state. But there were important differences between the Stalinist and Maoist methods. Instead of rejecting Trotsky's notion of a 'permanent revolution', Mao refined it into the notion of an ongoing 'cultural revolution' — one that would destroy the old mode of thinking, in much the same way that the initial revolution would reject the old (capitalist) mode of production.

Conducted mainly between 1966 and 1969, Mao's 'cultural revolution' became a campaign of persecution against any aspect of traditional Chinese culture (such as 'ancestor worship') that was thought to legitimise inequality and 'anti-socialist' values. Religion, deference to the elderly and the subordination of women were duly, and cruelly, discouraged. As with Stalin's Russia, millions died or disappeared in the process.

Despite its notoriety, the Marxist–Leninist method continued to be adopted and practised in the second half of the twentieth century, in countries nowhere near the level of economic development Marx had deemed necessary for revolution. During the 1950s, revolutionary societies in Cuba (under Fidel Castro), North Korea and North Vietnam all invoked the idea of vanguard communist parties, governing on the basis of democratic centralism.

As a result of its widespread application, Marxism–Leninism may now be referred to as 'orthodox communism'. Yet within these states, there has been little evidence of Marx's ultimate objective — communism — being even pursued, let alone attained. Far from withering away, the state in all these regimes became ever more pervasive. As a result, many believe that Luxemburg's critique of Marxist Leninism (offered long before most Marxist–Leninist regimes emerged) has been powerfully and tragically vindicated. For most of today's fundamentalist socialists, Luxemburg's ideas are therefore considered a more compelling brand of revolutionary socialism.

Rosa Luxemburg (1871–1919)

One of those who sought to uphold and develop the ideas of Karl Marx was Rosa Luxemburg. Through her membership of the German Social Democratic Party (SPD), Luxemburg made a distinctive contribution to the development of Marxist socialism.

- In one of her earliest publications, *Reform or Revolution?* (1900), Luxemburg accepted Marx's argument that capitalism promoted exploitation and was at odds with humanity's natural, fraternal instincts. She also agreed that evolutionary socialism was impossible: only revolution could create real change. Like Lenin, she had little sympathy for Marx's 'historicism' and denied that for revolution to occur, capitalism would have to reach an advanced stage of development. However, Luxemburg's analysis of how the revolution should come about would distinguish her from both Marx and Lenin.

- Luxemburg rejected Lenin's claim that revolution could occur only through the planning and leadership of a vanguard elite. Instead, she envisaged revolution arising 'spontaneously', after class consciousness had gradually been brought about through the proletariat's ongoing battle for progress in the workplace. Mass strike action would develop spontaneously from this and eventually ignite a much wider revolutionary movement that would overthrow the capitalist state. Yet Luxemburg rejected the Marxist–Leninist idea of revolution leading to a dictatorship of the proletariat. Instead, she advocated the immediate construction of a new democracy, underpinned by common ownership, open debate and elections.

- In many respects, Luxemburg was more faithful than Lenin to Marxist ideas. For example, she upheld Marx's internationalism by dismissing Lenin's interest in socialist nationalism, claiming Lenin overlooked the transnational character of both capitalism and proletarian interests. Socialist revolution, she contended, should be more than a form of national regime change; it should be a revolt against capitalism and nationalism globally — an argument which continues to be made today by groups like the International Socialist League.

- Luxemburg's concerns about nationalism were brought to a head by the outbreak of the Great War in 1914, which she stoutly opposed. Disgusted by the SPD's support for the German war effort, Luxemburg left the party and began organising anti-war demonstrations, certain that the war provided optimum conditions for revolution, while proclaiming that 'the enemy of socialism remains in our own country'.

- After the war, Luxemburg helped establish the German Communist Party (KPD). Conventional Marxists and Leninists were appalled by Luxemburg's belief that the KPD should contest elections to the post-war German Constituent Assembly, claiming this was a betrayal of Marx's rejection of evolutionary socialism and an heretical compromise with the status quo. Yet Luxemburg argued that having a foothold in the existing political system made it easier for communists to convey the case for revolution to proletarian voters. This argument portended Euro-communism in the late twentieth century and remains popular with modern communist parties in Europe.

Activity

Find out how Rosa Luxemburg died in 1919 and explain (in approximately 100 words) the political circumstances surrounding her death.

Debate 1

Is Marxism redundant?

Yes

- Far from communism marking the 'end of history', recent history has marked the end of communism.
- The collapse of the Soviet Union in 1989–1990 signalled the failure of an attempt (spanning 80 years) to bring Marxist principles to effective fruition.
- The attempts at implementing Marxist principles were not just unsuccessful; in the USSR, China and elsewhere they were catastrophic, leading to repression, torture and genocide.
- Capitalism has not imploded, as Marx forecast. Instead its reach has become ever wider, penetrating states that are either formerly or currently Marxist–Leninist (for example, Russia and China).
- In advanced capitalist states, the working class has not risen to revolution, as Marx predicted. Instead it has taken on the characteristics of the bourgeoisie (for example, acquisition of private property) while enjoying the benefits of market economies.

No

- Just as Marx deduced, capitalism remains unstable and volatile.
- Capitalism continues to leave a legacy of poverty and gross inequality, particularly in developing economies.
- Globalisation has weakened the power of national governments, reinforcing Marx's argument that economic power supersedes political power.
- The 'disappointing' record of socialist governments in capitalist states (such as François Hollande's in France after 2012) vindicates Marx's argument that radical change is impossible without revolution.
- Regimes such as the USSR and China were a distortion of Marxist principles — nowhere in Marx's writings is there explicit justification for the horrors that followed. Just because they were misapplied does not mean that Marx's theories were invalid.

Democratic socialism

In the UK and most other western European societies, the most influential form of fundamentalist socialism has been democratic socialism. It emerged during the late nineteenth century, developed during the twentieth century and (thanks to politicians such as Jeremy Corbyn and parties like Syriza in Greece) remains a feature of western politics in the twenty-first century.

Early democratic socialism

In the UK, democratic socialism was initially associated with the Fabian Society and bourgeois intellectuals like G.B. Shaw, Sidney

Webb and Beatrice Webb. It was also a strand of socialism that proved vital to the development of the Labour Party. Clause IV of Labour's 1918 constitution, heavily influenced by Webb, expressed the fundamentalist-socialist creed by aiming to 'secure for the producers by hand and by brain the full fruits of their industry and the most equitable distribution thereof...upon the basis of the common ownership of the means of production'.

What distinguished Webb's socialism from that of Marx and Lenin, however, was its rejection of 'big bang', revolutionary change. In her book *The Cooperative Movement in Great Britain* (1891), Webb argued that revolutions were 'chaotic, inefficient and counter-productive' and, for that very reason, 'guilty of the same problem besetting capitalism — *unpredictability*'.

Like other early democratic socialists, Webb, despairing of capitalism's volatility, looked forward to a more planned and 'rational' society where 'matters may be resolved sensibly...by rational, educated and civic-minded officials'. So, for Webb and other Fabians, the mayhem associated with revolution did not seem the ideal starting point for a bright and orderly future.

Early democratic socialists believed that the extension of the suffrage, from the late nineteenth century onwards, had facilitated a more orderly, election-based progression towards post-capitalist society. In a scenario Webb and other Fabians dubbed 'the inevitability of gradualism' (see Box 3.2), democratically elected socialist governments would steadily transform society via the existing parliamentary system, gradually replacing a society based on private ownership with one based on common ownership and public control.

Box 3.2

Democratic socialism and 'the inevitability of gradualism'

- Democratic socialist parties would campaign peacefully and gradually win the attention and trust of voters.
- The majority of voters (the working class) would gradually and inevitably realise they had no vested interest in capitalism.
- Voters would inevitably elect socialist governments.
- Democratic socialist governments would inevitably oversee the gradual replacement of private ownership with state ownership.
- Voters would gradually recognise the progress being made and inevitably re-elect democratic socialists to government.
- The continuous effects of democratic socialist governments would gradually and inevitably produce a socialist society.
- The benefits of such a society would inevitably be clear to all, thus making any reversal of socialism unlikely.

Beatrice Webb (1858–1943)

Beatrice Webb made a significant contribution to the development of early democratic socialism and its belief in the inevitability of gradualism (see Box 3.2). Webb's socialism was defined by four principles:

1 Capitalism was the principal cause of 'crippling poverty and demeaning inequality' in society and a 'corrupting force' for humanity, fostering 'unnatural' levels of avarice and selfishness among men and women.
2 Neither paternalism (see Chapter 2) nor philanthropy was a sustainable solution to the problems of poverty and inequality.
3 Poverty and inequality were most likely to be eliminated through vigorous trade unionism and extensive state intervention.
4 Effective reform tends to be gradual rather than revolutionary.

■ Along with her husband Sidney, Webb became active in the Fabian Society, an organisation committed to evolutionary socialism via reforms made at Westminster. She was instrumental in the Fabians' decision to align with the emerging Labour Party and was involved in drafting Clause IV of Labour's 1918 constitution. Although this committed Labour to 'common ownership' of the British economy, Webb helped ensure that Labour would pursue this goal via the existing political system.

■ Between 1905 and 1909, Webb served on a Royal Commission that examined the state's approach to poverty. Her celebrated Minority Report argued that the state should guarantee 'a sufficient nourishment and training when young, a living wage when able-bodied, treatment when sick, and modest but secure livelihood when disabled or aged'. Much of this anticipated the Beveridge Report of 1942, which was implemented by a Labour government after 1945. Webb's views on poverty and inequality therefore pre-dated both the agenda of a democratic socialist government and the emergence of a welfare state in the UK.

Activity

Explain, in no more than 200 words, why Webb rejected revolutionary socialism.

Later democratic socialism

Many regard the UK's post-war Labour government as a prime illustration of democratic socialism in action. After an overwhelming victory at the 1945 general election, Clement Attlee's government duly implemented a series of measures that had been carefully discussed and planned beforehand. The introduction of a welfare state and the transfer of several industries and services from private to public ownership all seemed to promote progress towards a fairer, post-capitalist society — underpinned, of course, by support at the ballot box.

Democratic socialist thinking was further updated by the writings of Tony Benn (1925–2014). In his *Arguments for Socialism* (1980), Benn restated his belief in fundamentalist socialism, arguing that the 'failure' of the Wilson–Callaghan UK governments proved the 'impossibility' of achieving socialism within a mainly capitalist economy. For Benn, the drastic cuts to public spending in 1976, made by a Labour government under pressure from the International Monetary Fund, underlined the danger of a 'socialist government seeking to rescue a flagging capitalist system'. In addition, Benn saw Labour's defeat at the 1979 general election as the inevitable punishment awaiting any socialist government that 'compromised with capitalism's contradictions'.

However, Benn did not accept that this invalidated **evolutionary socialism** — it merely strengthened the case for democratic socialists rethinking their tactics. Benn therefore argued that for fundamentalist socialism to be pursued peacefully, by a Labour government, a number of adjustments were needed. These included:

- the restoration of parliamentary sovereignty through the UK's withdrawal from the European Economic Community (as the EU then was) — for Benn and many other democratic socialists, the EEC, and then the EU, were simply 'capitalist clubs'
- parliamentary reform, so as to ensure an easier passage for socialist reforms — Benn therefore advocated the abolition of the unelected House of Lords and the subsequent strengthening of a socialist-dominated House of Commons
- stronger resistance by socialist governments to pro-capitalist vested interests — this could be achieved if socialist governments mobilised support from their own vested interests, within, for example, the trade unions
- the internal restructuring of a governing, socialist party — this should happen in a way that gave more power to individual party members outside Parliament, allowing them (for example) to select and de-select party leaders. This would encourage socialist prime ministers to 'stay true' to socialist principles and not be 'diverted' by non-socialist forces once in office.

Activity

Explain, in approximately 200 words, why later democratic socialists like Tony Benn retained their faith in parliamentary socialism.

Euro-communism

The belief that capitalism could be gradually decommissioned, via parliamentary methods and evolutionary socialism, was shared from the 1970s by a number of communist parties in western Europe. This gave rise to the phenomenon of Euro-communism.

By the 1970s, many communist parties in western Europe were keen to distance themselves from the excesses of the Soviet Union and wished to establish themselves as radical yet 'respectable' forces in mainstream politics. As a result, groups like the French Communist Party (PCF) and the Italian Communist Party (PCI) rejected the Marxist–Leninist case for revolution. Instead, they contested elections, took up seats won in national parliaments and occupied positions of executive power within the existing constitutional system. George Marchais of the PCF served in France's Socialist–Communist coalition government of the early 1980s, while George Napolitano of the PCI served as Italian president between 2006 and 2015.

In adopting this approach, Euro-communists were much influenced by Italian socialist intellectual Antonio Gramsci (1891–1937), who founded the PCI. Gramsci argued that capitalism could never be overthrown without mass public support. But he argued that such support was hard to achieve given that the ruling economic class had a supreme influence (hegemony) over society's culture. Socialist change, he contested, must therefore be preceded by the emergence of a counter-culture — not just in the workplace, as Marx and Lenin prescribed, but in artistic, literary and recreational life as well. To achieve this, Gramsci argued, socialists needed their own 'cultural vanguard', promoting new ideas from within existing society.

Euro-communists endorsed this idea, claiming that a socialist counter-culture would be more persuasive if parties like the PCF were legitimised by routine election campaigns and responsibility in government. All this meant, of course, that Euro-communism was a significant departure from orthodox communism. To summarise:

- Euro-communists argued that the existing 'liberal-bourgeois' state could accommodate meaningful, socialist change, including the transition from a privately owned to a publicly owned economy.
- As a result, Euro-communists rejected the inevitability and desirability of revolution. The PCF routinely referred to the 'disaster' of both the 1917 revolution in Russia and the 1949 revolution in China.

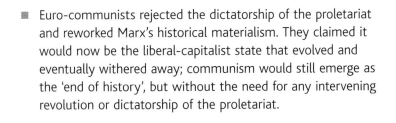

- Euro-communists rejected the dictatorship of the proletariat and reworked Marx's historical materialism. They claimed it would now be the liberal-capitalist state that evolved and eventually withered away; communism would still emerge as the 'end of history', but without the need for any intervening revolution or dictatorship of the proletariat.

Neo-Marxism

During the twentieth century, certain socialist thinkers, though respectful of Marx, nevertheless felt obliged to explain the survival of capitalism in western Europe. One of the most important contributions in this respect came from the so-called Frankfurt School, centred upon philosophers such as Herbert Marcuse (1898–1979) and Max Horkheimer (1895–1973).

Like Gramsci, Marcuse and others embraced the idea of a cultural hegemony when explaining capitalism's durability. As such, like Gramsci, they argued that capitalism's values do not simply infect the economy but also the arts, the media and education. Yet whereas Gramsci argued that this cultural hegemony could be countered if a socialist vanguard infiltrated key parts of society, the Frankfurt School felt that cultural hegemony merely vindicated Marx's belief in revolution. Echoing Marx, they argued that the violent overthrow of the capitalism system was necessary to smash both capitalism and the false consciousness that allowed capitalism to survive. That said, the Frankfurt School was not optimistic that revolution would occur; its spokesmen conceded that capitalism was proving more resilient and adaptable than Marx had envisaged.

Antonio Gramsci: critic of 'capitalism's cultural hegemony'

Consequently, these neo-Marxists rejected the Euro-communist belief that capitalism could be gradually reformed out of existence. Instead, they asserted that when the next economic slump came, socialists should advocate revolution rather than pursue a long-term project of cultural change. According to Marcuse, a society's economic system would always shape its culture; Gramsci was therefore wrong to suggest that the reverse could ever apply.

During the second half of the twentieth century, there were attempts by other neo-Marxists to update Marx's call for revolution. One of the most important was Ralph Miliband, whose key work, *The State in Capitalist Society* (1973), sought to demolish the idea that socialism could be achieved via gradual, parliamentary reform. Miliband argued that whenever democratic socialist governments had come to power, in the UK and elsewhere, they had been 'blown off course' and forced to dilute their socialist agendas.

For Miliband, this was wholly foreseeable — as Marx had predicted, the existing state would always protect the existing, dominant economic class. Examining the record of recent socialist governments in western Europe, Miliband claimed they were confronted and frustrated by a web of state-sponsored, anti-socialist forces, such as the senior civil service, the judiciary, the armed forces and the security services.

All these 'pro-capitalist' forces, Miliband stated, would conspire to divert socialist governments, especially during the economic crises to which capitalism was prone. Miliband thus concluded that a 'parliamentary road' to socialism, on its own, was impossible. It would have to be accompanied, or supplanted, by a revolutionary overthrow of the economic status quo, probably arising from the 'spontaneous' trade union action commended by Rosa Luxemburg several decades earlier.

Activity

With reference to the UK, find an example of a 'socialist' manifesto commitment that was subsequently ignored by a Labour government.

Box 3.3

Revolutionary socialism or evolutionary socialism?

Revolutionary:
- classical Marxism, Marxism–Leninism, neo-Marxism.

Evolutionary:
- democratic socialism, Euro-communism, all forms of revisionist socialism.

Activity

Explain, in no more than 200 words, why Marx and Engels thought socialism could be achieved only via revolution.

Revisionist socialism

Unlike all strands of fundamentalist socialism, **revisionist socialism** seeks to revise Marx's view that socialism is incompatible with capitalism. Furthermore, like some strands of fundamentalist socialism, revisionist socialism also revises Marx's view that socialism can be achieved only via revolution. Yet despite these two underlying principles, there are three important variations to revisionist thinking.

Key term

Revisionist socialism
This is the belief that socialism can be achieved without the destruction of capitalism and private property, and without the upheaval of a revolution. It is therefore a form of evolutionary socialism. Dating from the late nineteenth century, this view has been associated with Eduard Bernstein, post-war social democracy and the Third Way of the late twentieth century (see below).

105

Classical revisionism

The earliest form of revisionism came from German socialist Eduard Bernstein, in his book *Evolutionary Socialism* (1898). Bernstein noted that by the end of the nineteenth century, the condition of the working class was steadily improving under capitalism — especially in those states where capitalism was well developed. In short, there was little evidence that history was unfolding in the way Marx had prescribed, or that Marx's 'crisis of capitalism' was about to materialise.

This led Bernstein to argue that, if overseen by socialist governments, capitalist economies could provide an even greater improvement to workers' conditions, with capitalism's worst features forever contained. Furthermore, Bernstein contested that the widening of the franchise, and the advent of a working-class majority among voters, meant that socialist governments were increasingly likely. Such governments could then legally insist, for example, that employers regularly improved conditions for their workers, and that landlords continuously improved conditions for their tenants — all of which would curb the inequalities of a capitalist society, while eliminating the need for revolution.

Bernstein endorsed many of the ideas being promoted by early democratic socialists, such as the Fabians, and supported laws that would extend trade union rights and education for the working classes. He evidently shared the Fabian Society's belief in a gradual, parliamentary road to socialism and was friendly with some of its members. What made Bernstein different was that he did not hold such views alongside an irrevocable contempt for capitalism — in other words, he believed the struggle for socialism could co-exist with an economy based on private property.

Debate 2

Must socialism involve the abolition of private property and capitalism?

Yes

...according to fundamentalist socialists:

- Socialism's core values include equality; private property generates inequality.
- Socialism's core values include fraternity and cooperation. Private property promotes individualism and competition.
- Marx, Engels and disciples like Rosa Luxemburg believed that private property (capitalism) led to exploitation and oppression of working people. Marx and Lenin also believed the collapse of capitalism was historically inevitable.
- Gramsci and the Frankfurt School believed that capitalism's cultural hegemony promoted false consciousness among working people. This made the promotion of socialist values difficult.
- Early democratic socialists like Beatrice Webb believed public ownership to be more rational and efficient than private ownership.
- Later democratic socialists like Tony Benn believed that attempts to achieve socialism alongside Keynesian capitalism had failed.

No

...according to revisionist socialists:

- The debate about private/public ownership merely concerns the means not the ends of socialism — the true ends being equality and fraternity.
- Early revisionists like Bernstein noted that working-class conditions had improved under capitalism, as a result of capitalist economies growing in a way Marx did not envisage. With democratically elected socialist governments (passing laws favourable to trade unions, for example), Bernstein believed this was even more likely to happen.
- Social democratic revisionists, like Crosland, stated that increased public spending, not public ownership, was the key to more socialism. Steady increases in public spending were possible if capitalist economies grew steadily, which would occur if Keynesian economic policies were properly applied.
- Third Way revisionists, like Giddens, argued that a thriving neo-liberal economy could provide the state with a growing tax yield, thus financing the extra public spending socialism required.
- The globalisation of capitalism, and the spread of home ownership in states like the UK, simply forced socialists to reconcile their core values to a society where private property was ubiquitous.

Social democracy

During the late nineteenth and early twentieth centuries, the term 'social democracy' was associated with hostility to capitalism and even a belief in revolution. In the UK, for example, the Social Democratic Federation was formed by Henry Hyndman in 1881 after he was inspired by the works of Marx. By the mid-twentieth century, however, it was regarded as the most important and relevant form of revisionist socialism, far removed from the politics of Marx and Lenin. How did this occur?

The origins of the change lie in developments after 1945 within West Germany's social democratic party (SPD), one of western Europe's most influential socialist groupings. At its Bad Godesberg conference in 1959, SPD revisionists (such as the future West German chancellors Willy Brandt and Helmut Schmidt) persuaded the party to renounce its remaining links with Marxism by embracing both modern capitalism and the post-war West German state. Yet this development also had a British dimension, for Brandt and others had been emboldened to make such arguments by the work of a young British socialist, Anthony Crosland, whose book *The Future of Socialism* (1956) came to be seen as the key work of post-war social democracy.

Crosland argued that the reformed capitalism prescribed by English economist John Maynard Keynes — whereby the state actively sought to 'manage' market forces — had guaranteed full employment and steady economic growth. Crosland

Anthony Crosland redefined British socialism

Key term

Keynesian economics
Based on the work of liberal economist John Maynard Keynes, Keynesianism involves the state managing market forces so as to ensure steady growth and full employment. Social democrats believed that this would finance steady rises in public spending and thus greater equality.

Activity

Explain, in approximately 1,000 words, the differences between social democracy and democratic socialism.

contested that thanks to **Keynesian economics**, capitalism was no longer vulnerable to 'peaks and troughs' and could now be relied upon to finance a richer, fairer and more classless society. As Crosland noted, the end of capitalism's cyclical character meant a constant expansion of public spending, a constant expansion of state welfare and constant progress towards the ultimate socialist goal of greater equality.

Indeed, Crosland went on to argue that by resolving the problems of capitalism, and by establishing that socialism was not just about 'common ownership', Keynesian economics allowed socialists to look at other methods whereby greater equality could be secured, such as ending the 'unequal' forms of secondary education created by the 11-plus examination.

Despite their personal rapport, there were still serious differences between British social democrats like Crosland and continental social democrats such as those of the SPD, notably over European integration. Whereas the likes of Brandt and Schmidt spoke warmly about the prospect of a federal Europe, Crosland and other Labour politicians like Peter Shore warned that the application of Keynesian economics required national governments to retain autonomy over their economic strategies. As Crosland warned in his final book, *Socialism Now* (1974), a Europe-wide economic policy was more likely to promote austerity than full employment — an argument that would be echoed 40 years later by continental socialist parties such as Syriza (in Greece) and Podemos (in Spain).

Key thinker 4

Anthony Crosland (1918–77)

Anthony Crosland was a senior Labour Party politician, who served as a Cabinet minister during the Labour governments of the 1960s and 1970s. His book *The Future of Socialism* (1956) made a vital contribution to the development of social democracy in Britain.

- Crosland contested that public or common ownership had gone far enough, arguing that public ownership had never been the aim of socialism, merely a method for achieving it. The true objective, Crosland insisted, was equality, which could now be achieved within a managed capitalist economy.
- Crosland asserted that capitalism had been changed for ever as a result of economist John Maynard Keynes, whose belief in state-managed capitalism became orthodox in western Europe after 1945. Thanks to Keynesian principles, Crosland argued, advanced societies could now enjoy permanent economic growth and full employment, without requiring any serious extension of public ownership. Thanks to constant growth, these societies could enjoy a steady expansion of the welfare state which, in turn, would diminish inequality and advance socialism.
- Crosland also noted an important change in society. He argued that owing to economic change, society was less 'binary', less polarised between employers and employees, and 'infinitely more complex than Marx could

ever have imagined'. In particular, Crosland cited 'new classes', such as 'managers' and 'technocrats', whose perspectives were likely to be different to those of traditional workers.
- Crosland argued that socialism now required a 'mixed' economy. This mixed economy would mainly comprise private enterprise and private ownership, alongside key services and a small number of industries owned by the state, a situation which, for Crosland, had largely been achieved following the 1945–1951 Labour governmens. For Crosland, the future task of socialist governments was not more public ownership but more public spending and better public services.
- In his later books, *The Conservative Enemy* (1962) and *Socialism Now* (1974), Crosland focused on other issues affecting society, notably education. He argued for a new form of state education, known as comprehensive education, which would end the segregation of pupils at the age of 11 and create new schools catering for all abilities. Crosland believed these comprehensive schools would break down class divisions far more effectively than any extension of public ownership, while ensuring all pupils had equality of opportunity. Crosland pursued this idea while Secretary of State for Education between 1965 and 1967, initiating a process that made comprehensive education the norm by the time of his death.

Activity

Explain, in no more than 200 words, Crosland's view that capitalism was no longer an obstacle to socialism.

The Third Way

The most recent form of revisionist socialism, sometimes referred to as neo-revisionism, is the Third Way. Associated with the UK governments of Tony Blair and Gordon Brown, and German SPD politicians like Gerhard Schröder, it emerged in the 1990s at a time when the case for fundamentalist socialism was thought to have disappeared once and for all. The Soviet Union had collapsed, market economics were being embraced across Russia and eastern Europe, even surviving communist states such as China were allowing forms of private enterprise. However, this did not simply vindicate post-war social democracy; the globalisation of capitalism was thought to have rendered much of Keynesian economics redundant, while the apparent failure of nationalised industries in the UK — and the extensive privatisation of the 1980s — made support for a mixed economy seem dated. So a new form of revisionist socialism seemed essential for the twenty-first century.

Anthony Giddens (1938–) (see 'Key thinker 5' box) is widely credited as the main author of both third wave revisionism and Third Way socialism. Giddens' political philosophy arose from a desire to 'triangulate' social democracy's wish for more equality with a capitalist economy that was now less Keynesian and more neo-liberal. He also aimed to reconcile the task of socialist parties seeking office (such as Labour in the UK) with an electorate that was increasingly propertied, suburban and individualistic.

Yet for Giddens these changes merely augured 'the renewal of social democracy' rather than its abandonment. Far from raging against a free-market, neo-liberal economy, Giddens urged modern leftists to 'go with the flow' by encouraging further privatisation and further deregulation. Giddens argued that as this was the modern way to boost economic growth, it was also the best way to boost government tax revenues, and therefore boost government spending in the name of more equality.

However, the most important (and controversial) aspect of Third Way revisionism was its revised attitude to equality of outcome. According to Giddens, greater equality of opportunity probably required more, not less, inequality of outcome. His reasoning was that in a neo-liberal economy, increasingly unequal outcomes often went hand in hand with increasing rates of economic growth, and if outcomes became less unequal, it often indicated slower growth and therefore a smaller tax yield, lower public spending and less opportunity to ameliorate the problems of society's poorest.

Anthomy Giddens: sage of the Third Way

These arguments were a long way from both traditional socialism and previous versions of revisionist socialism. Nevertheless, between 1994 and 1995 the case for this Third Way was duly accepted by Tony Blair and Gordon Brown, who persuaded the Labour Party to renounce its Clause IV commitment to common ownership and thus herald the era of New Labour. One of New Labour's architects, Peter Mandelson, later provided a stark illustration of the difference between the Third Way and previous versions of socialism, stating: 'We are intensely relaxed about people getting filthy stinking rich…just as long as they pay their taxes.' To socialist critics of the Third Way, such as Tony Benn, this analysis represented little more than paternalistic conservatism, an effort to make inequality of outcome more palatable while consolidating the position of very wealthy individuals.

Yet it should be stressed that under New Labour governments, the tax burden rose far more than it would have done under an average Conservative government. This, in turn, allowed New Labour to finance a corresponding rise in public spending, from 39% of gross domestic product in 1997 to 47% in 2010. For some, this amounted to brazen economic mismanagement. For Giddens, however, New Labour's stewardship of the economy — involving deregulation of banks and financial services on the one hand, plus steep increases in public spending on the other — was a robust example of Third Way triangulation.

Economic policy was not the only distinction between social democratic and Third Way revisionism. The Third Way also placed much more emphasis upon cultural and political equality, reflecting the fact that society by the 1990s was much more cosmopolitan and diverse than it had been during the 1950s. Giddens also argued that because globalisation made governments less influential in the economic sphere, it was fitting that Third Way governments should address other, 'less economic' examples of inequality within society. As such, governments like Blair's passed various measures promoting greater racial, gender and sexual equality; the legalisation of civil partnerships for gay couples is one example. Blair's government also brought in measures designed to redistribute political influence, such as devolved government and a Human Rights Act. For Giddens and other Third Way exponents, these reforms — with their aim of equalising social and political power — were perfectly appropriate to socialism in a modern setting.

Activity

Explain, in approximately 100 words, the differences between Third Way revisionism and social democracy.

Anthony Giddens (1938–)

Anthony Giddens is known mainly as a sociologist. Yet his work on political theory helped create a new strain of thinking within revisionist socialism: the Third Way.

- In *Beyond Left and Right* (1994), Giddens first established his credentials as a socialist sympathiser, highlighting the 'corrosive' effects of capitalism and individualism upon community and fraternity. Yet he also stressed that capitalism and individualism were irreversible and that any future project towards greater equality would have to take account of this.

- Giddens developed this theme in his next book, *The Third Way: The Renewal of Social Democracy*, written at the time of the 1997 general election and published during the first year of Britain's New Labour government. He argued that the survival of social democracy required recognition that free-market capitalism had an unmatched capacity to empower individuals economically. However, he also argued that capitalism functioned best when there was a strong sense of social cohesion, which neo-liberalism seemed to overlook. So a triangulation — reconciling neo-liberalism's view of economics with social democracy's view of society — was required to make centre-left politics relevant in the twenty-first century.

- Giddens claimed this triangulation was especially important given the emergence of 'post-Fordist' capitalist societies. During the mid-twentieth century, Fordist capitalism, based on huge industrial units of mass production, had spawned tightly knit urban communities, based on a uniformity of income and employment. These communities, Giddens explained, complemented human nature's yearning for solidarity and fellowship by giving their members a strong sense of support and identity, which might then encourage them to challenge both economic and cultural elites (traditional trade unionism being one expression of this). Yet, according to Giddens, the post-Fordist capitalism of the late twentieth and early twenty-first centuries — involving the decline of heavy industry — had fragmented such communities, 'atomised' the modern workforce and left individuals feeling alienated.

- Giddens accepted that, in many respects, this post-Fordist (or neo-liberal) capitalism was liberating for individuals — they were now freer than ever to 'self-actualise' and carve out individual identities. Yet those individuals would also find it harder to develop, precisely because society was becoming increasingly amorphous and ill defined. Stripped of the communities that once gave them confidence, human beings were likely to be less sure-footed and more likely to be influenced by both economic and cultural elites. So, for Giddens, the great irony was that the 'individualisation' of society might actually result in less individualism. Giddens therefore argued that if human nature were to flourish in the twenty-first century, the state — while retreating from economic management — would have to be more proactive, investing heavily in infrastructure (for example, better public transport and community services) and a modernised system of education, designed to prepare citizens for the knowledge economy (one where physical capacity was less important).

- Giddens thus proved a key revisionist socialist in that he revitalised the case for further state action in an era of globalised capitalism. In doing so, he recognised that conventional Keynesian economics (which formed the basis of Crosland-style social democracy)

Continued...

Anthony Giddens (continued)

was obsolete and that socialism needed to reconcile itself to a more free-market brand of capitalism. In the process, however, he was accepting that greater equality of opportunity might have to be accompanied by greater inequality of outcome if the free market were to generate the sort of wealth needed to fund modern public services. His arguments had a profound influence upon the New Labour governments of Tony Blair and Gordon Brown and the German social democratic government led by Gerhard Schröder.

Activity

Explain, in no more than 200 words, how Giddens' Third Way was advanced by Tony Blair's government.

Debate 3

Does socialism require revolutionary change?

Yes

…according to some fundamentalist socialists:

- Marx argued that the pre-socialist state reflected the interests of the dominant economic class — it would not allow the promotion of socialist values. Marx also believed revolution was historically inevitable.
- Lenin believed revolution was necessary to pre-empt the horrors of capitalist development and stifle 'false consciousness' among the masses.
- Rosa Luxemburg believed revolution would inevitably and 'spontaneously' develop from trade union agitation.
- Trotsky believed that 'permanent revolution' was needed until all capitalist states had disappeared.
- Mao believed that to cement socialism, economic revolution would have to be followed by long-term cultural revolution.
- Neo-Marxists such as Ralph Miliband argued that attempts at parliamentary socialism had failed.

No

…according to other fundamentalist socialists:

- Early democratic socialists (such as Webb) believed in the 'inevitability of gradualism' — i.e. slow, steady change within the existing political system.
- Later democratic socialists (for example, Benn) believed that the existing state required reform rather than abolition.
- Euro-communists believed the capitalist state would eventually wither away but could accommodate major socialist reform in the meantime.

No

…according to revisionist socialists:

- Early revisionists like Bernstein believed that, with universal adult suffrage, the existing state could allow socialist governments and steady, socialist change.
- Social democrats like Crosland and Third Way revisionists like Giddens believed that, with the advent of a welfare state, the existing political system could ensure steady increases in public spending and therefore steady progress towards a fairer society.
- Giddens believed the existing state's structures could be reformed (via devolution, for example) so as to produce greater political equality.

Can socialist values be reconciled to liberal values?*

Yes

- Socialism and liberalism are products of the Enlightenment.
- Socialism and liberalism always believe in the possibility of progress.
- Socialism and liberalism stress liberty and equality.
- Socialism and liberalism reject hereditary political power and paternalism.
- Socialism and modern liberalism endorse 'positive liberty' and further state intervention.

No

- Liberals prioritise individual liberty, socialists a fairer society.
- Liberals think individuals shape society, socialists think society shapes individuals.
- Liberals see inequality of outcome as a sign of freedom, socialists think inequality of outcome precludes equality of opportunity.
- Liberals see capitalism as a condition of freedom, fundamentalist socialists see it as a threat to freedom.
- Socialists wish to extend state intervention, classical and neo-liberals wish to reduce it.

This debate is best addressed after reading both this chapter and Chapter 1. A similar debate about socialism and conservatism can be found in Chapter 2.

Summary: key themes and key thinkers

	Human nature	The state	Society	The economy
Karl Marx and Friedrich Engels	Human nature, originally fraternal and altruistic, has been contaminated by capitalism, instilling the 'false consciousness' of bourgeois values. Revolutionary socialism, however, will repair this.	The existing liberal-bourgeois state is a tool of the dominant capitalist class; it must be destroyed by revolution and replaced by a new socialist state: the dictatorship of the proletariat.	Capitalist society is sickeningly, yet fatally, defined by class interests and class conflict. A communist society will be the perfect 'end of history'.	Capitalism is corrupt, inefficient and ultimately self-destructive. It should — and will — be replaced by an economy based on collective ownership.
Rosa Luxemburg	Human nature has not been damaged to the extent Marx alleged. Fraternity and altruism still flourish in working-class communities punished by capitalist economics.	The existing capitalist state must be destroyed by revolution, but one arising from strike action. The replacement state should be a genuine democracy, complete with free speech and free elections.	Capitalist society is class-ridden and morally indefensible, yet alternative societies, or sub-cultures, exist within downtrodden proletarian communities.	Capitalism is more resilient than Marx allowed. Its necessary destruction, and replacement by an economy based on workers' control, will require determination and solidarity among the proletariat.

Continued...

	Human nature	The state	Society	The economy
Beatrice Webb	The damage inflicted by capitalism upon the human psyche will be compounded only by violent revolution. Humanity needs to be guided back, gradually, to its original, cooperative condition.	If harnessed to universal suffrage, the existing state could be used to effect a gradual transition to socialism.	The poverty and inequalities of a capitalist society continue to depress human potential while fostering regressive competition.	A chaotic capitalist economy will gradually be replaced by one which secures for workers the full fruits of their labour, based upon a common ownership of the means of production.
Anthony Crosland	Human nature has a powerful sense of 'fairness' and an innate objection to huge inequalities of outcome.	Democratic socialist governments (for example, Labour 1945–1951) prove that the existing state can be used to effect radical, socialist change.	Society is increasingly complicated, altered by the emergence of new social groups comprising 'meritocratic' managers and 'classless' technocrats.	A mixed economy, underpinned by limited public ownership and Keynesian capitalism, will finance the greater public spending necessary to secure equality.
Anthony Giddens	Human nature has been shaped by changing socio-economic conditions. The pro-fairness instinct is still present, but it now competes with a sharpened sense of individual aspiration.	The existing liberal state should be improved, redistributing and decentralising political power while encouraging greater political participation.	Society has undergone embourgeoisement — egalitarians must harness, rather than deny, these forces.	A neo-liberal economy, propelled by privatisation and deregulation, will provide huge tax yields. This will finance huge increases in public spending, which will secure greater equality of opportunity.

Tensions within socialism

- **Human nature:** all socialists believe that human nature is malleable and improvable, 'plastic' not permanent. Yet some socialists, such as Marx, believe that human nature is especially susceptible to whichever economic system it lives under. Therefore, people are likely to suffer a 'false consciousness' that can be cured only by revolution and authoritarian rule (the dictatorship of the proletariat). Other socialists, including revisionists like Giddens, argue that human nature can prosper under capitalism yet still appreciate the importance of core socialist beliefs such as cooperation, fraternity and collectivism.
- **Society:** by definition, all socialists see our social environment (i.e. society) as the crucial determinant of our personalities. So if society can be improved (i.e. made more equal and fraternal), improvements in our attitude and behaviour will follow. Yet socialists disagree about whether society can be improved gradually. Revolutionary socialists, like Marx and the Frankfurt School, believe existing society is so 'sick' and so inimical to socialist values that only a revolution can provide the necessary 'shock therapy'. Other fundamentalist socialists, like Beatrice Webb, believe society can be 'gradually' improved, and socialist values gradually more entrenched, by a series of reforms that gradually curtail private ownership. Revisionists like Crosland and Giddens also argue that society can be gradually improved and believe such improvements can occur alongside private property and capitalism.

- **The state:** unlike collectivist anarchists, socialists believe a state is vital to the promotion of core socialist values. But they differ dramatically about what kind of state is needed. Marx and orthodox communists believed the existing capitalist state would have to be destroyed by revolution and replaced by a dictatorship of the proletariat, which, in turn, would 'wither away' to produce stateless communism. Democratic socialists like Webb and revisionists like Crosland and Giddens believed that the existing state can be used to steer society towards socialist values and that the traditional state (in capitalist society) requires constitutional reform rather than abolition.
- **The economy:** fundamentalist socialists (like Marx, Luxemburg and Webb) believe socialism is incompatible with a capitalist economy based on private property. Marxists and orthodox communists believe that a new, non-capitalist economy should be created quickly, via revolution, while democratic socialists believe such a non-capitalist economy will be created gradually, via a series of elected socialist governments. By definition, revisionists believe that socialism is possible within a capitalist economy. Social democrat revisionists like Crosland believe that the economy should be mixed (i.e. allowing a degree of public ownership) and run along Keynesian lines by governments. Third Way revisionists like Giddens believe the economy should be neo-liberal, privatised and deregulated, claiming this will produce a greater tax yield and thus more public spending.

Conclusion: socialism today

By the start of the twenty-first century, many commentators believed socialism was a redundant ideology — a 'wasm' rather than an 'ism'. As we saw in Chapter 1, academics like Francis Fukuyama were arguing that contrary to what Marx had predicted, liberalism — not communism — was 'the end of history'.

During the 1990s, there was certainly strong support for this dismissive view of socialism. The collapse of the Soviet Union marked the end of a 70-year experiment in anti-capitalist, and officially socialist, government. Meanwhile, within western states like the UK, parties like Labour formally renounced common ownership — a key feature of democratic socialism — while embracing a Third Way ideology which many saw as indistinguishable from modern liberalism.

At the same time, socialism's support for collectivism seemed ill at ease with an increasingly individualistic society. By the 1990s, the number of UK trade unionists, for example, had been surpassed by the number of UK property owners. Far from seeing an increase in class solidarity, as socialists traditionally recommended, working people in western societies seemed to be undergoing *embourgeoisement*, taking on the characteristics of a propertied class and endorsing the values of a property-based society, which socialism historically opposed. Small wonder, perhaps, that the word 'socialism' was omitted from all four of New Labour's general election manifestos between 1997 and 2010.

However, the apparent dominance of capitalism need not necessarily spell the end of socialism. As we have seen, there is a whole school of socialism — namely, revisionism — that seeks to achieve socialism within a capitalist economy. With that in mind, the notion of a revisionist socialist government (one that pursues core socialist values through public spending rather than public ownership) seems far from fanciful in a modern society. Indeed, this was the message of the French Socialist Party when its leader François Hollande swept to power in 2012.

Furthermore, during the first two decades of the twenty-first century the case for capitalism did not seem as secure as Fukuyama *et al.* had imagined. The economic crash of 2007–2008 forced governments, such as Gordon Brown's in the UK, to increase state regulation of capitalism and, in some cases, extend public ownership. Problems in the Eurozone after 2012, plunging countries like Greece into levels of austerity not seen in Europe since the Second World War, again shook faith in the efficiency of both market economics and 'managed' capitalism.

In view of these traumas, it was unsurprising that in many quarters socialist ideas began to creep back into mainstream debate. Policies once confined to socialism's more extreme supporters, such as the nationalisation of banks, were solemnly implemented by Gordon Brown's government after 2007. In response to the Eurozone crises of 2013–2014, socialist parties — like Syriza in Greece and Podemos in Spain — began to gain electoral traction with a clear anti-capitalist message. Likewise, by the end of 2015, Jeremy Corbyn was leader of the UK's official Opposition, winning two Labour leadership campaigns with a message that restored socialism to the language of front-line politics. Even in the USA, where socialism had been off limits to 'respectable' politicians during the twentieth century, the term began to be used more freely. Socialist politicians were elected to office in states such as Washington and Vermont, riding a tide of hostility to market failure, while the socialist senator Bernie Sanders made a plausible bid for the Democratic Party nomination in the US presidential election of 2016.

This should remind us of two important truths. First, socialism emerged in the nineteenth century as a reaction to the problems caused by capitalism. So as long as capitalism proves problematic, the relevance of socialism will never entirely disappear. Second, even when capitalism seems relatively problem free, it is well to recall that socialism was never fundamentally defined by a desire to get rid of capitalism — such notions were always a means rather than an end. Instead, the essence of socialism has been a belief that society shapes individuals and that the best societies are those that promote fraternity, cooperation and equality. As long as those values appeal to large numbers of people, the relevance of socialism is likely to endure.

Nevertheless, we should always remember that in countries such as Russia, China and Cambodia, socialism in practice has often proved horrific. As recently as late 2016, when many socialists (including Corbyn) were lamenting the death of Fidel Castro, a report from Amnesty International recorded that in Cuba there had been 'more than 8,600 politically motivated detentions of government opponents and activists during the past year'.

We may conclude that socialism's core beliefs have a residual and renewable appeal, one that has clearly outlasted the sort of society attending its birth in the nineteenth century. Yet, judging by the history of the twentieth century, the implementation of socialist ideals can be hazardous and potentially disastrous. For this reason, socialism continues to provoke reactions that are both passionate and polarised.

Further reading

Benn, T. (1980) *Arguments for Socialism*, Penguin.
Cohen, G.A. (2009) *Why Not Socialism?*, Princeton University Press.
Heywood, A. (2016) 'Corbynism — the strange rebirth of UK socialism?', *Politics Review*, 25,4.
Kolko, G. (2006) *After Socialism*, Taylor & Francis.
McLellan, D. (2007) *Marxism After Marx*, Palgrave.
Sassoon, D. (2010) *One Hundred Years of Socialism*, Fontana.

Exam-style questions

Short questions

The following questions are similar to those in examinations set by AQA.
Each carries 9 marks.

1 Explain and analyse the socialist view of human nature.

2 Explain, analyse and exemplify socialism's support for collectivism.

Essay questions

The following questions are similar to those in examinations set by Edexcel (Pearson)
and AQA.

Edexcel (24 marks) or AQA (25 marks):

1 To what extent are socialists committed to equality of outcome? You must use appropriate
   thinkers you have studied to support your answer.

2 'Socialists have disagreed over means rather than ends.' To what extent is this true? You
   must use appropriate thinkers you have studied to support your answer.

AQA only (25 marks):

3 'Socialism is implacably opposed to an economy based on private property.' Analyse and
   evaluate with reference to the thinkers you have studied.

4 Is it possible for socialists to reconcile equality and liberty? Analyse and evaluate with
   reference to the thinkers you have studied.

Chapter 4

Nationalism

Introduction

It is tempting to assume that nationalism is one single movement. After all, it appears, at first sight, to mean nothing more than a love of one's national identity and a pride in the nation's history and culture. But when we understand how controversial nationalism has been over several centuries, particularly in the sense that it has been seen as a positive force,

a negative influence on international peace and understanding and even a force for evil, we begin to see that it is, in fact, a description of several different kinds of collective consciousness.

The names of important nationalist leaders in history provide us with clues about its varied manifestations: Adolf Hitler and Benito Mussolini were described by their own movements as radical nationalists, Fidel Castro in Cuba was a post-colonial, socialist nationalist, Winston Churchill was a conservative nationalist, **Giuseppe Mazzini** (1805–72) (see 'Key thinker 3' box), the great Italian leader who contributed to the unification of the country, was a republican nationalist, and today Scottish leader Nicola Sturgeon is best described as a liberal nationalist.

Even a casual consideration of these leaders demonstrates that they have little in common. To be sure, they all promoted love of their countries and fought to protect and promote their fortunes, but it is there that the resemblance ends. They differ markedly in how they viewed the relationship between individuals and the nation and between the nation and the state. This is not surprising as they came from very different ideological traditions — fascism, socialism, anti-colonialism, republicanism, conservatism and liberalism. It is largely the synthesis between these traditions and nationalism that explains the varied nature of the movement. These themes are explored further in this chapter.

The origins of nationalism

Various forms of political unit have existed throughout human history. In various places and at various times, these have been described as countries or as states, empires, kingdoms, principalities, territories and colonies or subject provinces. In parallel with these entities, history has seen descriptions of cultural units as varied as 'peoples', 'races', 'civilisations' and, of course, 'nations'. It was not until the eighteenth century, however, that two of these ideas came together to form what has become the 'norm' today. These ideas were state and nation. When they came together they were known as 'nation-states'.

Nations and states

The term 'nation' comes about from the Latin language and means a people who share common circumstances of birth. These circumstances have varied greatly throughout history. Some important examples have been:

■ The nation of Israel exists within a people who trace their ancestry back to a single individual (Abraham) and who share a common religion which comes to them through birth.

- The French, originally a tribal distinction (Franks), distinguish themselves largely through language. This was also mainly true of the Germans.
- The British see themselves as born into a common culture. As a nation they have complex ethnic origins but consider themselves as culturally separate from the rest of the world.
- Japan is a nation by virtue of its ethnic exclusiveness. Unlike England, Japan was little affected by waves of immigration so its ethnic identity has remained largely exclusive.

Through most of its history, however, the idea of the nation was not viewed as a political distinction. Nations were largely cultural groupings which sometimes governed themselves (the French and the English), sometimes were governed by external powers (the Italians and the Scots) and sometimes were spread out in a variety of states (the Jews and the Slavs). During the Enlightenment period of the eighteenth century, however, the concept of the nation began to be seen as a political as well as a cultural distinction.

Enlightenment philosophers such as **Jean-Jacques Rousseau** (1712–78) (see 'Key thinker 2' box) were interested in how political communities can come about. If the authority of a monarchy is removed, what can bind a people together closely enough to persuade them to set up government over themselves? The concept of nation offered itself as the answer. In particular, the nation was seen as 'organic'. Nationhood was a force, a single organism, that could create sufficient cohesion for people to agree on what kind of government they should accept. Earlier still, liberal philosopher John Locke (1632–1704) (see Chapter 1) had suggested that national identity often emerged from peoples who had been subjected to rule by a foreign power and who yearned for freedom. The American founding fathers created a new nation based on the idea of the 'American people', using it to express their freedom and their collective identity.

During the nineteenth century the ideas of liberal nationalism, as exemplified in the spirit of the French and American revolutions, spread throughout Europe. Its two main manifestations were in unification movements, notably Italy, and among peoples who were subjugated by the Austro-Hungarian Empire, such as Czechoslovakia and Hungary.

The linking of the concepts of nation and state by liberal thinkers gained reality in the form of the modern nation-state, that is a people who consider themselves to be a nation, forming themselves into a state and governing themselves.

It was an idea that reached its height at the end of the First World War, when US President Woodrow Wilson declared the principle that all nations were entitled to statehood. He was speaking in the context of the break-up of the Austro-Hungarian Empire and the Turkish Ottoman Empire, both of which had been defeated in the Great War. Many of their subject peoples were freed to form their own nation-states.

However, liberal nationalism was not the only form gaining ground in Europe. A form of conservative nationalism was also gaining adherents. Its main homes were Germany and Britain.

Conservative nationalism – the organic nation

This conservative form was not concerned with freedom and democracy expressed through the state, but rather with uniting peoples into strong cultural entities. This was an organic form of nationalism which stressed the national spirit and the power of patriotism.

In Britain, conservative nationalism was not concerned with liberation or unification, neither of which was relevant, but instead stressed nationalism as the more effective response to social divisions, especially class conflict. Benjamin Disraeli (Conservative Prime Minister, 1868, 1874–1880) stressed the organic nature of the British nation and saw this collective identity as a way of transcending class divisions. His ideas came to be known as 'one-nationism'. In Germany, however, nationalism had a greater cultural aspect and ultimately turned itself into a more powerful political force.

Liberal nationalists saw the nation as subordinate to the state. What was important was that the state should become the expression of the will of the people, should be their servant and should guarantee their rights and liberties. The nation was mostly a means by which the state could retain its particular identity. The German conservatives, meanwhile, saw the state as the servant of the nation. In other words, they proposed a reversal of their respective roles. Johann Fichte (1762–1814) was a key figure in this respect.

Fichte saw the nation as a cultural reality, largely based on a common language. He believed that a people, united by history and a strong sense of patriotism, could achieve great progress in terms of economic and intellectual civilisation. He ultimately rejected the ideals of liberal nationalism, particularly in France, on the basis that they weakened the collective will of a people by emphasising excessive personal freedom. He strongly believed that the German people had the greatest potential for such dynamism and so urged that they should be united into one single state (which was not achieved until 1871) and should lead the world towards greater human progress.

Meanwhile, his fellow German philosopher, **Johann Herder** (1744–1803) (see 'Key thinker 1' box), was also urging a revival of German nationalism, based on a romantic mythology of the people's historical roots. His ideas have usually been characterised as cultural nationalism, a romantic response to the rational ideas of liberalism. He referred to people with a strong cultural unity as *Volk* and the spirit that bound them as *Volksgeist* (spirit of the people).

Nationalism in the twentieth century

Both liberal and conservative forms of nationalism continued to flourish into the twentieth century. Indeed, the conservative form of nationalism became distorted into fascism in Italy, Spain, Hungary and parts of the Balkans, and into Nazism in Germany. It was also sometimes described as radical nationalism in those forms. More moderate forms of conservative nationalism have endured and are currently re-emerging in the form of nativism, which stresses that the interests of indigenous people (original inhabitants) should be placed above later immigrant groups. In a more benign sense, too, all conservative political associations in the West tend to stress national unity and patriotism. In the East, China and India are prime examples.

For much of the nineteenth century socialists, notably Marxists, opposed nationalism. They believed that nationalist sentiments drew attention away from the true plight of the working classes. Capitalism, they argued, had an interest in promoting nationalism and patriotism, to prevent class consciousness from developing. The oppression of the workers, it was asserted, is international so nationalism is not an appropriate response. As movements to free various peoples from colonial rule gathered pace, however, a form of socialist nationalism emerged, led by Cuba as well as regimes in southern Africa and South America. These movements often adopted socialism as the partner of nationalism as they believed that a capitalist future would cause the newly independent states to fall into the hands of international capitalism and thus be no freer than before.

Thus we see that although nationalism had relatively simple origins, it has, over the past two centuries, become a pluralistic movement with several contrasting manifestations.

The core ideas of nationalism

Human nature

The concept of nation

It is an essential feature of nationalism that people feel a strong sense of national identity. This may be compromised by other identities, such as religion or ethnicity, but nationality is seen as a fundamental form of consciousness. It can be based on a number of different common identities, including:

- **Language:** this was stressed by early conservative nationalist philosophers such as Fichte and Herder. Language was seen as a key aspect of culture and as such binds people together in an organic way. Furthermore, a common language indicates a long common history. This was applied especially to the German people, but has also applied to the French and the Italians.
- **Religion:** the classic example of a people bound together by religion are the Jews. Indeed, their nationality is defined by their religious identity. A number of Islamic leaders have also attempted to synthesise religion and nationalism, including Muammar Gaddafi (1942–2011) in Libya and Muhammad Ali Jinnah (1876–1948) in Pakistan.
- **Culture:** culture includes a shared history. The British are the perfect example. They are a multinational people, made up of a number of ethnic groups, a process that is continuing to this day. However, the British have a strong sense of cultural identity that binds them together. This includes traditions in the arts, pride in their history and a strong set of values to which all the people can feel attached.
- **Ethnicity:** the biological divisions of the world are not always translated into national differences, but when they are they make a powerful combination. Strongly ethnic nations include the Chinese, Japanese and Scandinavian peoples.
- **Geography:** this includes people who have occupied a specific territory and have long spiritual attachment to it. This applies to the Jewish people as much as religion. An exaggerated sense of attachment to land among the Jews is commonly known as Zionism. Russians, too, have a strong sense of identity with what they describe as the 'motherland'.

Johann Gottfried von Herder (1744–1803)

Johann Herder, a German philosopher, formed part of a romantic reaction against the rational ideas of the Enlightenment. His principal interest as a philosopher concerned the role of language in society, so it was not surprising that he should link language with nationalism. He also should be seen as part of a growing nationalist movement among Germans at a time when Germany was divided into many separate states. Indeed, the movement to unite the German people into a single state was certainly influenced by Herder's work.

To Herder, the world was naturally divided into nations, each one of which was defined by its own distinctive culture. National culture is developed through historical experience and its main characteristic is a common language. Herder's use of the German word *Volk* expressed this idea. *Volk* or 'folk' have a common experience and this binds them together. Though he was not one of Rousseau's followers, his idea of *Volksgeist* echoes Rousseau's concept of the general will. At first sight Herder's theories may be seen as a form of racism, but this is false. Herder was less concerned with the biological divisions among humans (a racist idea) than with cultural distinctions.

The role of language is the key to Herder's nationalism. He expressed its importance thus:

> 'Has a people anything dearer than the speech of its fathers? In its speech resides its whole thought-domain, its tradition, history, religion and the basis of life, all its heart and soul...the best culture of a people cannot be expressed through a foreign language, it thrives on the soil of a nation most beautifully.' (*Treatise on the Origin of Language*, 1772)

Interestingly, the stress on language and culture has influenced both liberal and conservative nationalists.

For many modern cultural nationalists, the defence and preservation of a threatened language has become a key element in national aspiration. This applies, for example, to Welsh nationalists and Catalans in Spain, both movements inspired by liberal values. However, many conservative and radical nationalists have claimed language as a justification for the forcible unity of a nation and discrimination (or worse) against peoples who do not share that language. Hitler's creation of a 'Greater Germany' was an example of this. Apart from it racial connotations, his form of national socialism defined the German people by their common language.

As an opponent of many of the ideals of the Enlightenment Herder argued that the fixed ideas of liberalism should not be applied to nationalist movements. This was because every national grouping of *Volk* was distinctive and developed its own values. This was in direct opposition to the French *philosophes* and Napoleon I who believed such principles were applicable to all peoples in all circumstances. Herder is therefore placed firmly in the conservative nationalist camp rather than among liberal nationalists.

Activity

Explain, in no more than 100 words, why Herder is seen as a conservative nationalist.

Cultural nationalism

The term 'cultural nationalism' refers to a kind of collective identity that relates to the organic unity of the nation. It has two main forms. One is a liberal ideal, the other extremely conservative in nature.

Liberal cultural nationalism flourishes among peoples who feel that their distinctive culture is threatened by a more dominant culture. This usually applies to a national group that exists within a state where there is such a dominant culture. Such nationalists may not seek independence but merely that their separate identity is respected and protected. Often their identity is related to their own language and culture. Welsh nationalism within the United Kingdom is a typical example. Most Welsh nationalists do not seek independence from Britain but do wish to see their language protected and supported. Language carries culture with it, so protecting language also protects a distinctive culture. Bretons in France are a further example of such cultural nationalism, as are Lapps in Scandinavia.

The ultra-conservative form has a similar concern to see the culture strengthened, but this is not in the interests of mere survival; instead it includes movements which believe their national characteristics are superior to others. This may translate itself into militarism and expansionism. Serbian nationalism between the world wars in the Balkans was an example, as was Arab nationalism in North Africa after the fall of the Ottoman Empire.

When such cultural nationalism meets a strong sense of ethnic nationalism, the combination can be dangerous. German fascism under Hitler was the most dramatic example, closely rivalled by Mussolini's radical Italian nationalism.

Racialism

Racialism refers to a belief that racial distinctions are the most important form of national identity. It can take a neutral form, in which case it simply implies that the basis of nationhood should be racial, though it can take a more radical form whereby one race should be favoured over others within the nation-state. This has been described in modern times as nativism. Nativism suggests that the original race that occupied a territory should be favoured, politically and economically, over racial groups that arrived later.

Racism

When a racial group feels itself superior to others and translates this prejudice into discrimination or even suppression or oppression, the term 'racism' can be applied. Racism can be both a state of mind — a sense of disdain or hatred by one racial group towards another — and a political movement. Political racists will openly favour one race over another.

Perhaps the most notorious example was Afrikaaner nationalism in South Africa under the apartheid regime. The white minority (largely Dutch-origin Afrikaaners) saw itself as superior to the indigenous black population, as well as those of mixed race (the so-called 'coloured' population) and immigrant groups from the Indian subcontinent. It therefore denied these populations civil rights (notably voting) and routinely discriminated against them socially and economically. Racism (based on tribal distinctions) is also a common feature of African states where one tribal people may enjoy a monopoly of political and economic power over minority tribal groups.

> ### Activity
>
> Explain, in no more than 100 words, the distinction between racialism and racism.

The state

Self-determination

The idea of the self-determination of peoples arose from the Enlightenment period. Its principal advocate at that time was probably Jean-Jacques Rousseau. His insistence, along with that of his fellow Enlightenment philosophers, on the self-determination of peoples was largely a reaction against absolute monarchy and became a touchstone for the creation of democratic states, emerging from both revolutionary activity (France and the USA) and constitutional reform (Britain). However, the aspiration of self-determination was often thwarted by the fact that many peoples of the world were subject to imperial rule. As the democratic spirit spread, however, during the nineteenth century, self-determination became the watchword for peoples seeking liberation from their imperial masters. In South America, Europe and Asia peoples who were describing themselves as subject nations were demanding self-determination.

While the Spanish Empire was largely dismantled by the mid-nineteenth century (Chile was independent in 1817 and Argentina became a unified independent state in 1861), the Austro-Hungarian and Ottoman Empires remained a stumbling block in Europe. The First World War finally brought the concept

Woodrow Wilson's 1918 declaration began the dominance of the nation-state

of the self-determination of peoples to a head when both these empires collapsed following defeat. It was US president Woodrow Wilson who finally expressed this principle to the world in a ground-breaking speech in February 1918 during the peace treaty negotiations. It is perhaps the best description of the self-determination of nations that we have. The key passage read:

> 'This war had its roots in the disregard of the rights of small nations and of nationalities which lacked the union and the force to make good their claim to determine their own allegiances and their own forms of political life... national aspirations must be satisfied...in the common interests of Europe and mankind.'

Wilson's principles have been followed in treaties made ever since, not least those that set up the League of Nations in 1919 and the United Nations in 1945. The principles of self-determination include:

- Any recognisable nation that aspires to self-government should be granted sovereignty.
- All states should respect the sovereignty of such nations.
- Threats to the sovereignty and independence of such nations constitute a threat to the whole international community.

Wilson's declaration represents the emergence of the nation-state as the dominant form of political community in the democratic world.

The nation-state

As the name suggests, the concept of the nation-state joins together the idea of statehood and the reality of collective national identity. While the state is a political entity — a political system which enjoys sovereignty and equal status with other states — the nation is a social reality, based on such collective consciousness as language, culture, ethnicity, common history or religion.

This is not to say that all nations are states or that all states are nations. There are exceptions:

- Some states are multinational — they contain more than one national grouping. The United Kingdom is a prime example, containing, as it does, English, Welsh, Scottish and Irish national groupings. The Russian Federation also contains a number of national minorities, as does China, even though all these states enjoy a common language.

Jean-Jacques Rousseau (1712–78)

Rousseau was a Swiss/French philosopher of the Enlightenment period. He was the leading member of the *philosophes*, a group of radical thinkers who were a major influence on the French Revolution and upon liberal thinking in general. Rousseau is well known for his theories on democracy, education and psychology, as well as on nationalism. His best known work was *The Social Contract*, published in 1762.

Rousseau is not normally thought of as a nationalist thinker, but his ideas on patriotism and civic pride did influence the creation of the idea of the nation-state in the eighteenth and nineteenth centuries. He was concerned with how political communities are created — how people might form themselves into units which would be capable of self-government, and which would be stable and capable of remaining united. States that were controlled by absolute monarchs — the norm in Rousseau's time — were held together only by the power of that monarch and by his armies and enforcement of law, but this could not be a justification for the existence of the modern state.

He therefore developed the romantic idea of the nation, a concept to which people could owe an allegiance which would hold them together. He was concerned not only with freedom of the individual but also with the collective freedom of the nation. To this end he wrote *Considerations on the Government of Poland* in 1771–1772. This work became something of a blueprint for writers of future constitutions. In claiming its freedom, Rousseau wrote, Poland would also create a new kind of state, held together by patriotism, reinforced by education and establishing a democratic form of representative government. For Rousseau, nationalism, freedom and good government went hand in hand. The third clause of the French post-revolutionary constitution of 1791 was influenced by Rousseau's ideas:

> 'The source of all sovereignty is essentially in the nation; no body, no individual can exercise authority that does not proceed from it in plain terms.'

The constitution went on to define French citizenship in a way never done before. It therefore established a series of rights and obligations based on that citizenship.

But Rousseau's principal contribution to political thinking was his concept of the general will. The true meaning of this idea has divided scholars ever since, but some have claimed that it was an inspiration behind some of the radical nationalist leaders of the twentieth century, including Mussolini in Italy and German National Socialists (Nazis). Rousseau's General Will could be interpreted to mean the collective will or spirit of the nation. As such it could not be expressed through conventional democracy but would have to be embodied in the mind of a single, all-powerful individual. While Rousseau almost certainly intended this device to be used for good ends, it was similar to the philosophy of a number of totalitarian rulers who used it to subjugate their people.

Activity

Explain, in no more than 100 words, why Rousseau's idea of the nation-state was revolutionary.

- Some states do not contain a single national identity. Their unity is based on shared political values, but their people may have many different national origins. The USA is perhaps the best example. The weakness of national identity is replaced by a strong sense of **patriotism** towards the state. It should be noted here that the term 'patriotism' refers to pride in one's state as a political entity, while 'nationalism' refers to strong identification with one's nation. Sometimes they come together. In South Africa, Nelson Mandela developed the idea of a 'rainbow nation' where different national groupings come together to create a new national identity based on their diversity.
- Some nations exist within another nation-state and either seek independence, as is the case with Scottish Nationalists within the United Kingdom, or are content to remain as a national grouping without statehood. Instead they seek respect for their national culture.

So the nation-state is not the only model for nationalist aspiration. However, it remains the dominant expression of national identity.

Society

Here we examine three social movements, all of which transcend nationalism. Civic nationalism seeks to create a new form of national identity where it does not exist as a result of any shared history, while liberal and socialist internationalism see the promotion of their aims lying in international cooperation rather than the division of the world into separate nations.

Civic nationalism

The model of civic nationalism is best exemplified by the USA. Here the claim to national identity is less important than the people's pride in the political institutions of the state. These political values are normally associated with liberal ideals, including respect for individual rights and liberties, a love of the democratic spirit and the importance of equal rights for all individuals and sections of society.

In the United States, citizens are encouraged, even at an early stage in their education, to develop a pride in the political institutions of the country. Thus, the US constitution and the office of the presidency are endowed with the same kind of spiritual status as national characteristics in states where the nation is the dominant collective feature. In this sense civic nationalism is also associated with patriotism.

Civic nationalism has also become an issue in modern states that have experienced a great deal of immigration in recent times. In the UK, France and Germany, immigrant groups are therefore encouraged to learn and support national civic values. Indeed, in order to gain citizenship, immigrant groups have to demonstrate their command of the language, political institutions, national characteristics and history of their new state. Civic nationalism therefore becomes a test of citizenship.

Liberal internationalism

The concept of liberal internationalism has two main elements. First, that the liberal democratic form of the state is intrinsically desirable and that it is to be promoted wherever possible, possibly including intervention in the affairs of sovereign states that do not conform to this model. In other words, it is a belief that liberalism is an absolute human value — whatever the kind of society in which they exist, these values deserve to be promoted. Second, that the most successful way of establishing and protecting liberal democratic values is through international cooperation. The most important example of this has been the European Union. Though the EU began as a force for economic cooperation, it eventually evolved into a political union. In order to qualify for membership, applicant states had to demonstrate that their political systems were truly democratic and that human rights were respected.

In general terms, liberal internationalists insist that states which do not conform to liberal principles are not members of the international community of nations. This effectively extends the concept of society to an international level. In European terms it opens the question of whether such a thing as a European society does or could exist.

Socialist internationalism

Fundamentalist socialists see class consciousness as the only valid vehicle for collectivist action. For them, class is everything. Other social phenomena, such as religion, ideology and nationalism, are merely reflections of capitalist domination and oppression. They are, in other words, means by which true socialist class consciousness can be inhibited by providing people with alternative, illusory, forms of consciousness.

The illusory nature of nationalism for the working class was expressed thus in the *Communist Manifesto*, written by Marx and Engels in 1848:

> 'The working men have no country. We cannot take from them what they have not got. Since the proletariat must first of all acquire political supremacy, must rise to be the leading class of the nation, must constitute itself the nation, it is, so far, itself national, though not in the bourgeois sense of the word.'

In other words, nationalism was to be replaced by socialist class consciousness. Pure socialists in general have converted this fundamental objection to 'bourgeois' nationalism into a belief that the working class of different countries have a common cause that transcends national identity. Thus they encourage international action to defeat capitalism and to establish socialist values. Nationalism is tolerated by socialists only if it is closely allied with working-class aspirations.

The economy

There is no intrinsic link between economic ideas and nationalism. Nationalism has been shown to thrive within different economic structures. Thus nationalism survived communist totalitarianism in Russia under Stalin and has coexisted with communism in China and Cuba, as well as living comfortably with capitalism. However, there are two prominent examples of nationalism being allied with specific economic systems.

Socialist nationalism

In contrast to socialist internationalism, socialist nationalists seek to synthesise nationalism with socialism. They have seen the two forces working to reinforce each other rather than as rival forms of consciousness.

Socialist nationalism has mainly thrived in Africa, where Julius Nyerere in Tanzania, Kenneth Kaunda in Zambia and Robert Mugabe in Zimbabwe all sought to establish socialism in their countries in order to combat international capitalist imperialism. Furthermore, by creating a collectivist economic system they sought to unite a people whose sense of national identity was weak. Fidel Castro recognised the same problem in Cuba after his successful revolution in 1959. Castro is perhaps the key example.

In Cuba, Castro saw an overwhelming need to create a sense of national pride, not around the country's colonial history but around the 'superior' values of socialism. However, this had an unfortunate consequence, which was that citizens who expressed opposition to socialism were also seen as unpatriotic. This led to a tyrannical form of ultra-nationalism where it was not possible to be a Cuban patriot without being a fundamentalist socialist, not to mention a challenger to the leader's will. A more extreme version of Castro's Cuba still exists in North Korea.

Nativism and protectionism

Nativism refers to a belief that the indigenous or original population of a country has a superior claim to nationality than groups who have arrived more recently. Thus while original settler Americans are favoured over Hispanics in the USA, original nationals over Arab immigrants in France, white English over European migrants in the UK, the main manifestation of this native sense of superiority is economic in nature.

Nativists believe that the original national group should have economic priority over other groups. This means, for example, that they should have first claim to employment and to social benefits such as health, subsidised housing, social security and education. It also means that domestic industries should be protected from international competition. Trade barriers (protectionism) should be erected to protect the job prospects

---

Debate 1

Is nationalism mainly a progressive or a regressive force?

Progressive

- Liberal nationalism has sought to establish the principles of democracy, tolerance and liberty.
- Liberal and socialist nationalists believe that it can be a force for progress, by uniting people around common values.
- Liberal nationalists and republicans believe that the freedom of the nation is synonymous with the freedom of individuals; individual freedom is also seen as a prerequisite for cultural and economic progress.

Regressive

- Conservative nationalists often seek to recreate a 'golden era' from the past, thus preventing further development. Nations which constantly look back to their history for inspiration may find it difficult to react positively to modern developments. This was a major problem for Japanese

nationalism after the Second World War, for example, as tradition clashed with modernity. China before communism was another example.
- Conservative nationalism is often defensive and xenophobic and so sacrifices progress in favour of militarism and isolationism. One may view Donald Trump's form of populist nationalism in the USA from this perspective.
- Racial forms of nationalism, such as Nazism and Afrikaans' apartheid, can often exclude racial groups they consider 'inferior' from prominent roles in society and so lose their potentially positive contributions.
- The rise of nativism threatens economic progress by inhibiting trade and by losing the efficiency that arises from competition.

of the native population. In addition, immigration should be controlled to protect the native culture.

Nativism is an ultra-conservative, regressive form of nationalism which looks back to a former age when the native national group and its culture were dominant. It also seeks to halt the progression of globalisation, in particular the free trade and movement of labour that goes with it. It has become a powerful nationalist force, notably in the USA and Europe, and stands in direct opposition to liberal internationalism.

Different types of nationalism

Liberal nationalism

It is generally accepted that the earliest form of modern nationalism was linked to the Enlightenment, the development of natural rights theory and the advent of liberalism, all of which took place in the latter part of the eighteenth century.

The influence of the Enlightenment and its stress on rational thinking and the right of individuals to determine their own free will led nationalists to believe that the nation-state was the ultimate expression of rational government. Until the nineteenth century, most states owed their existence to historical circumstances — they were derived from territories that had been governed by ruling families such as the Habsburgs, Bourbons and Hanovers for centuries. They had originally come into existence through conquest and thereafter the descendants of those original conquerors (even though succession was often disputed) continued to rule until they in turn fell from power, having been successfully challenged by another aspirant family. Subject peoples accepted this situation for three reasons: through fear if they rebelled, through a belief in tradition, or — and this is a key factor in this story — for lack of any credible alternative theory of government. During the Enlightenment, however, all this changed.

Rational philosophy provided a new justification for government. While there remained a general acceptance that the world fell naturally into separate, distinct nations, it was also established that such nations had to be converted into independent nation-states corresponding to those national identities. Furthermore, the philosophy of natural rights, to which all people were born, led to an understanding that hereditary rulers had denied those rights in favour of their own divine right to govern, based on religion and/or tradition. Rights could be restored only if the people themselves became involved in the establishment of government. This was characterised as 'self-determination'. If rights were to be sacrificed by individuals and granted to governments, this had to be achieved through consent and not through force.

These ideas were first incorporated into the establishment of the United States of America in 1787 and the first French Republic in 1791. Indeed, the first words of the American constitution express this idea clearly:

> 'We the people of the United States, in order to form a more perfect union, establish justice, ensure domestic tranquility, provide for the common defence, promote the general welfare, and secure the blessings of liberty to ourselves and our posterity, do ordain and establish this **constitution** for the United States of America.'

The opening words of the American constitution

Hidden in these words is the idea that the establishment of the nation-state by the people will create freedom both for the nation itself and for the individuals within it. Herein lies the fundamental liberal nature of this principle of self-determination. Furthermore, if a nation were not free, the people who made up the nation were also not free.

Giuseppe Mazzini, the great Italian nationalist of the nineteenth century, explains the link between liberty and nationalism:

> 'Young Italy, therefore, recognises the universal association of peoples as the ultimate aim of the endeavours of all free men. Before they can become members of the great association it is necessary that they should have a separate existence, name and power. Every people is therefore bound to constitute itself a nation before it can occupy itself with the question of humanity.'

Giuseppe Mazzini (1805–72)

Guiseppe Mazzini holds an almost unique position in the history of nationalism. This is largely because he combined philosophy with heroic political and military action in the pursuit of his ideals. Along with his close associate, Giuseppe Garibaldi (1807–82), he became the face of Italian nationalism and did much to create the idea of 'republicanism'. He was a charismatic figure who inspired a loyal following wherever he went. In the 1830s he formed a movement known as 'Young Italy', dedicated to the overthrow of the hereditary monarchies that dominated the fragmented Italian peninsula and to replacing them with a united Italy under democratic rule. He also fought against the domination of Italian states by the Austrian Empire at that time. He did not live quite long enough to see the unification of Italy under a new government centred in Rome. At the time of his death Italy remained a monarchy (under the Piedmont king) and had not completely thrown off Austrian influence.

Mazzini's form of nationalism has come to be known as republicanism. This is an imprecise term which has been claimed by many movements throughout modern history, but it can best be described simply as a synthesis between nationalism — the desire to see a nation united and free from external domination — and popular democracy. For Mazzini and his followers, the two aspirations were indivisible. A nation living under hereditary rule was not a free nation at all. His inspiration was the classical Roman republic. By freeing Italy from foreign domination, by unifying the Italian people and by establishing a form of representative democracy, he hoped to create a new Rome.

But the idea of nationhood was not a mere rational concept. Mazzini is often described as a 'romantic nationalist' in that he saw the forces that bind people together as being spiritual in nature. This is clear from this extract from *The Duties of Man* (1860): 'A country is not a mere territory, the particular territory is only its foundation; it is the sentiment of love, the sense of fellowship which binds together the sons of that territory.' Thus he saw nationalism in terms of both territory and nationalist spirit. Some of this spirituality was based on his religious faith.

Though he is sometimes claimed as a liberal nationalist, Mazzini did not see nationalism as a liberal value in that he did not believe that individual liberty should be allowed to interfere with the aims of nationalism. It was a collective enterprise for him, an enterprise ordained by God. Though he supported representative democracy as a political system, he saw the interests of the nation as standing above those of the individual.

Mazzini should be seen as a key example of a romantic but also dynamic form of nationalism, based on collective spirit and republicanism.

Explain, in no more than 100 words, what is meant by the term 'republicanism'.

The idea of liberal nationalism, the synthesis of the democratic state and a people who view themselves as a coherent and separate nation reached its ultimate expression within the fourteen-point peace plan proposed by President Wilson in 1918 at the end of the Great War. In his plan he insisted that all recognised nations were entitled to become free, self-governing states. On the whole, his plan was put into effect and many new nation-states came into existence.

The principles of liberal nationalism were now established:

- All recognisable nations are entitled to form a state if they so wish.
- The nation-state must be based on the self-determination of its people, i.e. their right to form a government of their own choosing.
- Each state should recognise the right of other free states to exist in peace with them and should not interfere with their internal affairs.
- All nation-states should have equal status in the world order.

In most cases, too, liberal nationalists were supporters of democratic government and respect for the rights and liberties of the citizens. Where they proposed the abolition of monarchy, they may also be described as republicans.

Liberal nationalism flourishes today largely in countries which are part of a larger state but wish to be free and independent. These include Scotland (where perhaps half the population are nationalists), Wales (where fewer are nationalists than in Scotland), the Basque Country and Catalonia, in both Spain and France, and Northern Ireland where about one third of the population are republicans. Nationalist sentiments also flourish among the Kurds in the Middle East, Chechens in southern Russia and various other ethnic groups in Asia, but their claims to be 'liberal' movements are more tenuous.

In liberal democracies nationalism is not normally specially emphasised. However, there is a link between liberalism and multiculturalism which involves one form of national identity. This is the idea that a nation should have a shared understanding of the values that bind it together. In common with liberal ideology these values usually involve equality, tolerance and respect for personal liberty. This common pride is sometimes described as **civic nationalism**. It is expected that new arrivals in a country should adopt this same form of national identity and pride. Naturally it also includes the principle that one nation should not interfere with the

Key terms

Civic nationalism This is a sense of shared national pride in the values of a nation. In most liberal democracies these are typically tolerance, love of liberty and equality between all groups and individuals.

value systems of another. Indeed, liberal nationalists accept that all nations have an equal right to their freedom and sovereignty.

Before leaving liberal nationalism, it is worth noting that many such liberals also have their own international vision. This is sometimes described as **liberal internationalism**. Far from being an aspiration to create supranational organisations, this idea stresses the equality of nations, that each nation's sovereignty should be respected, and that interference in the affairs of other nations, provided they do not pose a threat to others, should not be justified.

Conservative nationalism: the traditional form

For much of the nineteenth century, conservative nationalists were suspicious of liberal nationalism. They feared that it would lead to the destruction of traditional forms of authority (especially church and monarchy) and would therefore threaten order. Two great German nationalist philosophers, Fichte and Herder, both started by admiring the spirit of the French Revolution of 1789, but both became disillusioned as it led to conflict and a breakdown in the stability of the country. However, as an increasing number of nation-states came into existence, they saw that nationalism could be a force for order and stability. The politicians who adopted such a form of nationalism also saw it as an opportunity to further the interests and ambitions of the state.

Otto von Bismarck (1815–98), a German statesman, saw Prussian nationalism as the means by which the German people could be united and the deep historical values of Prussia could be advanced. He became the first chancellor of a united Germany in 1871 and proceeded to pursue two nationalist goals. The first was the creation of a new German *Volksgeist* and the second was the domination of the European continent by Germany. He expressed these two aspirations in the expression 'iron and blood', a phrase which was to return to Germany with devastating effect under Hitler. Meanwhile, to the south, Giuseppe Garibaldi was forging a new kind of Italian nationalism.

Garibaldi was an admirer of German nationalism and gradually his liberalism turned into conservatism. The unity of Italy was essential to his hopes for its people. As long as they suffered domination by foreign powers such as France and

Key terms

Liberal internationalism
This is the principle that each nation should respect the values and sovereignty of other nations provided they do not pose a direct threat to other nations.

Austria, Italy could never be a great country. His was a form of nationalism based upon both liberation and defensiveness. He also echoed Bismarck's ideal that nationalism could be forged through armed struggle and sacrifice. Famously during the armed struggle for unification he exhorted his followers to make the sacrifice with these words:

> 'I offer neither pay, not quarters, nor food; I only offer hunger, thirst, forced marches, battles and death. Let him who loves his country with his heart, and not merely with his lips, follow me.' (1849 speech)

These were words similar to those offered by Winston Churchill in the dark days of the Second World War. Churchill, too, was a conservative nationalist.

In France, **Charles Maurras** (1868–1952) (see 'Key thinker 4' box) was also urging a visceral, emotional form of nationalism. His brand of conservatism added xenophobia and anti-semitism to its call for the greatness of France to be restored after two crushing defeats by Prussia and Germany. Like Bismarck and Garibaldi, he appealed to the patriotism of the French people as well as their traditional Catholicism in an attempt to unite them. An anti-rationalist and anti-democrat, Maurras saw nationalist aspirations in terms of culture, race and religion. He never claimed to be a fascist, but his form of extreme conservative nationalism was very close to that of Hitler, Franco and Mussolini.

Today a key conservative nationalist is Vladimir Putin in Russia. Seeking to create a new unity out of the ruins of the Soviet Union, his ideology is based upon the collective will of the Russian people and on a determination to pursue their national interests both around Russia's borders and in the wider world. His obsession with demonstrating the strength of his leadership, both at home and abroad, is designed to inspire the people to put aside selfish interest and to work for the good of the homeland. Some have described it as 'communism without Marx'. Putin believes that Russia's national strength lies in the historical strength of its leaders, so that he is the heir of the great czars and of Joseph Stalin.

Imperialism and colonialism

Conservative nationalism often turns itself into imperialism and the pursuit of colonies which can be exploited to serve the national interest. The height of such nationalist aspirations occurred in the nineteenth century and involved the main

Charles Maurras (1868–1952)

Charles Maurras is a key example of what should be described as right-wing nationalism. His views remain prescient today and many of his ideas can be found within the contemporary nativist, populist wave of beliefs that flourish in the USA and various parts of Europe. In 1899 he founded a journal called *Action Française*, which was pro-monarchy, anti-semitic and anti-democratic. In the Second World War Maurras and *Action Française* supported the pro-fascist Vichy regime which governed half of France on behalf of the German occupiers. He described his brand of nationalism as integral nationalism.

Maurras believed that France had lost its greatness as a result of its abandonment of hereditary monarchy, its separation of church and state and its excessive attachment to democracy. His proposed remedy was the restoration of French nationalism and a stress on patriotism. He also believed that the French state and the Catholic Church should be united. He was an admirer of fascism, though not of the Germans, in particular admiring their belief that the Jewish people were responsible for the decline in French fortunes and for the introduction of decadent lifestyles.

The type of ultra-conservative nationalism favoured by Maurras featured a nostalgic yearning for a bygone age of glory, partly based on mythology, an acute xenophobia, notably concerning Jews, the establishment of a strong authoritarian state and the restoration of traditional values, including patriotic attachment to the nation. Much of his philosophy can be found in the Front national led by Marine Le Pen. Maurras, in colourful language, opposed all three principles of the French Revolution of 1789. Excessive freedom had led to a lack of respect for the authority of the state; equality had given too much power to the ignorant masses; fraternity had led French people to become too close to inferior peoples. He therefore proposed a return to pre-revolutionary France when the monarch and the Church imposed discipline upon the people and democracy had a very limited scope.

Leaving aside some of the more extreme details of Maurras' philosophy, his main contribution to nationalist thought was the idea that the interests and consciousness of individuals should be suppressed in favour of a collective identity, and the most powerful collective identity was integral nationalism. Integral nationalism accepts no collective identity above the nation and demands the people's complete obedience to the ideals of the nation. It is not quite fascism, but it has a great deal in common with it.

Activity

Explain, in no more than 100 words, why Maurras is described as a 'conservative' nationalist.

European powers. Indeed, national rivalry was expressed to some extent through a contest to collect subject peoples all over the world.

Britain, France, Spain, Germany, Holland, Belgium and Portugal were the main protagonists. All these states created their overseas empires at times when they were governed by conservative nationalist leaders. At the height of European imperialism, national identity was largely expressed through colonialism. Furthermore, to some extent, national pride was replaced by imperial pride.

By the time the Second World War was over, however, it was becoming clear that the imperialist era of history was coming to an end. The United Nations, on its introduction in 1945, outlawed colonialism (encouraged by the USA which had no overseas empire, it being forbidden under its constitution) and set about promoting the dissolution of the various European empires. By the end of the 1970s this process had been almost completed. Nation-states continued to engage in economic imperialism and commercial and military rivalry, but their colonies were dissolved.

Radical nationalism and fascism

There is a significant distinction between conservative nationalism and its twentieth-century corrupted form, fascism, sometimes described as radical nationalism. Fascism is distinct in that it advocates the complete subjugation of the individual to the will of the governing party of the state. Hitler in particular saw himself and his Nazi Party as embodying the *Volksgeist* of the German nation. This led to a leadership cult which allowed no dissension from his will. Those who challenged the will of the leader were therefore, by definition, traitors to their people. Conservative nationalism has had its share of powerful, dominant leaders, but none of them claimed to embody the national will. That will existed only in the collective identity of the people themselves. They were, in other words, the messengers but not the message.

Fascism is also distinct in that it places the power and will of the political state above the nation. While it is true that the nation is embodied in the state, they are not the same thing. Ironically, in common with liberals, fascists see the nation as the servant of the state and not the other way round as conservative nationalists tend to do.

It is also true that many conservative nationalists, though dictatorial in their character, have been democrats to a greater or lesser extent. This is especially true of British nationalists such as Disraeli and Churchill, but it also applies to the great nationalist

French leader Charles de Gaulle (president 1958–1969) and the Turkish nationalist Mustafa Kemal Ataturk (president 1923–1938). No fascist could ever claim to be a democrat of any kind!

Anti-colonial and post-colonial nationalism

Here we are considering nationalist movements which either emerged during colonial occupation (anti-colonial) or dominated the political agenda of countries after they had achieved full political independence (post-colonial).

One of the characteristics of nationalist movements within existing or former colonial possessions in all parts of the world was that they were underpinned by a variety of political traditions. In other words, there was no single pattern. Table 4.1 identifies a number of anti-colonial leaders, showing the political tradition from which they came.

Table 4.1 Anti-colonial leaders

Leader	Country	Colonial power	Political tradition
Kwame Nkrumah (1909–72)	Ghana	Britain	Pan-Africanism
Frantz Fanon (1925–61)	Algeria	France	Marxism
Mahatma Gandhi (1869–1948)	India	Britain	Liberalism/social democracy
Muhammad Ali Jinnah (1876–1948)	Pakistan	Britain	Islamic nationalism
Ho Chi Minh (1890–1969)	Vietnam	France	Maoist-style Marxism
Lee Kuan Yew (1923–2015)	Singapore	Britain	Conservatism
Patrice Lumumba (1925–61)	Congo	Belgium	Social democracy
Julius Nyerere (1922–99)	Tanzania	Britain	Community and kinship (*Ujaama*)
Robert Mugabe (1924–)	Zimbabwe	Britain	Moderate Marxism

Not surprisingly, once former colonies gained their independence their leaders continued the practice of synthesising nationalism with another political creed. The reason for this was largely because it proved extremely difficult to create a strong sense of national identity in states which were often artificial creations and which were divided along tribal, ethnic or religious lines. By adopting a strong political identity, therefore, the lack of national distinctiveness could be overcome. The most common political traditions adopted in post-colonial states included the following.

Marxism/socialism and post-colonial nationalism

This has probably been the most common synthesis among post-colonial nationalists. It is an unlikely combination in one sense. Marxism and nationalism do not sit well together.

Marxists normally oppose any form of consciousness (notably religion) which might inhibit the development of socialist consciousness. However, many nationalist leaders had been supported by communist regimes — normally either the Soviet Union or China — and were also aware of the danger that having removed their colonial master, they might fall prey to international capitalism and the so-called economic imperialism of multinational corporations. These states were all developing countries and so had a need for economic development which would make external investment an attractive proposition. To avoid this form of economic imperialism, therefore, nationalist leaders often adopted Marxist and socialist policies. Socialism also contributed to the destruction of local elites left behind by colonial administrations.

Fidel Castro (1926-2016) was revered as national hero in Cuba.

Robert Mugabe is a typical example in Zimbabwe, but the classic case is Fidel Castro in Cuba. Strictly speaking, Cuba was not a colonial state in 1959 when Castro seized power, but the Batista regime which he overthrew was effectively a tool of US economic imperialism, so the principle was the same. The synthesis of Cuban nationalism and strict Marxism worked well and US imperialism was indeed resisted. Despite unrest over the dictatorial methods of Castro's regime, Cuban nationalism has flourished and remained a powerful force.

Julius Nyerere (1922–99) of Tanzania was a typical African socialist/nationalist leader. He recognised the need to achieve two objectives in his newly independent country. One was economic development, which he hoped to achieve (with mixed success) by a programme of collectivisation of farms under state sponsorship. The other was to foster a sense of 'kinship and community', both strong values in that part of Africa. His policy, known as *Ujaama*, became something of a model for African nationalism. This combined economic development with the preservation of villages and family groupings. In so doing Nyerere created the idea of the nation as a 'community'. His policies were economically unsuccessful but he did create a unified, stable nation.

> **Activity**
>
> Explain, in no more than 100 words, why post-colonial nationalists have often also been socialists.

Religion

Most post-colonial nationalists in Islamic countries have adopted a form of religious nationalism. This has led to the concept of the 'Islamic state', in which nationalism is allied with Islamic values and law. This combination was a recognition that national identity could not be achieved without the binding force of religion to underpin it. Muammar Gaddafi (1942–2011) in Libya was such a leader, as was Liaquat Ali Khan (1895–1951), the first prime minister of the Islamic Republic of Pakistan. The principle of the Islamic Republic, a synthesis of religion and national identity, has become a common one in the Middle East and Asia.

Leadership cults

Democracy has found it difficult to establish itself in post-colonial states, as has national identity. A common political form, therefore, has been dictatorship and the cult of the leader, where the ruler seeks to create national identity by force. As occurred in fascist states, the leader has typically come to embody the 'spirit of the nation' in his single personality. Idi Amin (president of Uganda, 1971–1979) was a typical example. Robert Mugabe has created a similar leadership cult in Zimbabwe. Kenneth Kaunda of Zambia retained power from 1964 to 1991, having banned opposition parties, and so became Africa's longest-serving absolute ruler. However, by the time he lost power, Zambia had become a recognisable nation-state.

Expansionist nationalism

It would be wrong to assume that all conservative nationalists are also expansionists. This is partly due to the reputation of fascist states, notably Germany and Italy, and partly due to the assumption that the behaviour of the Soviet Union — which was led by the Communist Party, which was both conservative and nationalistic in character despite its Marxist roots — was based on a form of imperialism. Conservative nationalists are often defensive in their relationship to the rest of the world. Many nationalist leaders have underpinned their power by creating a general belief among their peoples that the country was under constant threat. This could be characterised as a form of 'defensive nationalism'. The Chinese regime under Mao Tse-tung after 1949 and Indian nationalism in the 1980s under Indira Gandhi (1917–84) were examples. Nevertheless, expansionist nationalism has flourished from time to time.

Expansionist nationalism takes on a number of forms. Among them have been:

- **Imperialism:** this is typically associated with conservative nationalism in the nineteenth century.
- **Pan-nationalism:** this is an aspiration to unite a people who are spread among many different states. The key examples have been pan-Arabism (associated with Gamal Abdel Nasser of Egypt in the 1950s, pan-Africanism led by Kwame Nkrumah of Ghana and pan-Slavism led by czarist Russia in the nineteenth century.
- **Militarism:** this is the most notorious form. It is based on the mythological character of the nation which harks back to a time when it was militarily dominant, a bygone classical age of conquest and heroism. Nazism was a classic example, as were Japanese nationalism in the 1930s and Italian fascism under Mussolini. Militarism and **chauvinism** (excessive patriotism) achieve two nationalist objectives. One is to rekindle past glories of the nation and so inspire the people. The other is to mobilise the people through the armed forces and thereby create a powerful sense of national unity.
- **Chauvinism:** this is an exaggerated form of patriotism, especially associated with Maurras and later in the twentieth century with French leader de Gaulle (president of France 1958–1969). It is so exaggerated that it demonstrates a certainty that the characteristics of one nation are superior to all others.

> **Key term**
>
> **Chauvinism** This exaggerated form of patriotism and national pride sees one nation as superior to all others.

■ **Racial conquest:** when racist nationalists come to believe that their own race is superior to others it can lead to a further belief that the race is entitled to territory currently occupied by other racial groups. This was an important part of the Nazi creed, but was also prominent in the Balkan wars of the 1990s.

Debate 2

Is conservative nationalism expansionist in nature?

Yes

■ Many conservative nationalist movements have practised imperialism. Imperialism is seen as serving the interests of the nation and arises from a sense of cultural superiority.
■ Conservative nationalists have often used militarism and conquest to create a strong sense of national unity.
■ Where conservative nationalism arises from a sense of either racial or cultural superiority it is inevitable that rivalry with other states will emerge, leading to conflict and the need to protect one's borders through domination of neighbouring states.

No

■ Nativism is the opposite of expansionist. It is isolationist and self-protective.
■ Moderate conservative nationalists are also usually democrats and respect the independence of other nations.
■ Expansionist nationalism was an historical form that has now largely disappeared. Globalisation has removed the need for national expansion and conquest, which have been replaced by economic competition.

Black nationalism

Black nationalism was a form of nationalism first introduced by the Jamaican political leader **Marcus Garvey** (1887–1940) (see 'Key thinker 5' box). It looked to the common ancestry of all black peoples in Africa and sought to foster a sense of nationalism among them. There is no suggestion that Africa ever was a nation in the true sense of the word, but Garvey campaigned for the creation of a new kind of nation which crossed boundaries and created a new collective consciousness.

Garvey's ideas were too early to take hold, but in the 1960s in the USA Malcolm X (1925–65) created a black nationalist movement that combined Islamic principles with racial identity. He called this idea the Nation of Islam. The great heavyweight boxing champion Muhammad Ali became a prominent adherent. Malcolm X divided the world into two races, black and white, and saw the black race as superior and pre-dating the white race. The traditional values of the black race he regarded as matching those of Islam. In the 1960s black nationalism threatened to take hold in the USA and other parts of the western world. It was, however, overtaken by a liberal movement which advocated equality for black people, as opposed to conflict with, and conquest of, the white race. As the radical spirit of the 1960s faded, so too did black nationalism.

Marcus Garvey (1887–1940)

Marcus Garvey was a Jamaican politician, writer and entrepreneur. (Jamaica was then a British colony.) Though a West Indian, he was primarily concerned with Africa. The basis of his beliefs was that the African people were one single race who had been scattered by slavery and divided within Africa itself by colonial rule. By uniting, the black peoples would be capable of throwing off colonial rule and creating a new, free and united Africa. His doctrine was known as Garveyism. He asserted that it had been a conscious policy of colonial rulers to divide the African peoples to be able to dominate them. He expressed this idea in his *Message to the People* (1937):

> 'This propaganda of dis-associating Western Negroes from Africa is not a new one. For many years white propagandists have been printing tons of literature to impress scattered Ethiopia [i.e. Africa], especially that portion within their civilization, with the idea that Africa is a despised place, inhabited by savages, and cannibals, where no civilized human being should go, especially black civilized human beings. This propaganda is promulgated for the cause that is being realized today. That cause is colonial expansion for the white nations of the world.'

As well as being described as a black nationalist, Garvey was a pan-Africanist, one of the first people to propose the unification of the continent. To this end he founded the Universal Negro Improvement Association, an attempt to counteract the lack of education that so many Africans and African Americans had experienced and which was holding back their progress. He also published a journal, *Negro World*, to encourage black education.

In the nineteenth century the state of Liberia had been set up in North Africa by anti-slavery campaigners in the USA as a new home for freed slaves. Garvey became interested in the project but lost interest in it when it became apparent it would be a failure. So by the 1920s his dream of a new African nation was nearly over before it had scarcely begun. He therefore turned his attention largely to black people in the USA.

Despite the lack of success in his own lifetime (he died prematurely in 1940) Garvey had a profound influence on future black emancipation movements, notably Malcolm X's Nation of Islam campaign. He was also a major inspiration behind West Indian Rastafarians from the 1950s onwards. Garvey had identified Ethiopia as the original breeding ground for human society, so it became a focus of interest in future black nationalist movements.

Activity

Explain, in no more than 100 words, the meaning of the term 'black nationalism'.

Debate 3

How close is the link between nationalism and race?

They are closely linked

- Most, though not all, nations claim some kind of ethnic identity which binds the people.
- Racial identity has been the binding force behind many radical nationalist movements, including forms of fascism. Race has been used as a means of differentiating one nation from others, even if the claim is tenuous.
- Many nations trace their history back to a single ancestor or group of ancestors, notably Italians (the original Romans), Jews (the original people of Israel) and Welsh (back to the Celts in Britain). This gives such nations a racial identity.

There is no intrinsic link

- Many nations are not derived from a single ethnic group and so are multi-ethnic (British, Indians, Australians).
- Even where common ethnicity is relevant it has had little impact on most nationalist movements (France, Greece, Turkey).
- Liberal nationalists in particular are less interested in race and culture than in shared values, and base their nationalism on the idea of liberty rather than organic unity.

Tensions within nationalism

Rather than speaking of tensions within nationalism, it is more useful to think of the main distinctions that exist between different forms of nationalism. Nationalism varies considerably in different contexts, so we can examine different manifestations of nationalism rather than specific examples. This section considers some of these distinctions.

- **Rational versus romantic nationalism:** this distinction arose at the dawn of modern nationalism towards the end of the Enlightenment period. Rational nationalists were concerned with the creation of sovereign political communities. The nation was seen as the most rational way of dividing people up into such communities. Any other way of dividing people would be arbitrary and therefore unstable. Above all, rational nationalists see the nation as serving the state rather than the state serving the nation.

  Romantic nationalism, exemplified by such philosophers as Herder and Fichte, stresses the importance of culture and language. The nation is an historic entity to which people have an emotional attachment. This also implies that nations have a future destiny. The nation is seen as organic in that people have a strong sense of community which binds them together. For romantic nationalists the interests of the nation stand above those of the state. The state exists to serve the nation and its organic unity.

- **Progressive versus regressive nationalism:** progressive nationalists seek to improve society and believe that nationalist sentiment can achieve desired aims. For example, economic progress may be fostered if there is a strong sense of national purpose. Such nationalists tend to be outward looking and accept the need to cooperate with other nation-states on an equal basis for mutual benefit. Though it has not achieved its aim of independence, Scottish nationalism is very much an example of a progressive movement. As an independent nation-state it is believed that Scotland could achieve economic and cultural progress.

  Regressive nationalists tend to be backward looking. They are conservative and reactionary, celebrating a past age when the nation was dominant, often referring to a 'golden age' in the past. They wish to return to traditional national values and institutions. Russia under

Vladimir Putin has been an example of a regressive state which believes that a return to strong central government and the power of the Church will serve the interests of the Russian people. Putin's nationalism also looks back to a golden age when Russia dominated eastern and central Europe as well as parts of southern Asia.

- **Inclusive versus exclusive nationalism:** inclusive nationalists do not see nationality as a reason for excluding people from the state. They are often also described as multiculturalists. Their view of national identity is that it is a flexible concept, based largely on shared values rather than shared historical experience.

  Exclusive nationalists, often described as nativists, stress the shared historical experience of a people. Such nationalists are reluctant to tolerate large-scale immigration and favour native peoples over newcomers to the state.

- **Expansionist nationalism versus nativism:** when nationalism becomes almost the whole historical destiny of a nation it can lead to a tendency towards expansionism. In the past this was converted into imperialism and colonisation, but this is no longer a realistic option. In its place some expansionist states have sought to dominate their region economically and culturally. The purpose of such expansionism is partly defensive — to create a protective ring — and partly a belief that the nation has an historical duty to become the principal regional power. This is true of current Iranian nationalism. Historically, Persia (Iran used to be called Persia) was the dominant power in the Middle East and it may seek to return to that position. Russia, too, is expanding its influence into the Crimea, Ukraine and possibly the Baltic states.

  Nativism, meanwhile, is inward looking. It seeks to cut itself off from the rest of the world (a doctrine known as isolationism) so that it can care for the interests only of its own people. The United States has passed through several such periods and may be heading that way again currently. The same may soon be true of some European states, especially if they become governed by populist, nationalist leaders.

- **Liberal versus conservative nationalism:** a key aspect of liberal nationalism was that it combined two elements. One was the achievement of the freedom of the nation as a whole, whether that entailed the unification of a people or their freedom from foreign control or domination. The other was that by achieving national freedom, the freedom of individuals would also be established. Thus the newly free nation-state was to be a liberal democracy. This was true of nineteenth-century movements seeking independence from imperial rule in such places as Czechoslovakia and Hungary, of the former states of the Soviet Union, such as Poland, Lithuania and Latvia, and of some contemporary movements in Scotland and Catalonia.

  Conservative nationalists also promote the creation of independent, unified nations, based on such features as shared culture, language, ethnicity or religion, but do not link this with democracy in the liberal sense of the word. This is not to say that conservative nationalists exist only in monarchies or authoritarian states; many conservative nationalists thrive in liberal democracies such as Britain and France, but for them, the organic unity of the nation is more crucial than the individual liberties of its people. It is something of a generalisation, but often true, that liberal nationalists tend to be progressive, looking to future development of their societies, while conservative nationalists seek to preserve the status quo or even a return to former national values and a past national identity.

- **Racialism versus multiculturalism:** racialists stress the division of peoples into ethnic groupings. For them, racial differences are important, sometimes to be celebrated, sometimes to be merely recognised and tolerated, sometimes to be converted into separate states for separate races.

Continued...

Whatever their attitude to race, they believe the state should take account of the differences. In a modern context this has become known as 'identity politics'. The UK Independence Party has adopted such a perspective, as has the 'Tea Party' wing of the US Republican Party.

Those who believe that ethnic distinctions are not important as far as citizenship is concerned are often described as multiculturalists. While a variety of cultures may enrich society, the state should never make distinctions of any kind on the basis of race.

- **Nationalism versus internationalism:** though nationalism became a dominant political idea in the twentieth century, a rival movement, known as internationalism, briefly rivalled it. Internationalism was largely a socialist ideal, based on the idea that the problems of the working class were international in nature. The First World War gave a fillip to internationalism as it was perceived by socialists to be a capitalist war in which the working classes of many nations made the sacrifices. In other words, members of the international working class have more in common with each other than with members of their own nation.

A further level of interest appeared after the Second World War when various European politicians cultivated an interest in international cooperation on a European basis. Jean Monnet, a French socialist, and Winston Churchill, the British Conservative prime minister, both proposed a political union which would eliminate the possibility of future national conflict. However, by the turn of the twentieth century it was becoming clear that nationalism was too strong a force for states to be willing to give up their national sovereignty to a supranational organisation. Furthermore, as globalisation has gathered pace, nationalist forces have strengthened against it, with right-wing nationalist parties making progress all over the western world.

Table 4.2 outlines the key distinctions within nationalism.

Table 4.2 Key distinctions within nationalism

Liberal	Conservative	Post-colonial	Expansionist
It proposes the establishment of a liberal democracy in new nations.	It tends to stress the organic nature of the nation rather than individualism.	It is less concerned with creating a democratic state, rather more concerned with nation building.	Expansionist nationalists do not respect the sovereignty of other nation-states.
The freedom of individuals is seen as synonymous with the freedom of the nation as a whole.	Patriotism is seen as a key social characteristic.	Post-colonial states are often socialist in order to combat economic imperialism from international capitalism.	There is usually a sense of racial or national superiority over other races and nations.
Liberal nationalists respect the sovereignty of other legitimate states.	Conservative states are either excessively defensive and seek to preserve national traditions or can be expansionist and seek to spread national values to other peoples.	Post-colonial nationalists often synthesise nationalism with another political creed, such as socialism or religious fundamentalism. National community is stressed.	Such nation-states are often highly militaristic. They stress ideas of historic destiny and mythical heroism.
The liberal state is more important than the nation. Nationalism should serve the state.	The state exists to serve the interests of the organic nation.	Post-colonial nation-states are often subject to dictatorship in the interests of nation building and self-preservation.	The nation and its historic destiny transcend individualism and democracy.

Conclusion: nationalism today

The subject of nationalism has scarcely ever been more important than it is today. This is largely because the context in which it exists has changed so dramatically. Three modern developments have seriously affected the world of nationalism:

1 Increasing globalisation has thrown the issue of nationalism into sharper focus. With the growth of multinational corporations, free trade, internet markets that do not recognise national boundaries, international crime, often cyber-crime, and supranational organisations, the independent power of nation-states to control their own affairs has significantly diminished. This has led to reaction among many conservative parties and politicians who fear that nations will lose both their economic independence and their cultural distinctiveness.

2 The division of the world into regional trading blocs, such as the European Union, the North Atlantic Free Trade Agreement and the Association of Southeast Asian Nations, has had a similar effect to globalisation. All these organisations have struggled to find a collective identity that can rival nationalism, but nevertheless are still seen as a threat to the traditional nation-state.

3 The rise of religious fundamentalism, especially in the Middle East, has cut across and threatened national identity. This has often given rise to the phenomenon of the 'failed state', a term adopted by anarchist Noam Chomsky, referring to states that have become hopelessly fractured and ungovernable as a result of forces, often religious, that have become rivals to national unity. Iraq, Afghanistan, Yemen and Somalia are prominent examples.

Faced with these pressures, nationalism has collapsed in many countries, but in western developed countries particularly, a different effect has been felt. This is the rise of populism, which has given rise to a new form of nationalism that has not been seen since the early part of the twentieth century. This is sometimes known as **nativism**.

In simple terms, nativism refers to a belief or movement that favours the native inhabitants of a country over groups that have arrived more recently. This preference may have more than one root cause. It may be simply an exaggerated form of patriotism, though some critics argue that it is a hidden form of racism. It can also be connected to cultural nationalism or a fear that a particular culture is under threat from rival cultures, usually brought in by immigrant groups. Above all, however, it tends to be economic in nature.

Key term

Nativism This is a form of nationalism or patriotism which distinguishes between the 'native' population of a country and immigrant groups who have arrived more recently. It manifests itself in demands to curb immigration and introduce economic policies that ensure the economic wellbeing of native groups, which are seen as threatened by immigration and free trade.

The economic roots of nativism lie largely in the belief that new immigrant groups threaten the economic position of the long-standing native population. Immigrant groups tend to be dynamic and highly aspirant, challenging the entrenched position of the existing population. At the same time the new influx of labour, often willing to work for low wages and put in long hours, is thought to be bringing down wage rates and creating unemployment. Globalisation and the increased competition that it brings is also seen as a threat to domestic income levels and employment.

Nativism has manifested itself in a host of new political movements, including the UK Independence Party, Donald Trump's following in the USA, the Front National in France and Geert Wilders' Party for Freedom in the Netherlands. The slogans of such movements are revealing, including 'America First', 'France for the French' and 'Make the Netherlands Great Again'. These parties and movements are universally opposed to excessive immigration and tend to be protectionist, proposing tariffs (taxes) on imported goods to protect domestic industry and employment from foreign competition.

Yet despite all the modern pressures on nationalism, its traditional forms continue to flourish. In Putin's Russia, for example, a typical conservative form of nationalism thrives, as it does in a number of former republics of the Soviet Union. Liberal feminism, too, persists in countries which seek the freedom of their peoples from domination by a more powerful culture. Movements in Scotland, Catalonia (Spain and France) and the Flemish parts of Belgium have all made considerable progress in recent decades. It remains a persuasive and potent ideology.

Summary: key themes and key thinkers

	Human nature	The state	Society	The economy
Johann von Herder	People see their own identity in terms of the collective identity of a cultural group with common language and history.	States can only be rightfully based upon the collective identity of a people with common cultural and linguistic heritage.	Society is a cultural concept. It is based on a shared sense of culture and national heritage.	Herder made no special relationships between nation and economy.
Jean-Jacques Rousseau	People are rational beings who desire their own freedom.	The basis of any legitimate state has to be the nation. The nation is the vehicle for self-determination.	Political society must be based on national self-determination.	Rousseau saw no particular relationship between nationalism and economic structures.
Giuseppe Mazzini	People have a romantic vision of their origins. They seek liberty, but it is contained in the liberty of the people to which they belong.	The state is a romantic ideal, the ultimate expression of the unity of a people.	Society must allow personal freedom to flourish. Individuals can be free only if a whole society is also free.	Economic freedom is a natural result of general freedom enjoyed by nations and their peoples.
Charles Maurras	Ethnic identity is a key aspect of our consciousness.	Various states do not have equal status. Some peoples and states are superior to others.	Society is based on a shared sense of ethnicity. Some societies are superior forms of civilisation to others.	The superior culture of one nation naturally leads to the economic dominance of that nation over weaker nations.
Marcus Garvey	All people are part of either a white race or a black race. Though the white race has dominated the black race, the latter can claim a superior history and culture.	States are largely artificial constructs, the products of white supremacy. The only meaningful state should be the united black peoples of the world.	Black society will be superior to white society once the colonial oppression of black people is defeated.	Garvey opposed both international capitalism, which leads to imperialism, and communism, which leads to dictatorship. Black peoples should set up their own form of capitalism for their own benefit.

Further reading

Five classic works on nationalism are:

Houston Chamberlain. *The Foundations of the Nineteenth Century*.

Frantz Fanon and Jean-Paul Sartre. *The Wretched of the Earth*.

Mahatma Gandhi. *India of My Dreams*.

Marcus Garvey. *Selected Writings and Speeches of Marcus Garvey*.

Jean-Jacques Rousseau. *Considerations on the Government of Poland*.

Important works about nationalism include:

Anderson, B. (2016) *Imagined Communities*, Verso.

Gellner, E. (2006) *Nations and Nationalism*, Blackwell.

Grosby, S. (2005) *Nationalism: A Very Short Introduction*, Oxford University Press.

Smith, A. (2010) *Nationalism: Theory, Ideology, History*, Polity.

Sutherland, C. (2011) *Nationalism in the Twenty-first Century*, Palgrave.

Exam-style questions

Essay questions

The following questions are similar to those in examinations set by Edexcel (Pearson) and AQA.

Edexcel (24 marks) or AQA (25 marks):

1 To what extent has nationalism been a progressive or backward-looking ideology? You must use appropriate thinkers you have studied to support your answer.

2 To what extent has nationalism been associated with racism? You must use appropriate thinkers you have studied to support your answer.

AQA only (25 marks):

3 'In the face of both globalisation and religious fundamentalism, nationalism is in terminal decline.' Analyse and evaluate with reference to the thinker you have studied.

4 With reference to the thinkers you have studied, analyse and evaluate the links between nationalism and liberalism.

Chapter 5

Multiculturalism

Introduction: a misunderstood concept

During the twenty-first century, the term 'multiculturalism' has played an increasingly prominent role in political discussion. For some, it is a term that denotes vibrancy, modernity and tolerance. For others, it is a word that distils much of what has gone wrong in diverse, western societies. Yet there remains widespread misunderstanding about what multiculturalism actually involves.

The main reason for this is that many people equate multiculturalism with the visible presence of a multicultural society — that is, a society with a multitude of communities, exhibiting a variety of cultural characteristics. This leads many to overlook a crucial fact which must be understood at the start of this chapter: a multicultural society, complete with ethnic and cultural diversity, is not the same as multiculturalism. Put another way, while multiculturalism may be impossible without a multicultural society, it is quite possible — indeed usual — to have a multicultural society without having multiculturalism.

To grasp the basics of multiculturalism, students must understand two further points. The first is that multiculturalism is a normative not empirical concept — initially at least, multiculturalism does not describe what is, it prescribes what should be. The second point is that multiculturalism's prescriptions have to be implemented by the state at either central or local level. It is this that makes multiculturalism a political ideology. Its diagnoses may overlap with other academic disciplines (notably sociology), but its prescriptions can be implemented only by politicians.

In summary, multiculturalism should not be seen as an adjective for modern, culturally diverse communities; instead it should be seen as a state-led strategy, designed to bring unity to a diverse, multicultural society. It is a strategy where politicians aim to unify society, not by crushing cultural variety but by actively promoting it. In short, multiculturalism seeks unity via state-sponsored diversity.

The origins of multiculturalism

Given that multiculturalism is a response to multicultural societies, its origins naturally lie in the emergence of such societies. Multicultural societies are no recent phenomena;

Culture A frequently used term, rarely defined with much precision. In the words of philosopher Isaiah Berlin, it refers to the 'sum of preferences and assumptions that create and sustain communities...normally relating to language, morality, religion and shared historical circumstance'. For Bhikhu Parekh, culture is defined by the 'primordo-historical' factors shared by groups of individuals, such as ethnicity or country of origin.

Assimilation A French-style response to a multicultural or multiracial society; one where the state vigorously promotes the 'majority' culture while encouraging those from minority backgrounds to avoid public expressions of their own culture in the interests of social cohesion.

Individualist integration A US/UK-style response to a multicultural or multiracial society; one where the state endorses a majority (and broadly liberal) culture, while recognising the right of minority cultures to exist in the private sphere.

Diversity Central to multiculturalism is the belief that as a result of tolerance, multicultural societies can glory in their ethnic and cultural variety, seeing it as conducive to a harmonious and united society.

they have existed across the world for centuries under all sorts of political regimes. Indeed, the first multiculturalist ideas were developed in Canada and Australia, nations that had long been anything but homogeneous in their cultural make-up. The distinctions between, for example, Canadian–British, Canadian–French and native-Canadian cultures had their roots in the Anglo-French colonisation of the eighteenth century, while the cultural ambiguities in Australia (involving those of both Aboriginal and European descent) had a similar historical pedigree, again largely as a result of Euro-imperialist expansion.

However, it was in the 1960s and 1970s that multiculturalism — as opposed to multicultural societies — began to gain traction within certain liberal democracies. There were four main reasons behind this development.

The first reason arose from the increased levels of migration seen after the end of the Second World War, especially from former colonies in Asia, Africa and the Caribbean to former imperial states like the UK and France. The black and minority ethnic (BAME) population of the UK, for example, duly rose from less than 1% in 1950 to more than 4% by 1970, a rise made much more notable by the concentration of BAME immigrants in particular urban areas. Furthermore, these new communities brought with them new and distinctive **cultures**, manifested by the very different languages, religions, dress and musical preferences of the countries from which their members arrived. As such, the cultural effects of post-war immigration were unusually intense and strikingly conspicuous.

The second reason arose from the way certain states — like the UK and France — were responding to such high levels of immigration; in other words, the way in which certain liberal democracies, with a traditionally 'mono-cultural' outlook, were reacting to their increasingly multicultural societies. We will examine these responses in some detail later in this chapter, but suffice it to say here that these responses — duly dubbed **assimilation** or **individualist integration** — were considered inadequate by 'multiculturalist' academics like **Tariq Modood (1952–)**, **Bhikhu Parekh (1935–)** and **Will Kymlicka (1962–)** (see 'Key thinker' boxes 3–5).

This led to the third reason: the perceived possibility of a new response to the challenge of a multicultural society. This response would be one in which the state would not just recognise but encourage and promote cultural **diversity**, based on a belief that this would produce greater social

Multiculturalist integration The notion that a culturally diverse society can be unified through the state highlighting and endorsing a variety of cultures, while according none of them primacy or preference.

Tolerance Rooted in the Enlightenment and the ideas of liberal philosophers such as John Locke and John Stuart Mill, tolerance denotes an acceptance of views and behaviour very different to one's own.

cohesion. This idea became known as **multiculturalist integration** and its principles obviously form the bulk of this chapter.

The final reason for multiculturalism's emergence relates to the broader political context in which it was advanced. For 'developed' nations like the UK, the 1960s and 1970s were decades when the 'conservative' view of culture and history was routinely challenged. Among so-called progressives, it was widely argued that 'imperialism' had left a poisonous legacy and that any 'dominant culture' with 'imperialist' influences needed urgent correction. As a result, far from just being a new prescription for unity in a multiracial society, multiculturalism became a way of purging post-imperial nations of their 'shameful' and 'racist' history. In the process, a new national culture would be fashioned — one that was less respectful of tradition and more attuned to progressive values like **tolerance**, pluralism and equality.

The core ideas of multiculturalism

Human nature

Communally embedded

Communitarianism Linked to Charles Taylor, this philosophy implies that individuals can make sense of who they are only with reference to the territorial communities of which they are part. These could be communities based on 'primordial' factors, such as race or religion, or 'material' factors relating to the local economy (as with farming communities or mining communities).

According to its advocates, multiculturalism is a progressive ideology with a generally optimistic view of human nature. However, it is fair to say that its view of human nature is much closer to that of socialism than that of liberalism. This is because, like socialism, multiculturalism sees human nature as malleable or 'plastic', heavily influenced by its social environment, and particularly by its communities.

In this respect, multiculturalism owes much to the **communitarian** theories of sociologists like **Charles Taylor** (1931–) (see 'Key thinker 1' box), who insists that human nature is 'communally embedded'. As Taylor states: 'It is impossible to understand ourselves and others…without understanding the communities in which we function' (*Multiculturalism and the Politics of Recognition*, 1994). In other words, human beings are shaped by, and products of, their communities. In this respect, multiculturalism's view of human nature is in sharp contrast to that of liberalism, which tends to see human nature as fixed at birth and developed independently of society.

Key term

Identity politics Linked to multiculturalist thinkers like Bhiku Parekh, this term indicates the belief that politicians should not focus just on what individuals do or say but on what individuals *are*, especially in relation to primordial factors such as ethnicity, gender and sexuality.

Activity

Compare multiculturalism's view of human nature with those of the three 'core' ideologies.

Identity

Multiculturalism is closely linked to the relatively recent phenomenon of **identity politics**: the notion that what we believe and what we want are largely determined by what we *are*. Taylor further asserts that human beings are driven by an urge to uncover and define their individual identity — that is, their 'true' self and personality. However, unlike classical liberalism, which argues that self-realisation can be achieved autonomously, multiculturalists argue that an individual's identity can only be ascertained *interactively*. As Taylor records:

> 'Our identity is not constructed from within and generated by each of us alone. It is only through dialogue with certain significant others that we negotiate who we are...those significant others being the individuals with whom we engage and evolve on a daily basis.' (*Multiculturalism and the Politics of Recognition*, 1994)

Kymlicka agrees with Taylor that communal identity provides 'an anchor for an individual's self-identification'. Yet Kymlicka also stresses that 'self and community identification' is much more likely when there is a multitude of varying communities with which individuals may or may not identify. This argument has been supported by Modood, who observed: 'To be among those of very different cultures makes one aware of what one *is not*, and thereby sharpens our understanding of what one *is*.'

Recognition

The third key aspect of multiculturalism's view of human nature concerns its supposed need for recognition. According to Taylor, it is not enough for us simply to locate our own identity and the extent to which it has been shaped by our communities. If we are to be self-confident enough to develop, it is also necessary for our communal identity to be recognised by those outside our community. This means that individuals seeking self-respect also require recognition of their community. By contrast, if a community's identity is not recognised, this can have grave consequences for the individuals concerned. As Taylor duly warned:

> 'Just as recognition of one's identity is a vital human need, non-recognition or misrecognition can inflict a grievous wound, saddling its victims with a crippling self-hatred, denying their desire for self-esteem and stifling a sense of their own authenticity.' (*Multiculturalism and the Politics of Recognition*, 1994)

Key thinker 1

Key thinker 1

Charles Taylor (1931–)

A Canadian philosopher, Charles Taylor's contribution to multiculturalist thinking came initially via a doctrine known as communitarianism. This doctrine was associated with a number of philosophers — notably Michael Sandel and Alasdair MacIntyre — and was significantly developed by Taylor's book on the subject, *Multiculturalism and the Politics of Recognition*.

■ Taylor refuted the liberal argument that individuals are autonomous or atomistic, and that communities are mere products of the individuals inside them. Instead, he argued that individuals are 'irreducibly social' and that communities make an inestimable contribution to individual well-being and self-confidence.

■ From this, Taylor developed theories highlighting the 'politics of identity', arguing that a person's sense of who they are is central to their overall character, including their opinions and preferences. This sense of identity is formed, Taylor argued, from ongoing dialogue with what he termed 'significant others' (citing family, friends, neighbours and colleagues as obvious examples). As such, Taylor argued that our identities are shaped 'dialogically', thus underlining the claim of earlier political philosophers (notably Rousseau and Hegel) that we become 'complete' individuals only 'intersubjectively' — in other words, via routine contact with others.

■ From Taylor's support for the politics of identity came his subsequent demand that the state should practise the **politics of recognition**. Indeed, Taylor argued that if individuals' identities were 'misrecognised' — by both other individuals and the state — this could lead to individuals suffering a serious lack of self-confidence and self-esteem; and if such misfortunes befell a large number of individuals, this could create a society lacking purpose and cohesion, which in turn might impede the effectiveness of state policy.

■ Taylor also criticised liberalism for its stress on 'universality' (as with its assumptions that certain rights were applicable to all). Although he sympathised with most of the rights liberals favoured, Taylor alleged that their application by a liberal state too often betrayed a dominant or majority culture, which then misrecognised the identities of those in minority communities (such as the Quebecois).

■ In the course of writing *Multiculturalism and the Politics of Recognition*, Taylor developed a new universal principle — that we should all have diverse individual identities which should be recognised by the state. But for this to occur, Taylor argued, there would have to be more 'diversity' and 'specificity' in the implementation of state policy.

Key term

Politics of recognition
Associated with sociologist Charles Taylor, this involves those with group identities seeking greater acknowledgement from the state, claiming it is crucial to their self-respect.

Activity

Summarise, in approximately 200 words, Taylor's views on why the state should recognise identity politics.

Key term

Essentialism Linked to ideologies such as feminism, nationalism and multiculturalism, essentialism argues that each individual's character is subject to fixed factors (such as gender or culture) which limit variation between those affected by them.

Essentialism

The fourth aspect of multiculturalism's perspective on human nature is its **essentialism**. Multiculturalists state that though there may be differences between individuals within communities, those individuals will still ultimately share essential characteristics and essentially similar attitudes and viewpoints. As Parekh wrote:

> 'Although individuals may critically evaluate their culture, and accept the criticisms levelled by those outside it, they are still deeply shaped by it; they can overcome some but not all of its influences, and will still view the world from within the culture they have inherited...Although they might personally loathe some of the fellow-members of their own culture, or find their views and values unacceptable, their mutual commitment and concern as members of a shared community remain unaffected.' (*Rethinking Multiculturalism*, 2005, p. 336)

Parekh's summary actually has huge implications for multiculturalism's view of human nature. For it means that even if individuals wished to 'escape' their community, their nature has been so fundamentally shaped by it that such escape will be impossible. This implies that though multiculturalism is associated with an 'optimistic' take on humanity, it also believes that rational choice plays only a limited role in human nature.

Society

Society is significant

The first thing to note here is that, for multiculturalism, society is fundamentally important. Multiculturalism rejects the neo-liberal idea that 'society' (in so far as it exists) is merely the sum total of 'atomistic' individuals, whose personalities have been shaped 'autonomously'. As already discussed in respect of human nature, multiculturalism believes that societies — or more specifically, their various communities — have a vital effect on how we think and what we do. But what do multiculturalists mean by 'communities'?

Communities are culturally based

Despite Taylor's influence on multiculturalism, it is important to note that multiculturalism and communitarianism are not identical. This is because of a significant disagreement over what constitutes a community (and therefore a society).

For writers like Taylor, communities (and the societies they cumulatively create) are forged by whatever leads to a group of people having shared interests. Therefore, communitarians may use the word 'community' in respect of region and geography and thus accept that communities are frequently defined by economic factors (as with the farming communities of East Anglia or the former mining communities of South Wales).

Multiculturalists, however, stress culture and psychology rather than economics or geography as the main criteria of 'real' communities. Indeed, in the formation and maintenance of communities, multiculturalism's key thinkers tend to argue that regional boundaries will always be transcended by the importance of cultural identity.

Such cultural communities are defined by what we might call primordo-historical factors. As such, they may involve innate, 'primordial' factors such as ethnicity, sexuality or gender (hence references to 'the gay community'). Or they may involve 'historical' factors, such as the countries we or our ancestors hail from (hence references to 'the Irish community' in cities like New York), or the religions we and our ancestors historically uphold (hence references to 'the Jewish community' or 'the Muslim community' in cities across the world). Sometimes, of course, there *is* a geographical aspect to cultural communities (the Asian communities of various UK cities being an example), but this is said to be the effect, not the cause, of wider cultural identity.

Box 5.1

The 2011 UK census: indications of a multicultural society

The 2011 census showed:
- 14% of the population were BAME
- more than 40% of Greater London residents were BAME
- 49% of Leicester residents were BAME
- 13% of residents in England were born outside the UK
- 21% of Greater London residents did not speak English as their first language
- more than 20% of residents in London, Birmingham and Bradford were Muslim
- 59% of the UK population were Christian (compared with 95% in 1961).

Activity

With reference to previous UK censuses, describe in up to 200 words how UK society has become more multicultural.

The merits of diversity

As we explained at the start of this chapter, multiculturalism represents a normative approach to society; it prescribes what should be rather than what is. Its prescriptions, however, are still based upon the empirical 'fact' of a multiracial and multicultural society. In the case of the UK, for example, this means that multiculturalists will highlight the growing cultural diversity of our society, using the sort of evidence provided by the 2011 UK Census (see Box 5.1).

According to both Parekh and Modood, such data represent a glorious opportunity to broaden the understanding of all citizens — and thus create a society where there is greater tolerance and wisdom. As **Isaiah Berlin** (1909–97) (see 'Key thinker 2' box) argued, exposure to other cultures makes us more conscious of those cultures, more aware of the distinctive character of our own culture, and more likely to consider ways in which it can be refined. Parekh agreed:

> 'The multicultural society sensitizes us to the fact that all ways of life are inherently limited and that one way cannot possibly embody the full-range of the richness, complexity and grandeur of human existence. By contrast, the mono-cultural society insulates its members from the perspectives of others, which then perpetuates ignorance.' (*Rethinking Multiculturalism*, 2005)

Drawing upon Berlin's theory of value pluralism, Parekh argues that every culture offers a particular version of what 'the good life' should be. Yet according to Parekh, each culture's version of 'the good life' has its problems and weaknesses. As a result of this belief, multiculturalism's view of society is linked to **cultural relativism**: the notion that no single culture is objectively superior to another, that concepts of right and wrong will inevitably vary from one culture to another, and that the best societies will explicitly accommodate this 'reality'.

According to Parekh, the co-existence of many cultures within a society promoting cultural relativism will have endless benefits. For example, it will promote a mature citizenry, free from the psychological restrictions of a mono-cultural society, and an end to the dangerous assumption that those of 'other' cultures are somehow defective.

Multicultural societies, Parekh observed, would be 'less a competition, more a conversation...in which each community would learn from each other'. As Parekh further argued, 'all but the most primitive cultures are internally plural, evolving, and represent a conversation among their own participants'. For this

Key terms

BAME This is an acronym, standing for black and minority ethnic. It is a shorthand term, used by social scientists to categorise all those in society whose ethnicity is non-European.

Segregation This is a term associated with multiracial societies where there is little mixing between those of different races and cultures, and where public services and public laws are designed to prevent racial integration. Until the 1960s, it was routinely applied to the public services (such as schools and transport) of southern states in the USA and, until the 1990s, underpinned the apartheid regime in South Africa.

Cultural diversity is conspicuous in most UK cities

reason, Parekh asserted that the emergence of multicultural societies should be welcomed, not just as opportunities to foster tolerance among individuals but as historic opportunities to enrich and develop each of the cultures concerned.

Modood also sees cultural diversity as an opportunity to create a more unifying concept of 'society'. In respect of the UK, Modood believed it could lead to a 'community of communities' rather than a faltering mono-cultural society that alienates many of its **BAME** citizens. Modood also argued that by 'recognizing its multicultural character', the UK has a chance to 'rethink its national story', acknowledge the range of BAME cultures that affected Britain through its imperial history and thus foster a more harmonious society.

The state

What multiculturalism rejects

Given that multiculturalism's theorists see benefits rather than problems in a multicultural society, it is unsurprising that they advocate a state that will promote cultural diversity. As a result, they strongly reject the two other types of state response that are possible following the emergence of multicultural societies.

The first of these is state-sponsored assimilation. This involves the state encouraging those from minority cultures to 'blend in' with the existing majority culture and to suppress their native culture, the aim being to cement a more cohesive, mono-cultural society, free of **segregation**. Exemplified by the actions of the French Fifth Republic, the state will promote this assimilation by according equal rights to all individuals, while preventing anything that supposedly threatens cultural uniformity. Faith schools, for example, are likely to be not just unsupported but proscribed, as will any public display of dress codes that conveys a message of 'otherness' (France's ban on Muslim women wearing the burkha in public places is a well-known example of 'assimilationist' practice).

The other state approach that multiculturalists reject is that of individualist integration, an approach practised by both the UK and the USA from the 1960s onwards and generally supported by mainstream liberals in both countries. As with assimilation, the individualist-integration state will insist upon a prevailing dominant culture — usually of a liberal-individualist character — and encourage those from minority cultures to adapt to it in return for all the trappings of a liberal state (such as equal individual rights). As with assimilation, there will be no state subsidy for anything that smacks of minority cultural practice (see Box 5.2).

However, because of its liberal pedigree, individualist integration is more tolerant and reciprocal than assimilation. The individualist-integration state may therefore acknowledge the existence of other cultures and argue that, though not funded by the state, those other cultures should still be protected by the law. The individualist-integration state would therefore not object to individuals worshipping 'alternative' religions or dressing in a way that denotes 'other' cultures, just as long as those individuals acknowledge that, in the public sector, a single set of cultural values (usually liberal) must prevail (see Box 5.2).

As part of the same plan to integrate individuals from 'other' cultures, the individualist-integration state might also illegalise overt racial or cultural discrimination. The aim here is to ensure that just as each individual is expected to uphold and respect the 'mainstream' culture, each individual will also be protected from the sort of prejudice that might hinder his or her individual prospects. This has been the rationale behind the UK's various Race Relations Acts since 1965 and its various watchdog bodies, such as the Commission for Racial Equality (1976–2010).

Box 5.2

State policy in a multicultural society: one scenario, four responses

Let us imagine that a group of community leaders proposes to establish a new medical centre, staffed by, and exclusively serving, members of an ethnic minority community. They approach the relevant state department, seeking approval and state funding. The state's response might involve one of the following:

- A state practising assimilation is likely to deny both approval and funding, on the grounds that the proposal is 'divisive'.
- A state practising individualist integration may approve the proposal on the grounds of 'tolerance', but deny funding on the grounds that this would threaten 'integration'.
- A state practising pluralist multiculturalism (see below) will offer approval and funding on the grounds that this would promote 'diversity' while validating minority communities.
- A state practising liberal multiculturalism or cosmopolitan multiculturalism (see below) may also offer support, although it may have concerns about the centre definitely excluding those outside the community.

Key terms

Value pluralism Linked to Isaiah Berlin, this term denotes that there is a range of 'absolute' values — such as liberty, equality and compassion — prevalent in liberal democracies. But it is not for the liberal state to decree any one of them as more important than another.

Formal equality Linked to liberalism's historic claim that all should be equal before the law, with equal political rights, this term is used by multiculturalism for an additional purpose: to ensure that the state accords equal respect to all cultures and religions in society and does not accord special treatment to any one cultural community.

Activity

Locate or suggest further examples of the 'pluralist' practices cited in Box 5.3.

What multiculturalism recommends

For multiculturalists like Kymlicka, state-led assimilation is fundamentally wrong, while individualist integration is inadequate. Instead, multiculturalists want a state that will not just tolerate but actively promote cultural diversity. This will involve the state acknowledging what Berlin termed **value pluralism** and then practising what Kymlicka refers to as group differentiated rights (see key term, p. 171). As a result, there might then be a series of state-led policies and initiatives designed to produce greater **formal equality**, such as those outlined in Box 5.3.

Box 5.3 suggests that most western states are still some way from practising 'pure' multiculturalism. However, elements of the multiculturalist state have been seen in both Australia and Canada (the latter institutionalising Anglo–French bilingualism, for example), while in the 1980s a number of Labour-led local authorities in the UK, including the Greater London Council led by Ken Livingstone, pursued versions of public-sector pluralism — such as subsidies for services (Muslim community centres, for example) or events (such as Sikh festivals) that advertised minority-culture communities.

Box 5.3

Multiculturalism in practice

Here are some examples of multiculturalism in practice:
- **Linguistic pluralism:** the state subsidises the publication of public documents (such as council tax bills or road tax notification) in a variety of languages.
- **Public service pluralism:** state agencies like schools and health services show greater sensitivity to issues such as the religious holidays and dress codes of minority cultures, while giving financial support to public services (such as faith schools) that cater specifically for minority religions.
- **Positive discrimination:** the state insists that governing bodies of public organisations (such as local education authorities) contain 'quotas' of representatives from a variety of cultural communities.
- **Legalistic pluralism:** the state allows its legal system to enforce separate religious laws in certain circumstances (such as **Sharia law**'s attitude to divorce and inheritance among Muslims).
- **Cultural federalism:** the state creates and supports new constitutional bodies (such as a Muslim parliament) that will reflect cultural diversity, discuss matters specific to certain cultures and pass laws applying to those of a certain cultural community.

The economy

The only generic view of economic policy, taken by all advocates of multiculturalism, is that economic policy must always respect the diverse needs of a dynamic, multicultural society. For that reason, the economics of democratic socialism and social democracy — with their stress upon centralised economic planning and 'one-size-fits-all' public services — may not sit easily alongside the principles of multiculturalism.

For Kymlicka, however, and cosmopolitan theorists like Jeremy Waldron, multiculturalism is the perfect complement to economic liberalism and modern capitalism. Indeed, Kymlicka and Waldron see multicultural societies as the natural consequence of global, free-market capitalism — an economic system which encourages free movement of labour, multiracial populations and a range of identities embraced by choice-conscious consumers.

Equally, Kymlicka accepts that free-market capitalism can generate huge inequalities, which then threaten the stability of liberal democracies. In such circumstances, Kymlicka argues, multiculturalism becomes even more important. Economic inequality, Kymlicka notes, can challenge the liberal principle of 'government by consent' — particularly among those sections of society suffering from inequality. Yet Kymlicka believes this problem will be easier to overcome if the state has explicitly recognised, and then endorsed, the range of cultural identities in a modern capitalist society, including those of communities where many find themselves economically weakened.

Key terms

Positive discrimination Referred to as 'affirmative action' in the USA, this involves the state correcting historical inequalities by discriminating in favour of those who have traditionally been discriminated against. This can lead to 'quotas', ensuring the presence of minority group representatives on key public bodies.

Sharia law This refers to the collection of laws governing the Islamic religion, as prescribed by Allah and the Prophet Mohammed. It provides instruction in respect of worship, government and everyday human activity.

Different types of multiculturalism

In this section of the chapter we shall examine the three recognised strands of multiculturalism:

- liberal multiculturalism
- pluralist multiculturalism
- cosmopolitan multiculturalism.

We will also examine the conservative critique of multiculturalism while considering whether 'conservative multiculturalism' is necessarily an oxymoron.

Liberal multiculturalism

This is the most practised strand of multiculturalism, one that has been framed largely by the writings of the Canadian political

Key thinker 2

Isaiah Berlin (1909–97)

Widely considered one of the most influential philosophers of the twentieth century, Isaiah Berlin is remembered chiefly for his specific contribution to the debate within liberalism. In particular, Berlin's seminal work, *Two Concepts of Liberty* (1959), is thought to offer the definitive distinction between 'negative' and 'positive' liberty (see Chapter 1).

- Berlin's work on liberty also led him to consider wider issues of culture and how various values could be accommodated within society. His connection to multiculturalism arose on account of his support for value pluralism (see key term, p. 167).
- Berlin asserted that there were certain values — 'absolutes' — that were common to all cultures. These absolutes included a commitment to truth, honesty, compassion, courage, liberty and equality. However, Berlin argued that this presented two problems for politicians in charge of the state.
- The first problem was that 'absolute' values are 'incommensurable': they cannot be ranked in any objective order. It is impossible, for example, to assert whether compassion is more important than courage, or vice versa. The second problem was that such absolutes would often conflict with each other. The quest for equality, for example, might erode liberty; yet, because liberty and equality are incommensurable, this conflict would be difficult to avoid.

- Berlin argued that it would be hard for politicians to resolve such conflicts if they deemed societies mono-cultural (defined by a single culture). Berlin also feared that the state could use the notion of a mono-cultural society to underwrite utopian political ideals (such as Marxism's 'dictatorship of the proletariat'). That, he argued, could lead to oppressive and tyrannical states.
- To avoid such dangers, while providing a way of resolving tensions between absolutes, Berlin advocated a value-pluralist arrangement. Here, the state would recognise a variety of cultures, with a variety of views about which absolutes were paramount. Berlin believed that such a society need not be one that was fragmented: the various cultures would still be bound by a common agreement about what the absolutes were and this agreement would be enshrined by the state.
- For Berlin, it was also crucial that individuals should not be trapped within a particular culture but should instead have the capacity to choose which culture they were part of. It was the state's duty to ensure that individuals had the opportunity to do this.

Activity

Explain, in approximately 200 words, Berlin's belief that value pluralism produced a stable and content society.

theorist Will Kymlicka. It is one that naturally champions diversity. But, as explained below, it does so mainly within a framework of liberal values. It is less comfortable, for example, in affirming cultures that are explicitly illiberal in their values. For this reason, liberal multiculturalism is sometimes dubbed 'shallow diversity' — its acceptance of cultural and ethical diversity goes only so far, and certainly not as far as some other multiculturalist thinkers (such as Parekh) recommend.

In putting forward a version of multiculturalism that is indeed liberal, Kymlicka links multiculturalist principles to the pursuit of self-determination, self-realisation and self-fulfilment. In short, Kymlicka connects multiculturalism to individualism and, in particular, the relationship between individualism and moral choices. In this respect, Kymlicka was extending liberalism's examination of value pluralism, an exercise first carried out by the liberal philosopher Isaiah Berlin some 40 years earlier.

Community-based individualism

Kymlicka also endorsed the communitarian position of Charles Taylor by conceding that an individual's character was significantly shaped by their community. Such communities, Kymlicka agreed, provide the 'contexts of choice' within which people 'frame, revise and pursue their goals'. Kymlicka also accepted the claim of other multiculturalist thinkers, such as Parekh, that communities were primarily determined by culture rather than by geography.

With reference to liberalism, however, Kymlicka also asserted that individuals would be stifled if they were from a community that was not just economically but culturally disadvantaged:

> 'If individuals are born into the dominant culture of society, they enjoy brute good luck, whereas those belonging to minority cultures suffer disadvantages in virtue of the brute bad luck of their minority culture status... the state must therefore accord such individuals **group differentiated rights** so as to rectify unchosen inequalities and problems for which the individuals themselves are not responsible.' (*Multicultural Citizenship*, 1995)

By recommending such group differentiated rights, Kymlicka was therefore advancing a liberal defence of positive discrimination: such measures were necessary, he argued, in order to give individuals the freedom of opportunity they might otherwise not enjoy. But he was also putting a multiculturalist slant on the 'modern liberal' justification for 'positive' liberty: it was only by granting rights that were specific to an individual's community

Key term

Group differentiated rights Coined by Will Kymlicka, this denotes a belief that state-backed rights should not be 'universal' in the way suggested by liberalism, but more sensitive to the specific cultural perspectives of minority communities. As a result, some communities should be accorded rights (such as the right to make comments mocking religion) that are not expected to be upheld in other communities.

that the 'enabling' state could correct the specific injustices that this community had suffered — and thus 'liberate' its individual members.

Yet Kymlicka insisted that the links between multiculturalism and liberalism predate the advent of modern liberalism. Indeed, he argued that multiculturalist ideas had their roots in classical liberalism and the Enlightenment. He was especially keen to note Locke's insistence that any 'enlightened' state was sustainable only if based on government by consent. According to Kymlicka, in a multicultural society — where individuals were largely defined by their cultural communities — such consent would be hard to secure unless the state had formally recognised and respected the differing values of various communities.

In Kymlicka's view, ignoring such communities (especially those with a powerful sense of their own cultural identity) would jeopardise the Lockean idea of a social contract between governors and governed — at the heart of which was the classical liberal prescription that individuals must always feel better off inside the state than outside it. According to Kymlicka, this condition of a liberal state was one that the alternative approaches to a multicultural society — notably assimilation and individualist integration — did not, and could not, meet.

Checks majoritarianism

In addition to adapting the principles of one classical liberal thinker — namely Locke — Kymlicka argued that multiculturalism updated those of another: John Stuart Mill. Specifically, Kymlicka believed that multiculturalism helped answer one of the great problems that Mill grappled with as democracy loomed in the mid–late nineteenth century: how could government by consent be reconciled with the principle of majority rule? How might a liberal state be mindful of what minorities, as well as majorities, were prepared to give their 'consent' to? In short, how could democracy avoid what Mill termed the 'tyranny of the majority'?

For Kymlicka, the dilemma Mill highlighted was more pressing by the late twentieth century, given the existence (in states like the UK) of assorted, minority-culture communities. However, he argued that a multiculturalist state, practising positive discrimination and other group differentiated rights, could ensure that minority cultures were always recognised and accommodated alongside majority opinion. If a liberal state employed some of the methods outlined in Box 5.2, Kymlicka suggested, the 'tyranny of the majority' could be avoided and a more nuanced form of democracy secured.

Will Kymlicka (1962–)

Like Charles Taylor, Will Kymlicka is a Canadian political theorist. Yet Kymlicka's importance to multiculturalism stems partly from his critique of Taylor's conclusions. This is largely because Kymlicka aims to harness recent multiculturalist ideas to timeless liberal principles, with his two key works — *Liberalism, Community and Culture* (1989) and *Multicultural Citizenship* (1995) — being central to any assessment of liberal multiculturalism.

- Kymlicka challenged Taylor on two grounds. First, whereas Taylor suggested that cultural identity was inextricably linked to communities, Kymlicka argued it was more abstract. Culture, he claimed, might or might not involve regular and extensive interaction between individuals; instead it represented a set of ideals and values which individuals could access either communally or 'autonomously', via television, literature and the arts.
- Second, whereas Taylor saw cultural identity as an end in itself, Kymlicka saw it much more as a means to advanced individualism. According to Kymlicka, culture provides the 'contexts of choice…options and scripts within which individuals can frame, revise and pursue their goals'. Without such 'cultural contexts', he argued, individuals may struggle to make sense of the options available to them in increasingly complex capitalist societies.
- Furthermore, Kymlicka stated that cultural identity allowed people to enjoy ongoing individual development. He argued that it gave individuals 'an anchor for self-identification', along with the 'self-confidence that arises from a sense of effortlessly secure belonging'. He therefore cited a strong connection between 'an individual's self-respect and the respect accorded by a constitutional state to the culture with which he or she identified'.
- However, the chances of an individual finding such a culture were reduced if society was mono-cultural. By contrast, a multicultural society — containing cultures that appealed to both majorities and minorities, each endorsed by a liberal state — gave individuals cultural choice and greater opportunities for individual enrichment.
- In a nod to conservatism, Kymlicka accepted that multicultural societies could emerge organically. But to survive and flourish, he believed they needed active and ongoing promotion by a liberal state. This might involve funding for minority-language schools, documentation that was multilingual, and affirmative action (guaranteeing the inclusion, within various state agencies and committees, of those from minority cultures).
- Kymlicka argued for group differentiated rights whereby the state would recognise a variety of distinct cultures and underwrite the various practices and preferences those cultures embodied.
- Kymlicka argued that by extolling the doctrine of group differentiated rights, the state would ensure higher levels of political and civic participation among all sections of society and thus achieve an effective integration of all cultures.

Activity

Explain, in approximately 200 words, Kymlicka's argument that multiculturalism was consistent with the values of the Enlightenment.

Tolerance updated

Liberal multiculturalists have also been keen to cite both Locke's and Mill's support for toleration. Kymlicka reminded us that for Locke and Mill, any assault on freedom of religion in particular was an erosion of the individual freedom that liberals inherently extol. Noting that many of the cultural communities in a multicultural society are, in fact, faith-based (as with the Muslim or Jewish communities), Kymlicka contested that liberalism's support for multiculturalism is perfectly consistent with classical liberalism's demand for religious emancipation and freedom of worship.

Furthermore, as a rationale for determining what should and should not be 'tolerated', Kymlicka drew upon Mill's distinction between 'self-regarding' actions (affecting only those who carry them out) and 'other regarding' actions (those having a more widespread effect). Kymlicka argued that many of the cultural practices in minority communities — such as distinctive dress codes and manner of religious worship — fall into the former category. It was thus illiberal, he argued, for the state to discourage such practices. Yet this is precisely what might occur under a government practising either of the alternatives to multiculturalism (assimilation or individualist integration) in a multicultural society.

Debate 1

Is multiculturalism at odds with liberalism?

Yes

...say writers like Amartya Sen (*Identity and Violence*, Penguin, 2006):

- Multiculturalism (MCM) 'miniaturises' individuals, by addressing them merely as members of a 'community'.
- Some of the communities MCM legitimises exalt religion over rationalism.
- Some of the communities MCM legitimises oppose social liberalism, especially on issues like sexuality.
- Some of the communities MCM legitimises are patriarchal and opposed to homosexuality, thus denying many individuals equal rights and opportunities.
- Some of the communities MCM legitimises might oppose free markets, favouring instead protectionism for the community's own producers.

No

...say writers like Will Kymlicka (*Multicultural Citizenship*, Oxford University Press, 1995):

- MCM's stress on 'diversity' is consistent with liberal individualism.
- Like liberalism, MCM emphasises tolerance of minority cultures and communities.
- By ring-fencing the rights of minority communities, MCM prevents the 'tyranny of the majority'.
- MCM helps secures government by consent from all communities.
- MCM practices (such as positive discrimination and group differentiated rights) are consistent with the positive freedom and enabling state advocated by modern liberalism.

Pluralist multiculturalism

Bhikhu Parekh: advocate of 'deep diversity'

If liberal multiculturalism is known as shallow diversity (owing to its insistence upon diversity within a liberal context), pluralist multiculturalism may be termed deep diversity, on the grounds that it rejects the idea of liberalism being the only tenable ideology within modern western societies.

Linked to the writings of Parekh, this strand of multiculturalism asserts that in an era of globalisation and increased migration, liberalism is just one set of ideas among many, and that liberal ideas have no intrinsic moral superiority. Its exponents therefore assert that liberalism gives expression only to certain aspects of human nature, such as the longing for individual freedom and 'rational' discussion. But there are said to be other features to the human condition — such as tribal loyalty and the appeal of religious faith — which figure more prominently in other, non-western cultures. The view of pluralist multiculturalists is that these other cultures are increasingly vocal in modern society and that instead of seeking to stifle them, the state should give them recognition and respect.

In criticising assimilation, individualist integration or indeed liberal multiculturalism, writers like Parekh insist that human beings are 'culturally embedded'. So it is naive, Parekh argues, for western states to think that those from minority cultures can simply shake off their cultural legacy and identify with the majority-liberal mindset. Parekh argues that if we want a truly inclusive society, where citizens do not feel alienated, then modern states must recognise the 'deep pluralism' of modern society by encouraging the full range of cultures in modern society. Only then will we have a society where state and society are in harmony; only then will we have a society that is tolerant and united rather than dangerously divided.

The pluralist-multiculturalist approach would thus involve the state not just permitting but subsidising a host of public services (such as faith schools) that clearly reflect a distinctive cultural identity. Furthermore, cultural pluralists suggest the state should allow greater 'legalistic pluralism', so as to acknowledge the varied but strong sense of right and wrong among citizens. Variations in the laws surrounding (for example) polygamy, divorce, abortion, homosexuality and inheritance might then be permitted. In faith-based communities, elements of religious law might also be allowed to co-exist with secular law (even though the difficulties of this are seldom overstated). As Parekh concedes, all this is a radical prescription for any modern state to absorb. But it would merely reflect (he argues) the radical diversity of modern society and, in doing so, forge a state that would be more realistic in its approach to the multitude of communities it would now oversee.

In the UK, pluralist multiculturalism has been supported by many on the so-called New Left — such as former London mayor Ken Livingstone and the Respect Party under the leadership of George Galloway. For such (generally metropolitan) socialists, pluralist multiculturalism offers a solution to the problem of their traditional constituency being in numerical and political decline. With the white working class no longer constituting an electoral majority, pluralist multiculturalism supposedly provides socialists with a new constituency — what Parekh terms a 'coalition of the disaffected' — that will include many hitherto marginalised BAME communities.

As of June 2017, the UK has its most diverse parliament

Activity

With reference to either the Greater London Council 1981–1986 or the Respect Party 2004–2016, describe in approximately 200 words how pluralist multiculturalism has been advocated in the UK.

Bhiku Parekh (1935–)

As a Labour peer, Bhiku Parekh is both an active politician and a political theorist associated with the case for multiculturalism. His key work, *Rethinking Multiculturalism* (2002), remains a vital reference for those who reject univeralist liberalism and advocate instead a pluralist model of multiculturalism (often referred to as 'deep diversity').

- Parekh's starting point is that human beings are 'culturally embedded'. In other words, our attitudes and preferences are heavily shaped by our cultural identity. However, Parekh was also adamant that, though heavily influenced by it, we should still be able to evaluate, criticise and, if necessary, modify our cultural identity — and an effective multiculturalist society will make this task easier.
- Parekh's pluralist multiculturalism was designed to ensure that each culture, far from being isolated and autonomous, should freely interact with, and thus be acutely aware of, other cultures. For Parekh, these various cultures should not be conflicting or competitive but complementary and cooperative.
- For Parekh, a multiculturalist society would be 'a continuous conversation' between and within the various cultures. This would engender, among the adherents of each culture, greater tolerance, sophistication and self-scrutiny, while discouraging complacency or arrogance. This, in turn, would promote diverse cultural development, whereby each culture would consistently evolve in a manner conducive to greater tolerance — both between and within society's various cultures. The outcome would be what Parekh terms 'a community of communities'.
- Like Tariq Modood, Parekh vigorously denied he was simply promoting minority cultures; he castigated societies that were not just 'Euro-centric' but 'Afrocentric', 'Asio-centric', 'Sino-centric', etc. He also argued that each culture had strengths and weaknesses and the best societies were those which encouraged their citizens to be aware of such subtle complexities via 'interactive and dynamic multiculturalism'.
- The role of the state is to encourage such a society through a number of proactive measures. It should avoid any indication that citizenship is contingent upon subscription to any single culture and should thus reject the 'American model' of universalising liberal values — for Parekh, this will hinder, rather than foster, the respect of a multicultural citizenry for the state under which they live.
- Instead, the multiculturalist state will confirm — via its constitution and legislation — that it cherishes a variety of cultures, religions and belief systems, while insisting upon mutual tolerance, mutual respect and ongoing dialogue between communities.
- It has been suggested that Parekh's philosophy represents not just cultural pluralism but ideological pluralism, aiming to synthesise that which is best in the liberal, conservative and socialist traditions inherent to many cultures.

Activity

Explain how 'deep diversity' both complements and challenges core liberal values.

Debate 2

Is multiculturalism at odds with socialism?

Yes

...say writers like Brian Barry (*Culture and Equality*, Polity Press, 2002):

- Multiculturalism (MCM) stresses cultural differences and thus undermines the solidarity of society as a whole.
- MCM fragments and divides working people and thus impedes the struggle for social justice.
- Positive discrimination and group differentiated rights represent favouritism and are a denial of equality.
- The faith-based communities MCM endorses are often hierarchical and paternalistic rather than egalitarian.
- The faith-based communities MCM endorses may have specific problems with gender and sexual equality.

No

...say writers like Bhikhu Parekh (*Rethinking Multiculturalism*, Palgrave, 2005).

- Pluralist MCM represents a redistribution of power from majority to minority communities.
- Pluralist MCM thus strives for equality between majority and minority cultures.
- MCM helps correct the legacy of imperialism, exploitation and racism.
- MCM bolsters the struggle for racial and religious equality in society.
- MCM provides a counterweight to the 'globalisation' of bourgeois-capitalist values.

Cosmopolitan multiculturalism

Key term

Cosmopolitan integration
Linked to the political theorist Jeremy Waldron, this term denotes a belief that diverse societies are most likely to unite if citizens are defined not by one community but by a lifestyle in which citizens access a range of the cultures present in society.

The third strand of multiculturalism is, in many ways, an extension of liberal multiculturalism. This is because it examines the potential of multiculturalism to enhance the development, and enrich the freedom, of individuals, while integrating them more closely with a multicultural society. As such, it is no coincidence that the chief advocate of **cosmopolitan integration**, New Zealand philosopher Jeremy Waldron (1953–), has expressed his arguments within books concerning liberal multiculturalism (such as *The Rights of Minority Cultures*, 1995, edited by Will Kymlicka).

The cosmopolitan creed essentially involves a 'pick and mix' society in which individuals do not exist narrowly within one community but instead access the wide diversity of cultures available in a multicultural society. Consequently, individuals in a cosmopolitan society might enjoy Asian cuisine, calypso music and tai chi exercise, yet still attend the Church of England for religious nourishment. For Waldron, the outcome would be a society where people are more eclectic in their tastes and beliefs, and therefore more tolerant and individualistic. As Waldron predicts, 'multicultural societies will spawn multicultural individuals'.

The duty of the state, meanwhile, would be to sustain and promote the communities which facilitate such a cosmopolitan lifestyle. As a result, cosmopolitan theorists like Waldron support the sort of group differentiated rights extolled by Kymlicka, including positive discrimination. However, in this respect we see a potential contradiction in the cosmopolitan-multiculturalism argument.

Waldron admits that for cosmopolitan individuals to thrive, there has to be a diversity of cultural communities. Yet for such communities to exist, they have to be sustained by individuals with a strong and specific sense of their cultural identity. The logic of cosmopolitanism, however, is to produce fewer such individuals and to produce instead a society of culturally hybrid individuals — people who, while accessing a range of cultures, have no strong attachment to any single cultural community.

Although such hybrid individuals might be pleasing to cosmopolitan theorists, their growth in number might be accompanied by a withering of the diverse communities which make multiculturalism possible. We would then be left with a cosmopolitan but less communitarian society — one where most individuals endorse the idea of 'cultural tourism', but without having a clear community of their own (an arrangement Parekh has dubbed 'plural-monoculturalism'). For this reason, Parekh argued that, far from being a 'strand' of multiculturalism, cosmopolitan integration may actually threaten the survival of a multicultural society.

Multiculturalism and conservatism

As highlighted in our 'Debate' boxes, criticism of multiculturalism can be found among both liberals (see Debate 1) and socialists (see Debate 2). However, in respect of the three 'core' ideologies, it is conservatism that has seemed most incompatible with multiculturalism, for three particular reasons.

First, multiculturalism's stress on diversity is seen as an inherent threat to 'one nation', a concept that has been dear to conservatives ever since Disraeli coined the term in the 1860s. More recently, Samuel Huntington (in his 1996 book *The Clash of Civilisations*) claimed that multiculturalism will lead to 'torn countries and cleft societies', while the former Conservative prime minister David Cameron once stated that attempts at multiculturalism led to 'not so much the big society as the broken society'.

Activity

Explain, in approximately 100 words, the differences between liberal and cosmopolitan multiculturalism.

Key thinker 5

Tariq Modood (1952–)

A British-Pakistani professor of sociology and politics, Tariq Modood's contribution to multiculturalism's literature comes mainly via two of his books: *Multicultural Politics: Racism, Ethnicity and Muslims in Britain* (2005) and *Multiculturalism: A Civic Idea* (2007). However, much of Modood's argument arises from empirical evidence concerning multiracialism in the UK, often garnered through his involvement with various state-sponsored inquiries (notably the Blair government's Commission on the Future of Multi-Ethnic Britain, 1997–2000).

- One of Modood's main objectives has been to separate the case for multiculturalism from what he terms 'minoritarianism', or a focus on the assorted concerns of minority interest groups. Instead, he has sought to make the multiculturalist argument applicable to *all* sections of society — both minority ethnic and religious groups and the white majority — with a view to unifying an ethnically and religiously diverse society. In Modood's words, he seeks 'unity through diversity'.

- As such, Modood has been keen to stress that multiculturalism does not represent 'the politics of fragmentation' and that it is precisely to avoid this that multiculturalism is necessary. He has therefore sought to confirm that, though a Muslim himself, he is not merely advancing the interests of a Muslim constituency in the UK, but seeking to strengthen the UK generally. He is keen to stress that most cultural identities have strengths that contribute to the 'good life' of a citizen (assuming that no citizen is coerced into such cultures). The state's task is to synthesise these cultures so as to create 'a vibrant national narrative'.

- Modood is also keen to stress his opinion that the UK has been more adept than most other European countries in handling the impact of immigration. Drawing a contrast with 'anti-multiculturalist' countries, such as France and Germany, he deploys evidence showing that the status of those from minority backgrounds in the UK is more favourable — British Asians, for example, suffer lower levels of discrimination, victimisation and abstention from political participation than their continental counterparts.

- Modood believes that multiculturalism is advanced partly through laws — such as New Labour's Equality Act 2010, which strengthened the legitimacy of faith schools — but mainly through the state fostering a more inclusive national narrative, one which offers a more inclusive and culturally varied account of a nation's past.

- Modood has also been linked to a new strain of pluralist thinking, one that may tentatively be described as 'conservative multiculturalism'. His notion that multiculturalism can re-forge 'one nation', his claim that a multiculturalist narrative complements rather than repudiates Britain's imperial past, and his observation that many ethnic minority communities recall the 'little platoons' extolled by Burke, all appear to put timeless conservative principles into a modern, multicultural setting. Between 2010 and 2011, Modood duly suggested that a renewal of multiculturalism in the UK would reinforce the 'Big Society' project then being extolled by David Cameron and Conservative ministers such as Sayeeda Warsi.

Activity

Explain, in approximately 200 words, Modood's theory that multiculturalism is consistent with national unity.

Second, multiculturalism is regarded by conservatives as the denial of a country's traditions. Multiculturalism's emphasis upon minority religions is considered especially incompatible with a state like the UK, which for more than 400 years has had a state-sponsored Christian church, whose ultimate defender (the monarch) is head of the UK state.

Third, conservatives fear that for multiculturalism to be practised, the state would have to be far more proactive and interventionist than most conservatives wish. 'Social engineering', of the sort a multiculturalist state would have to practise (see Box 5.2), is anathema to most conservatives, who see society as mysteriously 'organic' and therefore beyond the grand, 'normative' designs of idealistic, multiculturalist governments. Conservatives thus argue that far from contriving 'unity through diversity', the state should simply focus on more earthy concerns such as the day-to-day maintenance of order.

Yet despite this well-worn critique, Modood believes that conservatism and multiculturalism need not always be in conflict. In the case of the UK, Modood has argued that multiculturalism is an opportunity for a new and more inclusive 'national story', which might in turn produce a new model of 'one nation' in a multicultural society. For Modood, this new national story would portray Britain's multicultural society as the legacy of the country's 'extraordinary imperial history and global impact'. According to Modood, the contribution BAME cultures now make to Britain's national story might thus be squared with a respect for tradition and history, as well as equality and fairness — thus linking multiculturalism to conservatism as well as liberalism and socialism.

Modood also noted a connection between multiculturalism and the 'Big Society' project associated with David Cameron between 2010 and 2011. In the eyes of Modood and others, Cameron's vision of a 'Big Society' was in fact an updated version of Edmund Burke's support for 'the little platoons' — a society where a multitude of small, localised communities co-existed and self-assisted. Yet, as Modood pointed out, these 'little platoons' were not merely historical, they were powerfully manifested by many of the BAME communities now flourishing in modern, diverse Britain. In respect of various British cities, Modood's view received an interesting endorsement from the conservative-inclined *Daily Telegraph* newspaper:

> 'Yet in the tight-knit enclaves peopled by Kurds, Sikhs, Poles and others, a strong sense of community does survive…But it also provides an invaluable safety net that makes the state's assistance redundant. It is mutual obligations, not government incentives or punishments, that motivates members of such communities. Dependence on the state is largely seen as unacceptable…

> 'Equally importantly, the alternatives to the family so cherished by liberals have never taken root: marriage is the model they live by and aspire to. Divorce is almost nil, single motherhood ditto; extended families living together are routine. Strong immigrant families support their children, but also supply them with a lifelong moral compass.' (10 August 2011)

Such observations would explain, of course, why many progressives oppose multiculturalism. As the feminist academic Marie Macey has argued, multiculturalism would effectively empower certain communities that are faith-based, sceptical about gender and sexual equality, and generally drawn towards social and moral conservatism. In short, Macey argues that multiculturalism may — ironically — sustain rather than reform conservative societies.

> ## Activity
>
> Highlight, in approximately 200 words, the differences and potential similarities between multiculturalism and conservatism.

Debate 3

Is multiculturalism a recipe for discord?

Yes

…say conservative theorists like Samuel Huntington (*The Clash of Civilizations*, Simon & Schuster, 1996):

- It denies the concept of 'one nation' and fragments society into small communities.
- Many of the communities it encourages have potentially conflicting values (for example, Islamic, Jewish).
- It may encourage members of some communities to view non-members with suspicion and hostility.
- It can lead to discord within communities, between those who take an exclusive view of their community and those who want strong connections with the rest of society.

No

…say writers like Tariq Modood (*Multiculturalism*, Polity, 2007):

- As a result of the state recognising other communities, all citizens will become more aware, cosmopolitan and tolerant.
- As a result of being recognised by the state, those from minority communities will feel less alienated and more receptive to others.
- As a result of being recognised, those from all communities will accept the state's legitimacy.
- Multiculturalism will help stifle racism, bigotry and xenophobia, and instead promote greater understanding between cultures.

Summary: key themes and key thinkers

	Human nature	The state	Society	The economy
Charles Taylor	Humans naturally seek their identity, which is shaped and developed by their communities.	The state must practise the politics of recognition, thus validating its communities.	Stable and successful societies comprise a wide variety of communities.	Laissez-faire capitalism may have to be moderated to protect communitarian interests.
Isaiah Berlin	Individuals seek autonomy, but mirror the absolute values extolled by cultures.	The state must practise value pluralism and let communities decide which values are paramount.	The best societies practise value pluralism and thus allow tolerance and freedom.	Capitalism may clash with certain absolute moral values, such as equality.
Will Kymlicka	Individuals adore choice, but are confused without the 'anchorage' provided by their culture.	The state must offer group differentiated rights in order to secure the consent of diverse cultures.	Society is defined by cultures, which often transcend geographical areas.	Multiculturalism enhances capitalism by energising individuals from diverse backgrounds.
Bhikhu Parekh	Humans are culturally embedded, but are able to alter and improve the cultures concerned.	The state should recognise cultural pluralism by allowing some legal and governmental diversity.	The ideal society is one hosting an ongoing conversation between and within various cultures.	Multiculturalism checks capitalism by promoting values other than those of economic liberalism.
Tariq Modood	Individuals find comfort and security in the history of their culture.	Citing its various cultures, the state should foster a narrative that promotes unity through diversity.	Culturally pluralistic societies help reconcile citizens to their nation's diverse history.	Multiculturalism softens capitalist inequalities by creating a more realistic version of 'one nation'.

Tensions within multiculturalism

- **Human nature:** pluralist multiculturalists like Parekh argue that humans are driven by the interests of their communities. Liberal and cosmopolitan multiculturalists, like Kymlicka and Jeremy Waldron, maintain that humans, while valuing their communities, are still heavily influenced by self-interest.
- **Society:** pluralist multiculturalists like Parekh believe that society should be reordered, via its communities, to produce greater equality of outcome. Liberal multiculturalists like Kymlicka and cosmopolitan multiculturalists like Waldron see society's communities as a vehicle for individual progress.
- **The state:** liberal multiculturalists like Kymlicka argue for a state that promotes shallow diversity by insisting that all communities respect core liberal values such as individual liberty and the universality of the rule of law. Pluralist multiculturalists like Parekh argue for deep diversity via a state which allows cultural federalism and some variation in law between communities.
- **The economy:** liberal multiculturalists anticipate free trade and free movement of goods between communities. Pluralist multiculturalists believe that a degree of protectionism may be required to safeguard a community's integrity and economic well-being.

Conclusion: multiculturalism today

Although it has been discussed and practised since the 1960s, it has been during the twenty-first century that multiculturalism has received its most intense and sustained scrutiny. Globalisation, the accelerated pace of migration and the violent manifestation of religious extremism have all conspired to make multiculturalism perhaps the most controversial of all the ideologies covered in this book. But what of multiculturalism's central aim: the pursuit of unity, in a multicultural society, through the state-sponsored promotion of diversity? Is this likely to gain more or less support in the years ahead?

In the UK and elsewhere, there has been no shortage of commentators arguing that multiculturalism is an unfit response to an increasingly diverse society. Central to this claim have been two charges.

The first is that multiculturalism does nothing to prevent — and actually encourages — the fragmentation of urban areas into ethnically and religiously defined communities. Following the UK riots of 2001 (in Oldham, Bradford and Burnley), the government-backed Cantle Report noted that citizens in those towns were living 'parallel lives', rarely interacting with each other, and thus creating a 'fractured society'. Meanwhile, the notable rise of Islamist violence since 2001 — including the terrorism carried out in London on 7 July 2005 — fuelled the

Trevor Phillips: critic of multiculturalism

notion that any ideology which promotes anti-western cultures was simply 'an incitement to bloodshed and civil war' (*The Spectator*, 10 July 2005).

The second and related charge is that multicultural societies spawn problematically different views about what constitutes acceptable and unacceptable attitudes, and subsequent confusion about what is and is not legal. Drawing upon evidence collated by the ICM polling company, Trevor Phillips, former head of the UK's Commission for Racial Equality, related that a third of British Muslims, for example, consider polygamy acceptable and that 52% believe homosexuality should be illegal (*Race and Faith: The Deafening Silence*, Civitas, 2016).

Such concerns were underlined by recent criminal cases in Rotherham and Bradford, where men of Pakistani origin, charged with the sexual assault of children, claimed a 'cultural defence' for their actions, citing the starkly different views of acceptable sexual practice within the country of their origin. Liberal-minded journals have also reported the '6000-plus cases of female genital mutilation (FGM) reported to the NHS since 2015...mainly concerning women from within the Somali community' — this despite FGM being illegal in the UK since 1985 (*New Statesman*, 7 October 2016).

It must be emphasised here that multiculturalism cannot be directly blamed for such shocking episodes. Indeed, at the time they occurred, the UK government was explicitly rejecting multiculturalism in favour of individualist integration. What might be argued, however, is that the state's rejection of multiculturalism needs to be much more vigorous if ethnically diverse societies are to avoid getting mixed messages about what is morally and legally permissible. Noting ICM's finding that a third of British Muslims regarded themselves as Islamic rather than British, and recalling that the Islamist terrorists who carried out the London Underground bombing of 2005 were UK citizens, Trevor Phillips warned that countries which 'flirted' with multiculturalism were:

> 'sleepwalking to a catastrophe that will set community against community, endorse sexist aggression, suppress freedom of expression and reverse hard-won civil liberties'. (*Race and Faith*, 2016)

In December 2016, Phillips's critique of multiculturalism was endorsed by Dame Louise Casey's government-backed report, *Review into Opportunity and Integration*. Like Phillips, Casey argued that the UK (specifically Labour-controlled local authorities) had 'flirted' with multiculturalism — the result being that there was now, in many urban areas, 'segregation not integration', a 'disturbing confusion about what is right and wrong', and a worrying spread of 'condoned criminality'. For example:

> 'We have heard about discriminatory practices against women which are causing serious harm...There have been claims some sharia councils have been condoning wife beating, ignoring marital rape and allowing forced marriage...and local authorities have often ignored such reports for fear of being seen as racist or Islamophobic.' (Casey, 2016)

Casey went on to argue that in addition to fostering a sense of 'separateness' within minority-culture communities, multiculturalist practices (such as positive discrimination) had fostered growing resentment and racist hostility among those from the majority culture. The danger of identity politics, Casey noted, was that it raised the consciousness of both minority and majority groups within the population — with effects that were seen, perhaps, in both the Brexit vote and the election of President Trump. In short, identity politics and multiculturalist language may simply nurture a variety of immoderate views and an increasingly polarised society.

Like Phillips, Casey duly recommended a clear, state-backed renunciation of the multiculturalist practices outlined in Box 5.3. Like Phillips too, Casey supported a renewal of the individualist-integration strategy, as traditionally practised in the UK and the USA. For the UK, Casey specifically backed measures such as an oath of allegiance (to be taken as a precondition of UK citizenship), along with compulsory state-funded English language classes for all migrants seeking residency.

Casey's report, however, provoked criticism as well as support, its critics stating that the alternatives to multiculturalism (individualist integration and assimilation) remain fraught with difficulty. We should remember, for example, that countries such as France, which unequivocally rejected multiculturalism, have themselves suffered acute problems regarding social cohesion and internal security. Between 2015 and 2017, for example, France witnessed outbreaks of Islamist violence (such as the attack on the *Charlie Hebdo* magazine) and an upsurge of support for extremist parties (like Marine Le Pen's Front National), despite decades of vehement opposition to multiculturalism and despite stern assimilationist policies (including a recent ban on the 'burkhini'). Likewise, the worrying findings uncovered by Phillips and Casey in the UK are perhaps

Marine Le Pen: populist advocate of assimilation

less an indictment of multiculturalism than of individualist integration — the policy which, for almost half a century, has been the default option of UK governments.

All this has encouraged defenders of multiculturalism to continue arguing that, in multicultural societies, the rejection of multiculturalism creates intolerance among the 'majority' community, alienation among minority communities and an obstacle to the unity of society. In addition, both society and the economy have changed in a way that makes assimilation and individualist integration harder to pursue. The traditional 'heavy' industries (such as coal, steel, textiles), which brought a daily dose of shared circumstance to thousands of workers from different cultural backgrounds, have been in sharp decline, while the increasingly diverse nature of our media works powerfully against cultural homogeneity and subsequent assimilation. As Phillips conceded:

> 'Finally, the divisive influence of today's media architecture: TV stations from Africa, Asia and the Middle East invade suburban sitting rooms daily.

> 'Many minority Britons inhabit separate echo chambers populated largely by people from their own ethnic or religious background.' (*Daily Telegraph*, 5 December 2016)

Furthermore, although the views offered by Phillips and Casey represent a liberal critique of multiculturalism, other developments during 2016 may have prompted some liberals to reappraise multiculturalism's merits. Particularly for liberals in the UK and the USA, both the Brexit vote and the election of Donald Trump as president revived fears of a 'tyranny of the majority' — a scenario where, thanks to results at the ballot box, liberal values such as tolerance and pluralism become threatened. In response, liberals were quick to re-engage with traditional methods of containing 'illiberal' majorities (namely, the sundry checks and balances of constitutional government). However, if 'illiberal populism' remains a feature of modern politics, then multiculturalism — with its inherent stress on diversity and minority rights — may come to be seen by liberals as an additional ally in their battle against populism (or simply democracy).

As the twenty-first century progresses, culturally uneven societies appear to be an irreversible reality. Consequently, the debate about how the state should manage them is unlikely to disappear and may well intensify. This should ensure that both multiculturalism and its alternatives remain pressing and controversial topics for students of political ideology.

Further reading

Heywood, A. (2016) 'Multiculturalism — a recipe for tension and conflict?', *Politics Review*, 25,4.
Kelly, R. and Crowcroft, R. (2012) 'From Burke to Burkha: towards a conservative multiculturalism', in Edwards, J. (ed.) *Retrieving the Big Society*, Wiley-Blackwell.
Kymlicka, W. (1995) *Multicultural Citizenship*, Oxford University Press.
Lentin, A. and Titley, G. (2011) *The Crises of Multiculturalism*, Zed Books.
Macey, M. (2009) *Multiculturalism, Religion and Women*, Palgrave.
Parekh, B. (2005) *Rethinking Multiculturalism*, Blackwell.

Exam-style questions

Essay questions

The following questions are similar to those in examinations set by Edexcel (Pearson) and AQA. Each carries either 24 (Edexcel) or 25 marks (AQA).

Edexcel (24 marks) or AQA (25 marks):

1 To what extent can multiculturalism be reconciled to national unity? You must use appropriate thinkers you have studied to support your answer.

2 To what extent does multiculturalism support the 'politics of difference'? You must use appropriate thinkers you have studied to support your answer.

AQA only (25 marks):

3 Is 'liberal multiculturalism' a contradiction in terms? Analyse and avaluate with reference to the thinkers you have studied.

4 Is multiculturalism a discredited ideology? Analyse and evaluate with reference to the thinkers you have studied.

Chapter 6

Ecologism

Learning outcomes

This chapter will enable students to:
- understand how ecologism ideas developed in the twentieth century
- understand the core values of ecology as a political ideology and distinguish ecology from environmentalism
- understand the various types of ecologism, how they differ and the tensions that exist within the movement
- understand the ideas of ecologism's key thinkers

Introduction: environmentalism, ecology and ecologism

In 1798 the reverend Thomas Malthus published *An Essay on the Principle of Population*. It is a work that has had a profound influence on economists and environmental thinkers ever since. Malthus's thesis was that the population of the earth would increase exponentially (i.e. it would rise in an accelerating fashion) but food production would grow more slowly. The result, he

predicted, was that the human race would simply run out of food in years to come and the result would lead to untold misery and disaster unless the growth in population could be controlled. Malthus turned out to be right about population but wrong about food production, which did, with difficulty, keep pace with the increasing demand.

Although his theory was flawed, Malthus' fundamental idea has been taken up again more recently. Today, it has been amended to show that as the demand for resources in general grows, there will come a time when the earth will not be able to satisfy that demand. In other words, humans are treating the earth as though it has infinite resources when they are, in fact, finite. Even if the population ceases to grow, as Malthus' theory demanded, there will still be a tendency to feed the ever increasing economic growth that modern capitalism makes inevitable. This, together with mankind's tendency to see the earth's resources as its own to exploit, forms the basis of much ecological thinking today.

Before beginning our exploration of ecologism, we need to define some terms. The word 'environmentalism' should be reserved for those political beliefs and attitudes that are concerned with the preservation and improvement of the earth's natural environment. The term also implies that this can be achieved by political action and that such action is possible with existing political and economic structures. In other words, it is a reform movement. As such it is extremely important to the future fortunes of mankind but does not require revolutionary change, either in attitudes or in social systems.

'Ecology' is a scientific term. It means simply the study of the relationship between human kind and its natural environment. It is therefore a neutral, descriptive term and says nothing about what should be done about the environment. It has the same status as terms such as 'physics', 'biology' and 'chemistry'.

Ecologism, the subject of this chapter, can be described as either a philosophy or an ideology. It shares with environmentalism a concern for the natural environment, but proposes fundamental, perhaps even revolutionary, changes in the way we view our natural world and how we should go about protecting it. While ecology studies the relationship between humans and the natural world, ecologists seek first to explain and then to change that relationship.

Key term

Ecologism This philosophy or ideology seeks to explain mankind's relationship to the natural world and the earth in general, and proposes ways in which this relationship can be improved to protect nature and preserve the supply of resources.

Activity

Explain, in no more than 100 words, the distinction between environmentalism and ecologism.

The origins of ecologism

Ecologism is a relatively modern phenomenon. Before the 1960s there had been growing concerns about the environment, notably the depletion of natural habitats and the loss of some animal species, pollution of the air, rivers and seas and the dangers of nuclear energy, but there was no fundamental concern over the long-term future of the environment.

Three developments were especially significant in the growth of ecological thought. The first, in the late 1960s, was the discovery that human activity, notably the emission of CFCs (chlorofluorocarbons) into the atmosphere, was causing long-term environmental damage. In particular, it was damaging the ozone layer, which absorbs ultraviolet light, protecting life on earth in general. Similarly, it was found that the release of carbons into the atmosphere, mostly the result of burning fossil fuels such as oil and coal, was leading to the phenomenon of global warming.

Global warming became the key theme of these discoveries, in particular because the raising of the sea's and earth's temperatures would lead to uncontrollable environmental consequences. However, it was a book by an American scientist, **Rachel Carson** (1907–64) (see 'Key thinker 1' box), that perhaps had the most profound influence in early ecologism. *Silent Spring* (1962) showed how the release of dangerous chemicals in industrial processes was causing extensive damage to the environment. Carson extended her warnings to a general assertion that mankind had learned to treat the earth as if it were its servant and as if the consequences of our actions were not our concern. This, she insisted, was a dangerous development. We should treat the earth as a precious gift, she wrote, and not an inexhaustible resource. Other philosophies since have been deeper or more comprehensive but none had the same impact on public attitudes to nature as *Silent Spring*.

The second development was the crisis in the supply of oil that occurred in the mid-1970s. The main oil producers reduced the supply of crude oil onto the market, as a result of which oil and petrol prices quadrupled. This led to concerns about the fragility of energy supplies, causing a growth in interest in finding sources of renewable energy, notably wind and thermal energy. It also made carbon-neutral nuclear energy more attractive, leading to a debate about whether it was safe and the question of how to deal with its dangerous waste products.

The third development, and perhaps the most significant in terms of ideology, was the emergence of a series of philosophical theories about mankind's relationship with the natural world. Possibly the most influential came from British scientist James Lovelock (1919–). Lovelock's main theory was that both the earth's animate and inanimate parts were interconnected and formed a single complete organism. Any change in one part would therefore lead to a change in the whole. In particular, there is a balance in the whole 'biosphere' (the earth as a whole single entity) and if this balance is disturbed there is an adjustment to find a new balance. Thus, human activity may have unintended and unknown consequences. Lovelock's philosophy came to be known as the **Gaia hypothesis**, Gaia being the name of the ancient Greek goddess of the earth.

> **Key term**
>
> **Gaia hypothesis** This hypothesis or principle, originated by James Lovelock, suggests the earth is one single organism and any change in one part of it will cause changes in the whole.

Lovelock was, it should be emphasised, somewhat optimistic about how earth will cope with mankind's onslaught. He saw the Gaia as having self-adjusting mechanisms, just as the human body has — if one part is damaged, the other parts will compensate. We would, he accepted, need to change our environmental behaviour, but the long-term prospects were relatively secure.

Lovelock was criticised by other philosophers who took a more pessimistic view in arguing that the self-adjustments that Lovelock identified did not exist and in re-examining mankind's relationship with the earth. Norwegian Arne Naess (1912–2009) believed that humans have a deep spiritual relationship with nature which, in modern civilisation, has largely been lost. In other words, instead of being 'one with nature', mankind has become alienated from it.

Similarly, Austrian scientist Fritjof Capra (1939–) developed the idea of a 'web of life', wherein all living organisms, from the very large to the microscopic, are interconnected and communicate with each other in ways humans cannot comprehend. Thus, rather than being separate from nature, we are bound up in it in mysterious and fundamental ways.

Placed together these three historical developments have changed the ecological movement in three main ways:

1   They have caused society to consider the ways in which it is damaging the environment and so search for ways to reduce and eliminate the damage, perhaps even reverse it before it is too late.

Deep ecology This philosophy and set of theories suggest the need for mankind to change fundamentally its attitude to nature. By doing so it will change its consciousness of the world and accept the need for deep change in philosophy and society.

Shallow ecology This refers to theories about the natural environment that require significant adjustments to mankind's relationship to the natural world, but which stop short of proposing a fundamental change in that relationship.

2   They have led to an understanding that the earth's resources are not infinite, so that new sources of renewable energy have to be found if mankind is to survive.

3   They have led theorists, philosophers and activists to reconsider mankind's relationship with nature in ways which have not been seen since ancient philosophy considered the matter before the time of Christ.

> **Activity**
>
> Explain, in no more than 200 words, how ecologists have developed their ideas about the relationship between mankind and nature since the 1960s.

Between them, these and other ecologists came to be known as leaders of the Deep Green movement, a philosophy known as **deep ecology**. This term was used to distinguish them from shallow green theorists and scientists, followers of **shallow ecology**, who took a less philosophical and fundamentalist view of the problem.

The core ideas of ecologism

Human nature

Anthropocentrism

Anthropocentrism is a typical human characteristic that sees mankind as the centre of the natural world. One important explanation for the power of this belief is that it is part of the Judaeo-Christian teaching that God created the earth for the benefit of mankind. In the Book of Genesis in the Bible, these words describe God's intention:

> 'God blessed them and said "be fruitful and increase in number, fill the earth and subdue it. Rule over the fish in the sea and the birds in the sky and over every living creature that moves on the ground".' (Chapter 1, Verse 28)

Since Christianity dominated western civilisation for many centuries it is not surprising that such a belief came to be part of mankind's world view. The fact that a similar account is given in the Koran serves to strengthen anthropocentric attitudes. It has also led to a **stewardship** model of mankind's relationship to nature. This suggests that although humans

Key thinker 1

Rachel Carson (1907–64)

American biologist Rachel Carson is credited with helping to launch modern environmentalist consciousness. Her book *Silent Spring*, published in 1962, had a great impact not only on the scientific world but among the American people in general. Her study of harmful chemicals, including pesticides that were leeching into rivers and lakes, demonstrated the enormous damage being done to plant and animal life. Not only that, she added, but water pollution also threatened the health of humans themselves. She outlined the danger to humans in *Silent Spring*:

> 'A Who's Who of pesticides is therefore of concern to us all. If we are going to live so intimately with these chemicals eating and drinking them, taking them into the very marrow of our bones — we had better know something about their nature and their power.'

However, Carson's work went much further than a mere exposé of how much industry and agriculture were polluting the water supply. She also wrote about a new form of human consciousness and attitude towards nature. It was the philosophy in *Silent Spring* that caught the public's imagination. Her romantic view of our relationship with nature is captured in this passage from the book:

> 'Those who contemplate the beauty of the earth find reserves of strength that will endure as long as life lasts. There is something infinitely healing in the repeated refrains of nature — the assurance that dawn comes after night, and spring after winter.'

To Carson there was a sense of wonder in nature, and human actions that damaged the environment might well be destroying that wonder. Her vision of anthropocentrism was a simple one: by polluting the natural environment, mankind was making decisions about who should live or die in nature; which parts of the sea could be sacrificed, which species in the rivers would be destroyed in the interests of agricultural output. This was a form of arrogance, she added, a belief that mankind was superior to nature when this, to her, was clearly not the case.

Carson became an adviser to the US government and her influence led to the introduction of some of the first legal environmental controls over pollution. However, her main legacy remains the strength of the environmental movement that followed her. *Silent Spring* was the spark that lit the fire of modern environmentalism.

Activity

Explain, in no more than 100 words, the meaning of the term 'anthropocentrism'.

have a superior position in nature, they also have a God-given duty to care for the earth they have been given. For less radical ecologists the stewardship model is attractive, though for deep greens it remains offensive.

Rachel Carson offered one of the earliest visions of the problems created by anthropocentrism. In *Silent Spring* she started by revealing the extent of water pollution that was being allowed to happen but extended her analysis to explaining that this was symptomatic of a wider attitude that mankind had adopted in relation to the natural environment — mankind had become so used to exploiting the environment that we had ceased to understand the extent to which we were damaging it. It was one of the first visions of anthropocentrism.

The critical response to anthropocentrism is often known as **ecocentrism**. Ecocentrism asserts that there is no distinction between the human world and nature; we are all part of the same organism. It is also a contrast to traditionally scientific views of the world. Science separates the various parts of nature, while the ecocentric view sees nature as one single whole.

Ecocentrism also proposes that all the aspects of nature have equal value, i.e. there is no hierarchy in nature. If there is no hierarchy, mankind cannot be at the top of it. If there is an apex to nature, it is the earth itself, as a whole organism, which stands there.

Environmental consciousness

If as humans we can rid ourselves of our natural anthropocentrism we can begin to develop environmental consciousness, deep ecologists argue. This kind of consciousness sees nature as having equal status with humankind and often goes further, suggesting that humans are merely a part of nature and not separated from it by any sense of superiority. This is how Capra expressed it:

'Shallow ecology is anthropocentric, or human-centred. It views humans as above or outside nature, as the source of all value, and ascribes only instrumental, or "use", value to nature. Deep ecology does not separate humans — or anything else — from the natural environment. It does see the world not as a collection of isolated objects but as a network of phenomena that are fundamentally interconnected and interdependent. Deep ecology recognizes the intrinsic value of all human beings and views humans as just one particular strand in the web of life.' (*The Web of Life*, 1996)

Naess went even further, suggesting that humans need to be conscious of the natural world in a completely different way. In particular, we need to see nature as having

Key term

Ecocentrism This is a form of consciousness that places humans as part of the natural world and not separate from it. This leads to a philosophy that is nature-centred and rejects the concept that mankind has the right to control the environment.

Key term

Intrinsic value This means value in itself. In ecological terms it refers to how humans need to be conscious of the natural world. We should see it in terms of nature's own welfare rather than the welfare of mankind.

intrinsic value. By this, he means we should cease to see the natural world as an extension of ourselves and instead see it as valuable in itself. In this way we will stop seeing it as something we use for our own benefit and instead see it as something to be protected. In practice this means seeing environmental problems, such as resource depletion, destruction of natural habitats and pollution, not in terms of how they affect mankind but rather in terms of how they affect nature itself.

There is also a shallower green version of environmental consciousness. This simply argues that in all actions, humans should be aware of the impact they are having on the natural environment. Thus we should always recycle, where possible, conserve energy, avoid activities that pollute and oppose threats to endangered animal and plant species.

Debate 1

Does the natural world exist for the good of mankind or does it have intrinsic value?

For the good of mankind

- The Judaeo-Christian and Islamic traditions suggest that God gave the earth to man for his own good and that he gave humans 'dominion' over the earth. Mankind is expected to treat nature with respect, but ultimately it is for our benefit and our pleasure.
- Humans are clearly superior to other living beings in terms of skills and intelligence, so it is natural that we hold a superior position in nature. Mankind can also bring science to bear upon the natural world, both to exploit and to protect it.
- Inanimate objects (rocks, earth, elements, etc.) are not sentient beings, so we need not consider their welfare. The idea that the earth is wholly interrelated is rejected. Mechanism suggests that mankind can solve the problems of nature through its constituent parts.

It has intrinsic value

- If God did indeed create the earth and everything in it, we have a duty to nurture and protect it (the stewardship model). Though we may be superior, we are also the guardians of God's creation. In other words, it is ungodly to despoil the earth.
- Apparent human superiority is viewed only from a human perspective. There is no reason why nature should not have equal or even superior value.
- Human life on earth is probably only temporary, whereas nature is permanent. We are part of a constant cycle of nature — a Buddhist idea — so nothing is permanent.

The state

Sustainability

The aims of many states and the international community can be summarised in the single term 'sustainability'. A technical term for this is **homeostasis**, meaning that the natural world should be in a stable condition where it is not losing natural resources, the atmosphere is balanced and nature is able to replicate itself successfully. Donella Meadows (1941–2001), an American environmentalist, described sustainability as:

> 'a careful balance between long term and short term goals and an emphasis on sufficiency, equity and quality of life rather than on quantity of output.' (*Thinking in Systems*, 2008, posthumously)

Sustainability has a number of features, including:

- **Biodiversity:** this means the preservation of those species that already exist and so provide variety in nature. Biodiversity is seen both as an end in itself and as an assurance that the natural world remains in a balanced state. Conservation of habitats, preservation systems, and the outlawing of irresponsible destruction of animals and plants are typical examples of action.
- **Preserving natural resources:** this is usually pursued by developing sustainable energy production such as nuclear, wind, wave, tidal and thermal systems. It also includes recycling systems.
- **Preserving nature:** this means protecting the natural environment through tight planning laws, controlling industrial development and outlawing illegal degradation of the natural environment, such as logging in rain forests.
- **Controlling atmospheric and water pollution:** this is designed to preserve the state of rivers and seas as well as the atmosphere.

It is acknowledged that these sustainability issues cannot be addressed solely by individual states, so they have largely been the subject of international conferences and agreements. These have included:

1984   Geneva Convention on controlling air pollution.
1985   Helsinki agreement on controlling harmful emissions.
1987   Montreal agreement on measures to prevent depletion of the ozone layer.
1992   Rio Accord (United Nations, known as the Earth Summit) declared the aim of achieving sustainability.

1997   Kyoto agreement on measures to prevent long-term climate change.

2009   Copenhagen — a first attempt at a comprehensive agreement. This failed.

2015   Paris agreement — 196 states signed. Its main commitment was to halt the rise in global warming and to reverse the process if possible.

Paris in 2015 was said to be the most important environmental agreement ever to be signed. In particular, it brought China and India into the process of achieving atmospheric sustainability. The election of Donald Trump as US president, however, has put the Paris accord in danger as he sees such agreements as a serious challenge to industrial development in the USA.

Associated with sustainability is the principle of **sustainable development**. This states that any form of current development, industrial or otherwise, should take account of the needs of future generations. Two clear examples of this concern the preservation of stocks of whales and fish which, if depleted to irrecoverable levels, will deprive future generations, and the preservation of the rain forests, which provide timber for the current generation but which will rob tribal groups, animals and plants of their habitat and will affect the climate for future generations. On a broader scale, the use of renewable energy resources will preserve the availability of energy into the future.

The principle of sustainability is a special case as it affects humans yet to be born. It therefore becomes an ethical issue. The current generation may not be adversely affected by irresponsible use of resources, but future humans certainly will.

Environmental ethics

The concept of environmental ethics is a problem for states. This is because current politicians will not benefit from measures taken when adopting an ethical approach to the environment which will show results in the future. It is difficult to persuade people to vote for measures that will not benefit them directly. Nevertheless, it has become a key aspect of environmental politics and philosophy.

Ethics is a complex issue in relation to the environment, but two key elements serve to illustrate its importance:

1   The issue of stewardship suggests that the current generation has a moral (ethical) obligation to manage our planet in a way that will be of benefit to future generations. This concerns preserving resources and natural habitats, for example, and protecting the environment generally.

> **Key term**
>
> **Sustainable development**
> This refers to the principle that the current generation should not use up resources and degrade the environment to the detriment of future generations, not yet born.

2   The issue of animal rights is a controversial aspect. Some liberal ecologists and deep ecologists have suggested that animals have similar natural rights to humans. This lends itself to veganism in its extreme form, of course. However, less dramatically, it concerns preserving species and habitats, outlawing hunting for recreation, preventing cruelty to animals and banning experimentation on animals. This principle involves a new kind of consciousness, which accepts that animals have the same rights as humans and that we, as a superior species, have a duty to protect and care for them.

A key figure in the field of environmental ethics was **Aldo Leopold** (1887–1948) (see 'Key thinker 2' box). Leopold was mainly concerned with man's relationship to animals and to the natural world. His field of action was the preservation of wild species of animals and the preservation of natural landscapes. His philosophy that underpinned this was described by himself and others as land ethics.

Biodiversity is a key issue for environmentalists

Society

Post-materialism

The post-materialist criticism of modern society is that it is based on the assumption that people will become increasingly prosperous and therefore consumption of goods will inevitably rise. Furthermore, and on a more philosophical level, consumerism is seen as a form of consciousness — that people now see their existence in terms of what they consume rather than what they believe or how they behave. Until this consciousness is changed, consumerism will remain a threat to sustainability.

Key thinker 2

Aldo Leopold (1887–1948)

Born in the USA, Aldo Leopold was a scientist and naturalist whose work *A Sand County Almanac* (1949), published posthumously, became a hugely influential work of early ecologism. In the book Leopold stressed that humans have an equal place in the world with animals and that we are not superior to them as was commonly accepted. Furthermore, mankind has an ethical duty to protect the countryside in general, both for its own sake and as the habitat for wild creatures. Much of Leopold's life's work concerned natural preservation schemes.

Rejecting the Judaeo-Christian view of mankind's ownership of the land, he said in *A Sand County Almanac*:

> 'Conservation is getting nowhere because it is incompatible with our Abrahamic [Judaeo-Christian] concept of land. We abuse land because we regard it as a commodity belonging to us. When we see land as a community to which we belong, we may begin to use it with love and respect.'

Leopold also advocated **biodiversity**. In practice this meant measures to conserve endangered species and their habitats. For him the concept of 'wilderness' was essential. Wilderness represented the natural state of the landscape, untouched by the hand of mankind. As an extension of this philosophy he developed the idea of land ethic. Land ethic philosophy insists that humans should accept that the land does not belong to them but that they and the land are equal partners. Leopold understood that humans would have to use some of the land for their own purposes but it was vital that some of the land should be preserved in its natural, pristine state. He expressed this idea colourfully: 'Harmony with land is like harmony with a friend; you cannot cherish his right hand and chop off his left.'

In his lifetime Leopold was popularly known as little more than a conservationist, but since then it has become apparent that his was a major ethical philosophy. Some have added that his spiritual relationship with the land had a religious quality to it. In this sense he was close to the later ideas of Naess.

Key term

Biodiversity This is the desire to ensure that as many species of plants and animals survive as possible, maintaining richness in nature.

Activity

Explain, in no more than 100 words, the meaning of 'ethics' in terms of ecologism.

E.F. Schumacher (1911–77) (see 'Key thinker 3' box) provided one solution to post-materialist problems. He advocated a new kind of economics whereby people would form themselves increasingly into self-sufficient communities. These would inevitably be small-scale, hence the title of his best known work, *Small Is Beautiful* (1973). The switch to small-scale self-sufficiency was to have two beneficial effects on the environment. First, it would involve simpler technologies which would do less environmental damage. Second, it would lead to a halt in the apparently inevitable rise in consumerism.

E.F. Schumacher (1911–77)

Ernst Schumacher was a German-born economist who carried out most of his work in Britain. He became a major figure in the ecology movement in 1973 when he published a book entitled *Small Is Beautiful*. It had an immediate impact, especially within the anarchist-inspired 'commune' movement that was popular at the time. Its subtitle, *A Study of Economics As If People Mattered*, gives a clue to its contents.

The main thesis of *Small Is Beautiful* is that because of the way in which capitalism and consumerism were developing, the world would eventually run out of resources. In other words, such progress was unsustainable. This was a modern version of Thomas Malthus' population thesis of 1798 in which he had argued that the world would run out of food before long. Schumacher argued that this problem should be addressed in two ways. One was by voluntarily limiting capitalism's seemingly inevitable insatiable desire for economic growth. The other was by reverting to simpler technologies that will use up less of the earth's resources.

In *Small Is Beautiful* he expressed the first problem:

'An attitude to life which seeks fulfilment in the single-minded pursuit of wealth — in short, materialism — does not fit into this world, because it contains within itself no limiting principle, while the environment in which it is placed is strictly limited.'

On the second area, Schumacher described himself as a **Buddhist economist**. He explained his call for a simpler form of economic structure:

'From the point of view of Buddhist economics, therefore, production from local resources for local needs is the most rational way of economic life, while dependence on imports from afar and the consequent need to produce for export to unknown and distant peoples is highly uneconomic and justifiable only in exceptional cases and on a small scale.'

In practice, what he was advocating was the creation of small communities which were largely self-sufficient. This would lead to a more natural relationship between humans and the natural environment, he argued. He lamented the loss of rural life in favour of increasing industrialisation and urbanisation. The proposals in *Small Is Beautiful* would restore the primacy of rural life. His ideas are therefore sometimes described as **pastoralism**. Pastoral, simple life has a double benefit, Schumacher claimed. First, it will preserve the land, and second, it will create a more meaningful lifestyle for individuals, who will find themselves in harmony with the land.

Activity

Explain, in no more than 100 words, the meaning of the idea 'small is beautiful'.

Key terms

Buddhist economics This is a term associated with Ernst Schumacher. It implies that people will find simpler ways of living and working, with limited desires for goods and a more natural, spiritual relationship with the environment.

Pastoralism This is a call for people to return to the land and start living a simpler form of existence, leading to a higher form of environmental consciousness.

Holism

In her book *Thinking in Systems* (2008), Donella Meadows expressed the idea of holism:

> 'The world is a complex, interconnected, finite, ecological-social-psychological-economic system. We treat it as if it were not, as if it were divisible, separable, simple, and infinite. Our persistent, intractable global problems arise directly from this mismatch.'

In the world of ecologism, holism proposes, as Meadows shows us above, that all of nature is interconnected. In other words, it is a single organic whole. This implies that if humans take an action which affects one part of nature, it will affect other parts, often in ways that cannot be predicted. Two alternative ideas stand in opposition to holism.

One is that nature is divided into its constituent parts and that they can be treated separately. In environmental terms, this implies that damage to one part of the natural world will not necessarily lead to damage elsewhere, especially if remedial action is taken. Holism challenges this view by asserting that the natural world is organic and it is not possible to keep separate its constituent parts. As a single organic whole, damage to one part will lead to damage to the whole organism.

The second is the **mechanistic world view**. This arises from traditional science and suggests that nature is like a machine and has separate parts which operate in predictable ways. Thus, if human action affects one part of nature, it is possible to predict its outcomes and take action to prevent further damage. Again, holism opposes this view with its organic outlook on nature. Nature is not like a machine, holism suggests, but is a single organism. Changes thus become uncontrollable and unpredictable.

Capra was one of the most important holistic thinkers. He suggested that eastern religions had discovered the idea of the oneness of nature and that mankind is but one part of the whole. Lovelock's Gaia theory — that the earth itself is a single organism — is similar. However, Lovelock is more optimistic than most holistic thinkers in believing that the earth has the ability to repair itself, so damage wrought by humans may be reduced or even eliminated by the earth itself.

Key term

Mechanistic world view
This suggests that nature is like a machine, its different parts operating in predictable ways. Environmental damage can be controlled by attending to different parts of nature.

The economy

Ecology and capitalism

There are many ecologists who believe that capitalism is incompatible with their environmental objectives. This is for a number of reasons. They argue:

- Capitalism has an inbuilt need for economic growth. If growth stops, capitalism automatically falls into recession, so there is an insatiable drive for increases in output. This kind of growth means that capitalist enterprises will continually use up natural resources in the race for growth.
- The drive for profit, which is intrinsically part of capitalism, means that if there is a choice between environmental considerations and keeping down costs of production, enterprises will always choose the latter. In other words, it is perceived that environmental protection incurs additional costs.
- There are many in the capitalist world who believe that environmental problems will have technological remedies. Their thesis is that environmental damage ultimately creates a demand for remedies and once the demand for remedial action becomes great enough, free-market capitalism will develop remedies to meet that demand. In other words, capitalism will protect the environment once it can be shown that there is a profit in it. However, ecologists assert, there is no reason why environmental protection should ever turn a profit, so the technology will never be created. In addition, ecologists say, the damage done will become irreparable, so technology will become powerless to prevent it or turn back the tide.
- Capitalists, say ecologists, take a mechanistic view of the world. This implies that they believe that any environmental damage they do is limited to those parts of the natural world directly affected. Action by themselves or by the state, therefore, can reduce or eliminate such damage. Holism, however, suggests that such damage will not be limited, that the whole of the environment is damaged if a single part of it is damaged.

So, it is largely the case that ecologists recommend either the destruction of capitalism — and these are naturally often socialists or anarchists — or a revolutionary change in the way in which capitalism operates to take account of environmental protection.

Probably the most fundamental critique of the role of capitalism in the destruction of the natural environment was proposed by **Murray Bookchin** (1921–2006) (see 'Key thinker 4' box). Bookchin, whose philosophy is usually described as social

Murray Bookchin (1921–2006)

Murray Bookchin has the distinction of being a leading thinker in two ideological movements — anarchism and ecologism. Certainly his ideas represent a synthesis of the two traditions. His philosophy came to be known as social ecologism. The term derives from his belief that we cannot differentiate problems and conflicts in society from conflicts between mankind and nature. This means the solutions to ecological problems must have social solutions.

Bookchin opposed capitalism on two grounds — that it is exploitive towards workers and that it exploits the natural environment. It is not possible, he asserted, to remove the exploitation of nature without also dealing with the exploitation of workers. He criticised shallow green campaigners who believed that capitalism could be persuaded to reform itself by limiting its insatiable desire for economic growth:

> 'To speak of "limits to growth" under a capitalistic market economy is as meaningless as to speak of limits of warfare under a warrior society. The moral pieties, that are voiced today by many well-meaning environmentalists, are as naive as the moral pieties of multinationals are manipulative. Capitalism can no more be "persuaded" to limit growth than a human being can be "persuaded" to stop breathing. Attempts to "green" capitalism, to make it "ecological", are doomed by the very nature of the system as a system of endless growth.' (*Post-Scarcity Anarchism*, 1971)

Bookchin's response to this problem was to promote the idea of anarchism with no state and the creation of small-scale communes based on common ownership and egalitarianism. With no state and no capitalism, humans would cease to exploit nature for their own purposes, he claimed. His economic thesis was that such a society would cease to pursue growth in production. The concept of scarcity would be abolished since demands would be severely reduced in a non-capitalist society. Without scarcity, the dynamic growth of capitalism would come to an end and there would be no incentive or need to exploit nature in an unsustainable way. Free-market capitalism was the principal culprit in environmental degradation. Looking for other causes was futile, he said:

> 'Unless we realize that the present market society, structured around the brutally competitive imperative of "grow or die," is a thoroughly impersonal, self-operating mechanism, we will falsely tend to blame technology as such or population growth as such for environmental problems. We will ignore their root causes, such as trade for profit, industrial expansion, and the identification of "progress" with corporate self-interest.' (*Post-Scarcity Anarchism*)

Bookchin was influential in the 1960s and 1970s but his political views were so extreme that his ecological theories were largely overtaken by ecologists who concerned themselves with changing human consciousness rather than economic systems. Nevertheless, he still has some influence over the anti-capitalist, anti-globalisation movements that exist today.

Activity

Explain, in no more than 100 words, the main ideas of social ecologism.

ecologism, opposed capitalism, on both socialist and ecological grounds. It exploits the environment, just as it exploits workers. Therefore, he argued, capitalism must be destroyed if the environment is to be saved.

Key term

Decentralisation In terms of ecologism, decentralisation means the transfer of enterprises to small-scale, local production on the assumption that such small enterprises will be affected for the better by their proximity to the natural world.

Green capitalism

Here we examine three perspectives which suggest that capitalism and environmental concern can co-exist.

First, Ernst Schumacher was one of the earliest advocates of a complete change in the way capitalism operates (see pages 200–1). He advocated **decentralisation** of production. This would mean the creation of small-scale productive units on the basis of living in small communes. He suggested that these productive units should be as self-sufficient as possible. By bringing production closer to nature, therefore, concern for the environment would prevail. However, it could be suggested that this is no longer capitalism but a free form of communism.

Second, British economist and former leading member of Friends of the Earth Tom Burke (1947–) takes a more optimistic view of capitalism and the environment. He insists that it is possible to create an ethical kind of capitalism which is committed to environmental protection. But more than this is needed, he accepts. Governments (and the international community) will have to take action to regulate capitalism so that it takes account of environmental issues. Among such methods would be:

- a carbon tax to be levied on companies that release carbon into the atmosphere — it will eventually become more profitable for them to stop carbon emissions than to pay the tax
- massive investment in industries devoted to developing sustainable energy
- global action to ensure that all governments develop plans to convert industry into resource-sustainable enterprises.

He created a 'Green Alliance' of companies that agreed to be environmentally responsible. If large numbers of private companies become responsible in this way, it may lead to a widespread movement throughout the capitalist world.

A third perspective on green capitalism is sometimes known as the consumer choice model. This idea depends upon the prediction that as environmental concerns become more serious and urgent, there will be a rise in consumer demand for environmental protection. In a free-market capitalist world, consumer demands are inevitably converted into supply to meet those demands. This means that capitalism itself will automatically become environmentally sensitive and will start to produce on the basis of sustainability.

Debate 2

Is capitalism compatible with ecological concerns?

Yes

- The consumer choice model suggests that as the public become more environmentally conscious and concerned, they will create a demand for environmental protection and sustainability. Private companies will inevitably respond to such demands positively.
- There is no intrinsic reason why capitalists should not begin to behave ethically, especially if a 'critical mass' of companies adopts environmentally responsible activities.
- Government action can regulate capitalism to ensure it protects the environment. This may include both regulatory laws and selective taxation.

No

- Capitalism's insatiable appetite for growth means that it will always sacrifice environmental concerns for increased output.
- Capitalists believe that paying for environmental protection will eat into their profits. Ultimately capitalism is driven by the profit motive, so environmental costs will be set aside.
- Governments rely on capitalist enterprises to implement their economic policies. They therefore will be reluctant to regulate businesses in the interests of the environment for fear of losing their cooperation.

Different types of ecologism

Deep green ecologism

Deep ecologism refers to a kind of environmental philosophy which proposes that we change our fundamental consciousness of the world. Unless we do this, ecological measures will always be superficial and will ultimately fail. As we have seen, there are several main elements of deep ecological thinking:

- **Holism:** this is the idea that all nature is one single organism and that humans are but one part of this whole. This implies that damage to one part is damage to the whole and that remedies to environmental damage must also be holistic. Lovelock is a key thinker.
- **Biocentrism:** this places nature rather than humans at the centre of our concerns. We should view the world from nature's point of view rather than a human point of view. Capra is an important example of such a thinker.
- **Anti-capitalism:** it is assumed that capitalism automatically poses a threat to the natural environment because of its obsession with growth and its tendency to abuse the environment in the pursuit of profit. Bookchin is a typical advocate of this view.

- **Naturalism or pastoralism:** this philosophy suggests that we have lost our connection with nature and we need to reconnect with the natural world in a spiritual way. Leopold was one of the first thinkers to promote this idea.
- **Social transformation:** deep ecologists insist that society itself must be transformed if ecological concerns are to be addressed. **Carolyn Merchant** (1936–) (see 'Key thinker 5' box) argued this from a feminist perspective while Schumacher advocated decentralisation and simpler, self-sufficient forms of production.
- **Ethics:** this argues that the protection of the environment and the rights of animals are ethical issues. We should protect them because it is the ethical thing to do. It also places humans on the same level as the natural world.
- **Spiritualism:** some deep ecologists view environmental consciousness in religious or spiritual terms. This sees nature as a permanent cycle of life, of which humans are but one part. If we damage the natural environment, we are interfering with the natural cycle and are sacrificing our place in it. Naess developed this philosophy during his travels and studies in the East.

Shallow green ecologism (environmentalism)

Shallow ecology does not share the holistic, spiritual character of deep ecology. This type of ecology does not require any transformation in our consciousness or in society. Instead it suggests that the natural world can be protected and repaired by political, technological and social action. Shallow ecologists are, therefore, social reformers rather than revolutionary thinkers. The main concerns of shallow ecologists include:

- **Emissions control:** this involves the control of carbon and other harmful emissions. It makes the assumption that private enterprise can be persuaded or forced to consider environmental damage in production methods.
- **Biodiversity:** there is concern that many species of plants and animals are in danger of extinction for a variety of reasons. These should be protected and, if possible, allowed to recover sustainable populations. This is an aspiration that shallow ecologists share with deep ecologists. It is seen as an end in itself and also as a way of protecting the 'web' of nature as described by Capra.

- **Preservation of the countryside:** this is a human-centred aspiration as it is seen as a benefit to mankind to live in a beautiful environment. It involves strict planning controls and the control of industrial and housing developments. Some ecologists, such as Leopold and Carson, have also suggested that there is a spiritual element to our connection with the natural world.
- **Sustainable energy:** this is a largely a technological issue. By developing new technologies mankind may cease to use up finite resources and instead generate energy which does not use up such resources, notably through wind, wave, thermal and nuclear power.
- **Energy conservation:** this policy involves using less energy through improving production methods and the insulation of buildings.

Shallow ecologists argue that all these policies are attainable within existing political and economic structures.

Sustainable energy production will conserve resources and improve air quality

Social ecologism

Social ecologism refers to a collection of traditions, all of which propose that environmental protection can be achieved only if there is some kind of social transformation. Bookchin is a prime example. His anarchist perspective demanded that capitalism be replaced by a communist system of small-scale, self-sufficient production. However, there are a number of other social traditions, including socialism, that see capitalism as the main cause of environmental degradation, and feminism, that sees patriarchy as an accomplice in the exploitation of the environment. Below we consider three forms of social ecologism.

Ecosocialism

In common with anarchists, ecosocialists see capitalism as the main cause of environmental problems. It follows from this that capitalism must be replaced by an alternative economic system if the environment is to be saved. Socialism, some argue, can be the solution. The assumption is that socialism does not include capitalism's desire for growth and industrial investment.

There is, of course, no intrinsic reason why socialism should not be as exploitive of nature as capitalism. Indeed, the environmental record of socialist states such as the Soviet Union and China is a poor one. Ecosocialists respond by arguing that the creation of real equality and common ownership will indeed take away the constant desire for growth. The socialist states that abused the environment were not genuinely egalitarian and simply replaced the capitalist drive for growth with the state's desire for increased output. In other words, the desire for growth came from the state rather than from consumers. True socialism, however, can be ecologically responsible in that there is no motivation for enriching the population.

Eco-anarchism

Eco-anarchists, such as Bookchin, take up this criticism of ecosocialists. The culprit, they insist, is not just capitalism but also the state. Thus the partnership between capitalism and the state must be broken by abolishing the state and transforming capitalism into communism.

Small-scale communist organisation brings mankind closer to nature. For example, the local extraction or processing of natural resources will foster greater care for the environment. One of the results of industrial capitalism is that there is a gap in the final consumer's consciousness of the natural source of what they are consuming. Specifically, if consumers are more directly involved with food production, they will have a vested interest in the protection of the land in a way that consumers under capitalism do not.

Ecofeminism

The ecofeminist perspective on ecology sees patriarchy as the cause of the irresponsible exploitation of nature. Men, as Merchant argued, are exploitive by nature. They will exploit women and they will exploit natural resources in the same way. In other words, they see society and nature from an egocentric

Carolyn Merchant (1936–)

Carolyn Merchant is an American philosopher, best known for her ground-breaking book *The Death of Nature*, published in 1980. In this book she argues that before the Enlightenment period, human identity was seen in terms of membership of wider organisms, one of which was mother earth herself. Individualism did not develop until Enlightenment philosophers began to see humans as rational beings who pursued their own interests as individuals. Merchant added that the development of modern science led humans to the belief that they could begin to explain and therefore control the natural world. This meant that the earth ceased to be superior to mankind and became inferior, something to be used for mankind's own purposes. In a 2002 interview for *California Monthly* she expressed this idea:

> 'Since the scientific revolution of the 17th century, the mainstream story of western culture is that humanity can recover the Garden of Eden through science, technology, and capitalism by remaking the whole earth into a garden. By cutting down forests and making the desert blossom as the rose, and by creating farms on the land — and ultimately agribusiness and then shopping malls and gated communities. All of this is part of a "progressive" narrative that technology can be used to interact with and to dominate and control nature.'

Merchant gives the earth a female identity, likening its relationship to humans to that of a mother with her children. In contrast, the scientific revolution, which began in the eighteenth century, was male-orientated, dominated by a mechanistic view of the world that suggested that each separate part of the world could be exploited for human purposes. This had led to the death of nature, the end of the consciousness of the natural world as the protector of all living things.

For feminists, society is based on patriarchy, the domination of all aspects of life by men. Merchant embraced this analysis and extended it into ecological concerns. Thus patriarchy also included the domination of nature by men. Similarly, capitalism is a male-dominated world so that human domination of the natural world was also an extension of economic domination.

It followed from this analysis that if a new, natural form of consciousness of nature is to be achieved and if mankind is to cease exploiting nature irresponsibly, there will also have to be a revolution against patriarchy. A healthy, egalitarian relationship between men and women will result in a new environmental ethic. In the same interview Merchant demonstrated some optimism for her vision:

> 'A partnership ethic means that women and men can work together as equal partners; it means that nature is still active and a subject, but in equal interaction with humanity. It tries to bring the pendulum back to a dynamic that's rooted in the relationship between people and the environment, between men and women, between minorities and whites. I believe that a partnership ethic is one way of getting to where we need to be. A new narrative that is not the death of nature and not mechanistic science but one of a sustainable partnership with nature and between human groups is part of the social reconstruction that is required. Over the next half century, I think we're going to see something new emerging.'

point of view — they both serve their own interests. By contrast, women are nurturing and caring by nature.

It follows from this that a world where women have equal status with men and where the genders learn to respect each other will be one which also develops a caring, female attitude to nature. Merchant goes one step further than this by suggesting that nature herself is female in character. If patriarchy can be combatted and if men learn to treat women as equals, they will also treat nature as equal to humankind.

Debate 3

How radical is ecologism?

Radical and revolutionary

- Ecologists such as Naess and Fritjof have proposed a fundamental change in human consciousness. Our attitude to nature will change only if society is transformed, placing it subordinate to nature, not superior to it.
- Many ecologists, notably ecosocialists and ecofeminists, propose fundamental changes in the nature of society in order to pursue ecological values. This often concerns economic change.
- Anarchists have a clear vision of an ecological society whereby anthropocentrism is replaced by biocentrism.
- Most deep ecologists say environmental problems all have socially based solutions.

Moderate and reformist

- It is possible to pursue environmental aims without radical reform of society. Good environmental practice can be achieved within existing social and economic structures.
- Shallow ecologists argue that the natural environment can be protected even within an anthropocentric society. If mankind is superior to nature, we can also protect it.
- Some ecologists such as Lovelock believe the environment will bring itself back to equilibrium so people need to concern themselves only with environmental issues that affect themselves.
- Shallow ecologists believe technology can solve many environmental problems.

Summary: key themes and key thinkers

	Human nature	The state	Society	The economy
Rachel Carson	Humans tend to see nature in terms of something useful to them rather than having value in itself.	The state must take active steps to protect the natural environment, especially the seas and rivers.	Society must change its attitude to the natural world radically, to one of protectiveness rather than exploitation.	Industry pollutes because it wishes to avoid 'unnecessary' costs. Therefore pollution must be prevented legally.
Aldo Leopold	We have become separated from nature and need to re-establish our natural affinity with it.	It is the state's duty to protect the environment.	Urbanisation and industrialisation have separated us from nature and threaten the natural environment.	The drive towards industrial growth has degraded the natural environment.
E.F. Schumacher	We have lost our sense of humanity and our connection with the natural world because of centralisation of living and of industry.	The overbearing state should be reduced in scale and political systems should be decentralised.	Small-scale societies can deliver both positive human development and a stronger relationship with the natural world.	Self-sufficiency on a small scale should replace large-scale capitalism, bringing mankind closer to nature.
Murray Bookchin	We have lost our individual sovereignty in modern society and therefore lost our individualistic relationship with nature.	The state is the enemy of both individual liberty and nature. It should be abolished and natural communities formed to replace it.	Natural forms of society have been destroyed by capitalism and the modern state. Voluntary forms of society are more natural and closer to the natural world.	Modern capitalism unacceptably exploits both workers and the natural environment. It must be replaced by an anarchist order.
Carolyn Merchant	We live in a society where we have come to accept patriarchy as normal. Patriarchy tends to exploit women and nature while women have nurturing qualities.	The state reinforces patriarchy and patriarchy naturally tends to exploit rather than nurture nature.	Society must discover new forms of equal relations between men and women. The increased influence of women will improve human environmental consciousness.	Capitalism is patriarchal and so exploits both women and nature for its own purposes. A non-patriarchal economic structure will liberate both women and nature.

Tensions within ecologism

On a general level the main schism among environmental thinkers and activists lies in the distinction between deep green philosophy and shallow green aspirations. Deep ecologists criticise the liberal-based environmental movement on the grounds that it has failed to understand fundamental truths about mankind's relationship to nature. In particular, deep ecologists argue that we must take a holistic view of the natural world. Furthermore, we must accept that humankind has an equal status with the natural world, and we are part of it, not separate from it. This principle is known as **biocentric equality**. Liberal shallow ecologists see mankind as separate from nature, responsible for its welfare but enjoying a higher status.

This distinction has implications for action. Deep ecologists argue that in order to protect the natural world, there need to be fundamental changes in society. For some on the socialist and anarchist wings of the movement, this involves the destruction of capitalism; for ecofeminists there needs to be a destruction of patriarchal society if progress is to be made. All of these ecologists promote a new form of eco-consciousness. Shallow ecologists argue that environmental protection does not depend upon social change. For them the state and capitalism can both reform themselves to take greater account of environmental protection.

On a more specific level, there are a number of key issues that divide ecologists (see Table 6.1). The principal examples are:

- **Anthropocentrism versus biocentrism:** either mankind is the centre of the natural world and superior to it or mankind has an equal status in nature with other living organisms.
- **Holism versus the mechanistic world view:** holism sees the natural world as a single whole, as expressed in Lovelock's Gaia theory, in which all the parts are interdependent and connected. The mechanistic view divides the natural world into separate, constituent parts.
- **Consciousness versus science:** more radical thinkers advocate a change in human consciousness that will allow a new, healthier relationship between humans and the natural world, which can result in improvements in the environment. The scientific approach suggests that environmental problems can be treated separately and can be solved by scientific understanding and technological solutions.
- **Anti-capitalism versus green capitalism:** many ecologists believe that environmental protection and improvement cannot be achieved within a capitalist environment. Green capitalists argue that capitalism can be reformed and regulated so that the concerns of the environment are balanced against growth and profit.
- **Causal measures versus technological solutions:** this issue does not match the deep/shallow dichotomy. The causal outlook insists that environmental problems must be solved by attacking the sources of the problem. This includes such measures as emissions control, anti-pollution legislation, energy conservation and species or habitat protection. The technological approach accepts that the environment is under threat but argues that society will develop technical solutions which will promote environmental recovery. These include the development of renewable and carbon-free energy generation, scientific ways of reducing global warming, and conservation of animal and plant species which are in danger.

The environmental movement is not at a crossroads despite these tensions. Progress is being made on both the deep and shallow ecology fronts. However, there will continue to be a dialogue between those who see environmentalism as ideological and those who see it as a liberal reform movement.

Continued...

Tensions within ecologism (continued)

Table 6.1 Features of deep ecology (ecologism) and shallow ecology (environmentalism)

Deep ecology features	Shallow ecology features
It is an ideological movement.	It is merely a reform movement.
Human consciousness, especially anthropocentrism, must be radically changed.	It is possible to sustain the environment from an anthropocentric point of view.
Deep ecologists take a holistic view of nature.	Shallow ecologists tend to take a mechanistic view of nature, separating it into constituent parts.
Deep ecologists often ally themselves with other radical ideologies, such as anarchism, socialism and feminism.	Shallow ecologists are usually from a liberal tradition.
The ethical view of ecologism sees nature as an equal partner with mankind and grants rights to animals as well as humans.	Shallow ecologists see mankind's relationship with the natural world as 'stewardship', i.e. mankind is superior but has a moral or religious duty to protect nature.

Conclusion: ecologism today

For today's ecologists there is much cause for optimism. A number of developments have been encouraging. These include:

- The Paris agreement on climate change in 2015 was widely praised. It was the first realistic international agreement to deal with the problem in a concerted, targeted way.
- Most of the scientific and political world has come to accept that climate change is indeed man-made.
- The ozone layer appears to be repairing itself (as Lovelock had predicted).
- In particular, China joined the company of nations dedicated to restore the atmospheric balance. In early 2017 the Chinese government announced a huge state investment in renewable energy research and production.
- The production of renewable, carbon-free energy is gradually increasing.
- The need for species protection is now accepted by most countries where this is a particular problem.
- Fish and whale stocks are gradually increasing after many years of depletion.
- Recycling is now a common feature of all developed economies.

Nevertheless, a number of concerns remain, not least of which is the reluctance of human civilisation to adopt what deep ecologists see as a new relationship between mankind and the natural world. More specific problems include:

- President Trump has declared himself hostile to environmental concerns, claiming that (a) there is no proof that climate change is man-made, (b) excessive environmental regulation of industry and agriculture will cost jobs and economic growth, and (c) technology will ultimately solve most of the world's environmental problems.
- The new populist movements tend to be anthropocentric, believing that employment and production stand above environmental concerns.
- Despite China's apparent conversion to environmentalism, the country remains one of the world's most serious polluters.
- Renewable energy production remains expensive compared with the burning of fossil fuels.

Despite this, the ecologism movement has made huge progress in the short time since it began to blossom in the 1970s. From relatively little concern shown in society, politics and economics before 1970, environmental concerns are now firmly established on the political agenda of most developed countries.

Further reading

Six classic works of ecologist thinkers are:
Murray Bookchin, *Toward an Ecological Society*.
Fritjof Capra, *The Web of Life*.
Rachel Carson, *Silent Spring*.
James Lovelock, *Gaia: A New Look at Life on Earth*.
Arne Naess, *Ecology, Community and Lifestyle*.
E.F. Schumacher, *Small Is Beautiful*.
Important works about ecologism include:
Baxter, B. (1999) *Ecologism: An Introduction*, Edinburgh University Press.
Dobson, A. (2007) *Green Political Thought*, Routledge.
Kelsey, E. (2016) *You Are Stardust*, Wayland.
Klein, N. (2014) *This Changes Everything: Capitalism vs. The Climate*, Simon & Schuster.
Lovelock, J. (2000) *Gaia: A New Look at Life on Earth*, Oxford University Press.
Townsend, C. (ed.) (2008) *Essentials of Ecology*, Blackwell.

Exam-style questions

Essay questions

The following questions are similar to those in examinations set by Edexcel (Pearson) and AQA.

Edexcel (24 marks) or AQA (25 marks):

1 To what extent do ecologists criticise anthropocentrism? You must use appropriate thinkers you have studied to support your answer.

2 To what extent do ecologists believe that capitalism can co-exist with environmental protection? You must use appropriate thinkers you have studied to support your answer.

AQA only (25 marks):

3 'The problem of ecology is that mankind considers itself separate from nature.' Analyse and evaluate with reference to the thinkers you have studied.

4 'Ecologism is an ethical question.' Analyse and evaluate with reference to the thinkers you have studied.

Index